## THE CENTRE FOR ENVIRONMENTAL STUDIES SERIES
*General Editor:* Christopher Foster

# THE POLITICS OF HOUSING IN BRITAIN AND FRANCE

This book is one of a series edited at the
Centre for Environmental Studies and published
on its behalf by Heinemann Educational Books
Ltd. The series will present work in the fields
of planning, and urban and regional studies.
The Centre is an independent research
foundation charged with the furtherance and
dissemination of research in these fields. Further
information about this series and the Centre's
work can be obtained from the General Editor.

In the same series

**The Future of Planning**
PETER COWAN

**London: Urban Patterns, Problems, and Policies**
*Edited by* DAVID DONNISON *and* DAVID EVERSLEY

**The Organization of Housing**
MICHAEL HARLOE, RUTH ISSACHAROFF, *and* RICHARD MINNS

**Swindon: A Town in Transition**
MICHAEL HARLOE

**Gypsies and Government Policy in England**
BARBARA ADAMS, JUDITH OKELY, DAVID MORGAN, DAVID SMITH

**Cities for Sale**
LEONIE SANDERCOCK

**Leaving London**
NICHOLAS DEAKIN, CLARE UNGERSON

# The Politics of Housing in Britain and France

ROGER H. DUCLAUD-WILLIAMS

 Heinemann: London

*Heinemann Educational Books Ltd*

London Edinburgh Melbourne Auckland Toronto
Hong Kong Singapore Kuala Lumpur New Delhi
Nairobi Johannesburg Lusaka Ibadan
Kingston

ISBN 0 435 85222 1
© Centre for Environmental Studies 1978
First published 1978

Published by Heinemann Educational Books Ltd
48 Charles Street, London W1X 8AH

Filmset in 10pt Baskerville by
Oxford Printcraft India Private Ltd., Gandhidham - 370 230.
Printed in Great Britain by
Richard Clay (The Chaucer Press) Ltd, Bungay, Suffolk

# Acknowledgments

I am particularly indebted to Professor B.D.H. Graham of the
University of Sussex for his constant encouragement and support
during the preparation of this work.

My thanks are also due to many politicians and civil servants, in
Britain and France, who have given generously of their time. I have
been unable to cite them in the text but the insight and information
they have made available to me have been invaluable.

# Contents

Acknowledgements iv
Abbreviations vii

**Part I: Introduction**

I The Approach and its Justification 3
II An Outline of British and French Housing Policy,
1945–72 15

**Part II: The Privately Rented Sector**

III Introduction 27
IV The Privately Rented Sector: France 33
    i The 1948 Rent Act and its origins 33
    ii The application of the Rent Act, 1948–58 43
    iii Application of the Rent Act after 1958 51
V The Privately Rented Sector: Britain 64
    i The continuation of control, 1945–56 64
    ii The Rent Act and its aftermath, 1956–65 65
    iii The 1965 Rent Act 79
VI Conclusions 87

**Part III: The Public Sector**

VII Introduction 111
VIII The Public Sector: France 124
    i 1945–53 124
    ii Rent levels 127
    iii Tenant selection 130
    iv The *Sur-Loyer* 138
    v Financing the HLMs 140
    vi Selling to tenants 142
    vii Differential rents 143
    viii Abbé Pierre 146
    ix Conclusions 147

IX The Public Sector: Britain 154
   i 1945–51 154
   ii 1951–55 158
   iii 1955–61 160
   iv 1961–64 162
   v 1964–70 165
   vi Policy since 1970 170
   vii Tenant selection 176
X The Public Sector: Conclusion 180
XI Repairs and Improvement 201

## Part IV: The Owner-Occupied Sector

XII Owner-Occupation: France 215
   i The semi-public sector—Crédit Foncier 215
   ii Other forms of aid to owner-occupation 226
   iii Conclusion 231
XIII The Owner-Occupied Sector: Britain 235
XIV The Owner-Occupied Sector: Conclusion 245
XV The Politics of Housing in Britain and France 257
Bibliography 272
Table IV.1 61
Table VIII.1 148
Table IX.1 177

# Abbreviations

| | |
|---|---|
| ANAHE | Agence Nationale pour l'Amélioration de l'Habitat Existant (previously FNAH) |
| CAF | Caisse d'Allocations Familiales |
| CFDT | Confédération Française Démocratique du Travail |
| CGC | Confédération Générale des Cadres |
| CGL | Confédération Générale du Logement |
| CGT | Confédération Générale du Travail |
| CIL | Comité Inter-professionnel du Logement |
| CNAHE | Confédération Nationale pour l'Amélioration de l'Habitat Existant |
| CNL | Confédération Nationale du Logement (previously Confédération Nationale des Locataires) |
| CNPF | Conseil National du Patronat Français |
| CPACT | Confédération pour la Propagande et l'Action Contre les Taudis |
| FNAH | Fonds National pour l'Amélioration de l'Habitat (now ANAHE) |
| FNB | Fédération Nationale du Bâtiment |
| FNCP | Fédération Nationale des Constructeurs Promoteurs (later renamed FNPC) |
| FNPC | Fédération Nationale des Promoteurs Constructeurs (previously FNCP) |
| HLM | Habitation à Loyer Modéré |
| ILN | Immeuble à Loyer Normal |
| INSEE | Institut National de Statistiques et d'Études Economiques |
| Logeco | Logement économique et familial |
| MRP | Mouvement Republicain Populaire |
| PCF | Parti Communiste Français |
| PLR | Programme à Loyer Réduit |
| PRL | Parti Républicain de la Liberté |

| | |
|---|---|
| PS | Parti Socialiste (previously SFIO) |
| PSR | Programme Social de Relogément |
| PSU | Parti Socialiste Unifié |
| RGR | Rassemblement des Gauches Républicaines |
| RI | Républicains Indépendants |
| RPF | Rassemblement du Peuple Français |
| SCIC | Société Centrale Immobilière de la Caisse des dépôts et consigrations |
| SEM | Société d'Economie Mixte |
| SFIO | Section Française de l'Internationale Ouvrière |
| SMIC | Salaire Minimum Inter-professionnel de Croissance (previously SMIG) |
| SMIG | Salaire Minimum Inter-professionnel Garanti (now SMIC). |
| UDR | Union Démocratique de la République |
| UDSR | Union Démocratique et Socialiste de la Résistance |
| UNAF | Union Nationale des Associations de Familles |
| UNFO-HLM | Union Nationale des Fédérations d'Organismes d'HLM |
| UNPI | Union Nationale de la Propriété Immobilière (previously UPBF) |
| UNR | Union pour la Nouvelle République |
| UPBF | Union de Propriété Bâtie de France (later UNPI) |
| AMA | Association of Municipal Authorities (previously AMC) |
| AMC | Association of Municipal Corporations (later AMA) |
| BSA | Building Societies Association |
| NATR | National Association of Tenants and Residents |
| NFBTE | National Federation of Building Trade Employers |

PART I

# Introduction

# The Approach and its Justification

The aim of this book is to present a comparative study of public policies. It is intended to advance knowledge in the field of policy studies and comparative politics. I have had three primary concerns. In the first place I have tried to examine the political characteristics of housing as an area of policy, without too much reference to particular institutions and problems. In the second place, I have tried to place French and British housing policies in their political context, and in tracing their development, examine the relation between politics and policy, between the struggle for power, and the use which is made of it. Finally, and this is perhaps the core of the book, I have tried to compare the patterns of policy development which pertain in each country and provide a political explanation for these different patterns of development. The approach adopted will become more clear if I compare it with other approaches to the study of policy which are already well established [1].

One approach to the study of policy-making is to concentrate one's attention on the process by which decisions are reached. In so doing one may well throw considerable light on policy outcomes. But studies of this sort are often limited in scope, concentrating much more on the process than on the outcome [2]. My emphasis is the reverse of this.

Another important tradition of writing which bears on policy-making is that which seeks to explain policy outcomes by reference to the activities of pressure groups [3]. Many of those who have worked in this field have been seeking to answer exactly the same question that I have posed myself—why is one policy pursued in preference to another? It is important to underline this point because much work in the field of political science is interested in public policy only indirectly. For example, much of what has been written about political parties has not been concerned to examine the role of the political party in policy formation [4]. But the pressure group approach does have this as one of its aims. Some writers suggest that the examination of group activity will go a long way towards explaining policy outcomes [5]. In their view, government remains often very passive and hence one only has to examine the power of the groups in contention, their differing resources, their means of access, and other important variables, and one will be provided with an explanation of particular policies and decisions.

There are critics of this approach who argue that its advocates are often vague as to how passive they believe government to be and therefore as to how far they can take the pressure group mode of explanation [6]. It is also argued, with some force, that many studies make the jump from the demands of the groups to the governmental response rather too easily and do not explain convincingly why the public authorities feel it necessary to adopt some of the solutions which are pressed upon them [7]. This is not the place in which to undertake a critical review of the achievements and shortcomings of the pressure group literature. I shall content myself instead with explaining my own particular reasons for not using this approach. Before doing so, I should make it clear that I do not reject this approach out of hand. In the course of this study I shall have occasion to refer to the activities of those groups that are active in the field of housing policy, but a discussion of pressure group activity forms a fairly small part of this work [8].

The criticism which is in my view most pertinent to the pressure group approach is that it takes as its starting point the activities of the groups themselves. Frequently the focus of interest is on a particular issue, or piece of legislation, in which private interests have a considerable stake [9]. Even if this particular difficulty is avoided and instead a broader and more systematic approach is adopted, there is a bias in the method itself which inclines to the finding that groups are a very important determining influence on policy. If one concentrates on interest groups, one is almost certain to find examples of successful campaigns. The question which must then be logically posed is: are these examples typical of the process of public policy formation as a whole? But in order to answer such a question, one must surely examine public policy and not simply the attempts of groups to influence it. It is precisely to avoid this danger that I have chosen to make public policy the centre of my study. It seems to me necessary to describe policy in a particular field before seeking to explain the course of policy development. If one does not follow this course, one has nothing to explain.

But objections of a methodological character were not the only reasons for allowing a fairly small space to pressure groups in this study. The main reason for this is empirical. As the research advanced, it became clear that changes of policy over time, and contrasts in the pattern of policy development as between one country and another, could not be satisfactorily explained by reference to the activities of groups.

Another tradition of inquiry which sometimes seeks to explain policy outcomes is the decision-making theory [10]. Many of those who have worked within this tradition have been concerned to isolate particular decisions, or chains of decisions, and to identify factors which appear to explain the choices made. In contrast to this approach, my concern has been not only with particular decisions but also with policy maintenance. Again, with respect to much of the writing in this tradition, I would make the point that I have not rejected it as much as chosen to follow a somewhat different path. It seems to me that close examination of the most important decisions associated with housing policy would add greatly to a study such as mine. A close and detailed focusing on a particular turning point is likely to turn up material which is bound to escape a student who seeks to take a broader view. But I am concerned to identify general patterns of policy development, and it is only possible to do this if one stands back a little so as to gain in historical perspective. It seems to me that one falsifies reality if one considers housing policy as a series of decisions spread over a period of more than twenty-five years. It is more realistic to recognize that policy is guided by certain general orientations, which are changed from time to time. Once a new general orientation has been set, the bulk of decisions taken for some time thereafter will be logically linked to it. This is not to say that detailed application always conforms exactly to the general policy previously laid down, but nevertheless it is important to maintain the distinction between the great decisions, or as I have called them policy orientations, and the smaller decisions which flow from them. One falsifies events if one considers each decision in isolation. My aim is to link decisions and see whether it is not possible in so doing to identify a pattern of policy development.

Another branch of decision-making theory, represented for example in the work of Lasswell, has been much concerned to escape from an approach which is thought to be too dependent on the formal structure of decision-making bodies [11]. Lasswell suggests instead that we identify clearly at the outset the logically separate steps involved in the taking of any decision. Thus one might start by examining the first step of problem identification, and then pass successively to the drawing up of options and the selection between them, arriving finally at a stage when, after appraisal, the original decision would be either maintained, revised or repealed. Judged theoretically, this approach seems to have much to recommend it. But when one begins to try to use it, one encounters great practical difficulties. However logically necessary the steps may be, it seems difficult to describe the reality of a developing policy in these terms.

A simple example taken from the field of housing may serve to make this point. It is suggested that the analysis of any decision must begin by isolating the process of problem identification. Let us suppose that the problem in question is the balance to be struck, either at the national or local level, between public and private forms of housing provision. If one were to ask when and by what means was this problem first identified, the answer would be that the problem has existed for as long as these two forms of provision have existed. It may be possible to avoid this sort of difficulty by defining problems much more narrowly, but in this case one is led to examine smaller and smaller problems which are less politically significant. It seems to me that such an approach may be useful in an organized administrative environment, where it is possible to trace a particular decision through all its stages from problem to solution, but that a rationally and deductively derived model such as Lasswell proposes is difficult to use in the less organized world of politics. It must be admitted though, on behalf of such an approach, that it can aid by pointing to logically separate steps in a process. In this way it may help the observer to avoid missing aspects of his subject which, because they are less conspicuous, might otherwise be overlooked.

Another important tradition of writing which aims to relate politics and policy is represented by those writers who, working mainly in the fields of American city and state governments, and using statistical methods, seek to establish correlations between social, political and economic factors and the policies to which they give rise [12]. My approach differs from this in that it is much more explicitly dynamic. I am concerned not simply with the state of policy at a given moment but also with the pattern of its development over a number of years. Since I have chosen to try and explain development and not simply policy commitments at a given moment, it is quite evident that statistical methods are inappropriate. This is not to say that I reject either the findings or the methods employed by writers in this tradition, but I do not find them appropriate in answering the questions which I have posed myself. It is quite evident, in fact, that economic and demographic conditions impose quite severe restraints on the range of housing policies effectively open to any government. David Donnison has, in a European context, suggested an extremely interesting typology using these variables [13]. I feel his approach to be totally consonant with mine. In referring to the importance of certain demographic variables, he is only suggesting that the broadest outlines of housing policy are fixed by these factors. Throughout he supplements this approach by reference to the significance of the political environment.

I have said enough about the approaches which I do not intend to use, for it to be necessary at this point to pass on to a fuller statement of my own aims. My basic concern has been to describe the housing policies adopted by successive French and British governments, and to describe the political conflicts surrounding these policies. I shall also attempt to explain why certain policies have been followed and not others. I have sought to identify patterns of policy development which are typical of the two political systems under study, and to explain why each country appears to have its own characteristic pattern of policy development. I am concerned both with the explanation of policy outcomes in each country, as they develop over time, and also with the total cross-national comparison.

I have stressed above that I have tried to use throughout an explicitly dynamic approach. I have not attempted therefore to characterize British and French policies in general and then to explain the differences existing between them by reference to political factors but tried instead to concern myself with the different ways in which policy has developed through time in these two countries. The importance of adopting this more dynamic approach may be brought out well if we compare the aims of this study with those adopted by J.R. Pennock in his article on agricultural subsidies in Britain and the USA. In some ways the approach which he adopts is extremely close to that which will be followed here but one important difference emerges. Whereas he takes as his starting point a basic difference between the agricultural policies pursued in two countries, that is, the fact that the subsidies given to farmers are in fact much more important in Britain than they are in the USA, the starting point in the present study is not an individual fact of this type but rather a series of facts taken together. The reason for his having based his comparative study on an observation of a particular individual phenomenon rather than agricultural policy in general over a period of years is not too difficult to find. As a student of politics, he had learned that the American federal system with its separation of powers and checks and balances was more amenable to pressure group activities. In contrast, he had also learned that the strongly disciplined political parties of Great Britain and the high level of centralization which existed within the country would limit severely the effectiveness of pressure group activity. As a student of agricultural policy, however, he observed that measured in whatever form, the subsidies which were given to farmers in Britain were very much more important than those received by American farmers. Therefore, it is apparent that although his study appears to take as its point of departure a certain policy area, in fact the point of departure was the received view as to the relative efficacy of pressure groups in the two systems. I have not followed this approach of first seeking out the received notions on a particular point and then confronting them with the observed facts. Instead, as I have explained in discussing the pressure group approach, I have sought to focus on a policy area and to work back from there to the political system.

As I have stated, my approach takes as its starting point an area of policy rather than any point in the political process. This provides what I might call an automatic perspective. If one takes as the central point of a study a particular element in the political process, one is faced with the problem of assessing its importance by comparison to other elements in that same process, If, however, one adopts a policy sector as the point of departure, provided always that the area chosen is an important one in the country concerned, one is not faced with the above difficulty. Different types of activity fall into place as either important or unimportant according to the contribution which they make to the process of policy formation. It must be admitted that although starting from a policy sector helps place different parts of the political process in perspective it involves the disadvantage of not answering the question: 'How typical is this sector of policy-making as a whole?' This sort of difficulty is unavoidable. Since everything cannot be examined at once, boundaries have to be drawn, and this leads to the question as to whether the area studied would not have looked very difficult if they had been drawn differently.

One of the assumptions of this study is that it will be possible to reveal contrasting political patterns by examining the way in which a single problem is treated in two political systems. This will only be so if the problem in question is, as nearly as possible, the same in each. Problems may vary physically and also in the way in which they are perceived. The first type of difference is the most serious for, if the problem is in fact very different in the two countries, there will obviously be great difficulties in coming to any sort of conclusion about the political responses which one is able to observe. Comparison of political systems is obviously extremely difficult, if not impossible, if the problems which these systems are obliged to face are in no way comparable. For example, it would be most unwise to attempt to draw conclusions about the politics of a developing and a fully industrialized country by comparing their respective educational policies. Problems in the two cases would differ so radically that it would be impossible to know whether policy differences were attributable to political or other factors.

As for the difficulties of different political perceptions of basically similar problems, these do not constitute a real obstacle to study. On the contrary, if one can show that a similar problem is perceived in different political terms in two countries, then one has succeeded in bringing to light an important political fact which will merit investigation. At numerous points in this study, there will appear examples of similar, if not identical, problems being treated, and sometimes perceived, in different ways.

Taking as the basis of the study the political systems of Britain and France, there would appear to be certain policy areas which would not lend themselves to a study of the sort which I have carried out. If one were, for example, to attempt the political study of the agricultural policies of the two countries, one would be immediately faced by the problem of the much greater importance of the agricultural population in France, the much greater importance for the French economy of the agricultural industry and the different historical inheritances in the area of agricultural policy which exist in the two countries. These difficulties might be surmountable, but it obviously seems desirable, if this is at all possible, to choose an area of study where the problems posed are very similar. The choice of housing avoids these difficulties, but, in order to justify this choice, it is necessary to examine in somewhat more detail exactly what is meant by housing policy.

The area of housing policy is essentially concerned with two things, firstly the production of houses and secondly the use which is to be made of them once they are available [14]. On the production side the principal questions which have to be decided are those of who is to do the building and, more importantly in our two cases, how this operation and the eventual purchase of the house is to be financed. With regard to use, the most important questions are firstly legal. One must decide whether the house is to be owned by the occupant or whether it is instead to be rented and if rented, whether by a public or private authority. If it is rented, one must also determine the terms of the tenure and the manner in which the rent is to be fixed. We shall at a later point be obliged to go into these different aspects of housing policy in much greater detail, but here our concern is to indicate very generally what is involved and to show that the problems are extremely similar in Britain and France.

If we turn from the discussion of what makes up housing policy generally to listing the particular problems which have presented themselves to the British and French governments in the past twenty-five years, we may see very quickly that there are great similarities. Both countries began the post-war period with an extensive and fairly rigid form of rent control which had necessarily to be modified at some time as a consequence of inflation, deteriorating standards, or simply because there were political objections to the continuance of control over the landlords' freedom of action. Both countries have a large publicly financed housing sector which is an important part of public investment and whose size must constantly be determined with regard to other demands on available resources. Both governments have been faced by the conflicting demands of tenants and landlords in the fields of security of tenure and have had to strike a balance, which has varied from time to time, between the demands for security and for the free disposal of privately owned property. Both governments have been faced by a problem of poor quality and insufficient quantity in the housing stock, which they have attempted to deal with by policies designed to encourage the repair and main-tenance of the existing stock and its enlargement by the expansion of house-building. We shall see as we enter more into the details of the study that, at some point, this basic similarity tends to dissolve into differences of detail, but sufficient has been said to show that there are important shared problems.

One might suppose from this description of basic problems which exist in the field of housing that it would be possible to conduct a comparative study of the politics of housing involving any advanced Western countries. This is in fact not the case. The limitations of housing as a possible tool in the study of comparative politics may be illuminated if we take as an example the possible study of the United

States housing policy and its comparison in political terms with policies adopted in other advanced European countries. Such a study would rapidly be confronted by the fundamental difference in approach between that of the US federal authorities and those of any European central government regarding the approved scope for state regulation and direction in housing matters. It would emerge very quickly that the public housing sector is insignificant in economic and social terms in the United States, whereas it has enormous importance in almost all European countries. It would also emerge that questions of rent control are not posed in the United States, and there would also be difficulties involved in comparing unitary and federal systems.

The problem here is an extremely interesting one for the illumination which it provides of the potential usefulness of the comparative study of policy fields. If one finds immediately that the policies followed are extremely different and that the terms in which political debate is conducted vary also greatly as between the countries considered, then the study immediately loses a great deal of its interest. One is almost certain to arrive quickly at the conclusion that one is observing a difference of a very basic nature in economic and social circumstances. In this situation, housing becomes very rapidly simply an example of a wider economic and social contrast. In this case, for instance, one would immediately be struck by the much smaller importance of the state's activities in the area of housing and the lack of any real controversy as to the extent of this involvement. One would then be thrown back on an examination of American society as a whole and its comparison with other developed Western societies, and the subject of housing as such would lose much of its interest.

In the case of Britain and France, this difficulty does not present itself since the degree of involvement of the state in the two cases under study is roughly comparable. Existing assumptions as to the role of the state in economic and social life are also roughly comparable, and hence one has a situation of comparability and also one in which the housing question is always on the agenda. The problem is always present, the state is always involved in adopting new policies and in modifying existing policies in the area under consideration, and hence the opportunity exists for the student to observe the interaction between the political life of the country and the policies which are adopted.

My examination of the politics of housing in Britain and France is confined to the decisions taken and the conflicts which exist at national level. I have chosen not to concern myself with local politics in Britain and France. This may be considered an important disadvantage since in both Britain and France there is some local direction in the implementation of housing policy, particularly in the former case. The existence of local politics as an element in housing policy and the varying importance which local government has in the housing policies of the two countries is not however a substantial obstacle in the way of our study because of the important and decisive role which remains for central government in both countries. It is the business of central government in both cases to define the terms on which public finance is made available for the building of public housing for rent, and hence indirectly to determine the level of rents which may be charged in the public sector. It is also the business of central government in both countries to define the legal framework within which the private rental sector operates, although a minor role is accorded in France to the local authorities in the local application of nationally applicable statutes in this field. The existence of this decisive role which belongs to central government in both countries is of course a necessary condition of the success of our study.

I have explained in principle why a comparative study of national housing politics and policies seems a sound method for obtaining information about the working of two political systems. But perhaps these arguments will be rendered more convincing if I anticipate a little some of my conclusions, without attempting to support them. Writers on French politics have often concluded that government instability means that any necessary continuity in policy can only be obtained by allowing power to pass from politicians into the hands of the administration. My examination of the way in which the politicians have been careful to guard against hostile public reaction to the process of rent decontrol during the 1960s does not bear this out [15]. Continuity there has been, but always as a result of decisions taken by politicians, not bureaucrats. Politicians under the Fourth and Fifth republics have been aware of popular hostility to the withdrawal of rent controls and their respect for this sentiment, not bureaucratic power, has brought about a situation in which rent policy changes always slowly and almost imperceptibly. The last word, even on detailed questions, is necessarily left with the politicians because it is understood that the decisions are political and not technical. The technicians' view of desirable policies has little relevance because of the gap between the desirable and the possible.

Again, many observers stress the importance of local autonomy and the partnership between central and local government in Britain and contrast it with the absence of such a relationship in France. A comparison of the Conservative Housing (Finance) Act of 1972 with the long struggles between the French government and its public housing authorities over tenant selection will show such a contrast to be quite false, or at least extremely over-simplified.

Yet again, much of what I have to say, particularly in discussing owner occupation, stresses the importance of established financial institutions, such as the Building Societies. The textbook accounts of British Governments do not discuss institutions of this sort, presumably because they are not regarded as political institutions. It will be clear by now that for me, if an institution has important effects on policy or the character of political conflict, then it is the concern of the student of politics. In this sense, the Building Societies are political institutions, although not necessarily primarily so.

In conclusion, it will be useful to explain the way in which I have chosen to present my material. It has seemed convenient to treat each sector of housing provision separately. Hence, Part II deals with the privately rented sector, Part III with the public sector, and Part IV with owner-occupation. There is no logical place in such a plan for the treatment of repair and maintenance but I have found it convenient to add a chapter on this subject to Part III. In the two most substantial parts of the work, Parts II and III, the same basic arrangement has been adopted. Both commence with a study of the character of the sector's politics, and the main aim is to analyse the basic issues which are inherent to the sector. When this has been done, a more or less chronological account of policy and political conflict in Britain and France is provided. Each part is then concluded by an attempt to explain the pattern of policy development in each national case and to compare these explanations so as to throw light on the national political systems. The presentation in Part IV, which deals with owner-occupation, is essentially the same, except that no introductory chapter was felt to be necessary. As will be seen, the empirical procedure of passing from description to explanation is followed. The body of the work therefore lies in these three parts but, since there is a certain inevitable overlapping, a brief introductory chapter (chapter 2) has been provided, the object of which is to familiarize the reader with the essentials of policy in Britain and France.

*References*

1. R. Rose, 'Comparing public policy—An overview', *European Journal of Political Research*, Vol. I, April 1973, p. 67. This article summarizes the immense variety of approaches to the study of policy, and contains a large amount of useful bibliographical information.

2. A. Wildavsky, *The Politics of the Budgeting Process* (Boston, Mass., Little Brown & Co., 1964).

3. A.F. Bentley, *The Process of Government* (1908), reprinted with an introduction by P.H. Odegard (Cambridge, Mass., Belknap Press, 1967); D.B. Truman, *The Governmental Process* (New York, Knopf, 1951).

4. R.T. McKenzie, *British Political Parties* (London, Heinemann, 1955).

5. E.C. Banfield, *Political Influence* (New York, Free Press, 1961).

6. J. Dearlove, *The Politics of Policy in Local Government* (Cambridge University Press, 1973), chapter 3, pp. 47–60.

7. ibid., pp. 53–8.

8. *See* chapter VI especially.

9. E.E. Schattschneider, *Politics, Pressures and the Tariff* (Hamden, Conn; Archon Books, 1963); H.H. Wilson, *Pressure Group: The Case of Commercial Television* (London, Secker and Warburg, 1961).

10. J.A. Robinson and R. Majak, 'The theory of decision-making', in J.C. Charlesworth (ed.), *Contemporary Political Analysis* (London, Macmillan & Co., 1967); C.E. Lindblom, *The Policy-Making Process* (Englewood Cliffs, N.J., Prentice-Hall, 1968).

11. Harold Lasswell, *The Decision Process: Seven Categories of Functional Analysis* (College Park, University of Maryland, 1956).

12. R.E. Dawson and J.A. Robinson, 'Interparty competition, economic variables and welfare policies in the American states', *Journal of Politics*, Vol. XXV, 1963, pp. 265–89. D. Lockard, *New England State Politics* (Princeton, Princeton University Press, 1959).

13. D.V. Donnison, *The Government of Housing* (Penguin Books, 1967), pp. 86–112.

14. Because a line must be drawn somewhere, I have defined housing policy so as to exclude town planning and issues associated with land speculation.

15. *See* chapter VI.

# An Outline of British and French Housing Policy, 1945—72

In this chapter I shall attempt to provide an introduction to the legal, financial, and administrative arrangements in Britain and France and also to outline in the broadest possible manner the policies that have been pursued in these two countries. Such a procedure is desirable for a number of reasons. In the first place, as I have already explained, I have found it necessary to analyse housing policy by subdividing it into three sectors. If, therefore, I were to plunge straight into the examination of policy in the first sector, there would be a danger of obscuring general contrasts because these would not appear until much later. In addition, the bulk of the study consists of a detailed examination of the development of policy on particular points, and it has seemed to me that the overall picture will be much clearer if I provide some general introduction to national policies at the start and also indicate what I consider to be the basic contrast between the French and British patterns of policy development.

The main feature of French policy has been its gradual and incremental development along predetermined lines in one direction and without any sharp or fundamental reorientations. This pattern is strongly contrasted with what may be observed in Britain. Here, one finds that policy is frequently fundamentally modified and that there are oscillations between alternative solutions. Since the contrast between the two national patterns takes this form, it is convenient to begin by describing the three important post-war French statutes, each of which laid the foundations that were to prove enduring in its sector. These three statutes taken together constitute what might be regarded as a platform upon which all subsequent development has been based.

### French post-war housing policy

The first legislation imposing a freeze on rents in the private sector dates, in France as in Britain, from the First World War. During the inter-war period bills were passed from time to time which allowed increases in percentage terms but in France the basic principle of control of all rents in this sector was maintained throughout this period [1]. The continuance of this control was rendered impossible by the rapid inflation which France suffered in the late forties, and therefore totally new legislation, in the form of the Act of the 1st September 1948, was enacted to supersede all earlier legislations. This statute constitutes the first of the three pillars to which I have referred. No attempt will be made here to examine the political significance of this Act or to acquaint the reader with the technicalities which surround it but some indication of its underlying principles is necessary.

The Act embodied a commitment to continue control but to do so in a more flexible manner. It was envisaged in this legislation that six-monthly increases in rent would take place up to the point when rents reached previously determined ceilings. These increases were to have the effect of raising both the nominal and real value of rents and also enlarging the share of the average family budget devoted to rent. The size of each increase was determined in the legislation as twenty per cent of the previously practised rent but the point from which the increases would start was to be fixed by the minister in the light of general principles laid down in the act. As with all forms of rent control, the control over rent level was coupled with the granting of security of tenure.

Rent policy has developed slowly from this point onwards but always in the same direction. The Act itself embodied a gradualist philosophy and gave the responsible minister wide discretion as to the manner in which it was to be applied. Rents were to rise but only very slowly, if steadily, and the solution to the problem of excessively low rents was only envisaged in the very long term. This aspect of the Act is brought out very well in the distinction which is drawn in the Act between what is termed *le prix technique* and *la valeur locative*. The former was the rent which might be demanded on the 1st January 1949 when the Act came into force. The latter was the rent which was thought to correspond to the value of the service being provided which would be reached in 1954, that is to say that the legislator expressly implies in the terms of the Act that rents will not reach the level which is considered reasonable until after six years of slow increase. This does not mean, of course, that the rent in 1954 was intended to correspond to a market rent, or even a cost rent, but would simply be the government's estimation of the value of the service being provided in the renting of a particular dwelling. The legislation set out certain principles for the determination of rents but delegated important functions to the responsible minister. When we come to examine the situation in the privately rented sector after twenty-five years of evolution we shall find that there have been important changes in many respects, but those twenty-five years reveal no watershed and the Law of September 1948, as subsequently amended, remains the basic text of reference for all matters concerning this sector. Such policy developments as there have been during this period have been carried out without major political clashes and have left unaltered the basic features of the Act. There continue to be increases in rent which are determined by the minister, even if they are now annual rather than six-monthly, and, even if the scope of the Act has been reduced considerably so that fewer and fewer houses fall within its orbit, this has been done with extreme gradualness and by way of the decree powers that were enumerated in the Act. Even this cursory account of policy in the privately rented sector shows up a stark contrast between the French and British patterns of development. In the former case there were no abrupt changes such as occurred in Britain with the Rent Acts of 1957 and 1965, and in France rents were very successfully kept out of the political arena during most of the post-war period.

The second pillar of housing policy was provided by the Law of the 21st July 1950 which established what has since come to be called the intermediate or semi-public sector of housing construction. This sector is defined by the fact that it draws the bulk of its financing from the *Crédit Foncier de France*. Provision was made in this legislation for the payment to owners of newly constructed houses of a subsidy of six francs per year per square metre of floors area for a period of twenty years. This payment was to be received by the purchaser of the dwelling without regard to his income. These subsidies, it was thought, would generally be associated with loans which would cover a proportion of the purchase price of the house, and which would also be provided by the *Crédit Foncier*. In the course of time the loans have become more important than the subsidies but both continue to exist and the essential features of this system remain unchanged. The benefits of the annual subsidies and the initial loans are destined primarily for the owner-occupier. These benefits are not considered a form of social aid and are therefore generally available without restriction as to income. Conditions are often imposed, however, as to the physical characteristics of the dwelling to be built. Another important feature of this sector, which as we shall see later has political significance, is that the number of subsidies or loans that are made available in any one year may be limited by the Minister of Finance and therefore a sort of rationing system has always prevailed. The number and types of loans and subsidies to be made available in a year are fixed in advance in the budget.

It may be readily understood that the politics of this sector have been mainly concerned with the number and size of the loans and subsidies to be made available, the conditions to be attached to them, either as to the income of the recipient or as to the structure being financed, and the limitations to be placed on those who built dwellings with *Crédit Foncier* finance as an investment and therefore rented them. As has already been indicated, this last sort of conflict was less important than the others mentioned because the intermediate sector has always been dominated by the future owner-occupier rather than the investor in housing. The politics which surround these conflicts are of great interest and will be examined in detail in later chapters when we come to deal with this sector. What was said of the privately rented sector is even more true here since the basic features, already described, persist to this day.

Something must be said by way of explanation of the *Crédit Foncier* [2]. It is juridically a private bank but its directors and governor are appointed by the Minister of Finance and it serves in fact as the government's errand boy in the field of housing finance. It is therefore one of those semi-public semi-private institutions so frequently found in the French economy. The major source of finance to which the *Crédit Foncier* has access is the public financial market. It does not, as yet, have the facilities necessary to collect short-term liquid savings in the way which the Building Societies do in this country. An additional handicap under which it must labour is that its issues must be approved by the Minister of Finance and therefore, although it never has any difficulty in raising all the finance for which it asks from the market, it is only allowed to float an issue when the minister feels that this is desirable in the interests of the economy as a whole. In more blunt terms, therefore, when the minister feels that there is a shortage of capital for investment in industry, which he very often does, he is inclined to limit the demands which the *Crédit Foncier* is allowed to make. The *Crédit Foncier* is not solely concerned with the system of subsidies and loans which has been described here but also carries on some other business of its own which resembles more closely the activities of any other important bank. These however have little to do with housing and do not concern us.

The third piece of legislation which must be discussed concerns the *Habitations à Loyer Modéré*, (housing at moderate rents), which are the agencies charged in France with public building for sale and to let. These institutions are obviously of first importance in French housing provision and will be examined separately later. The Law of the 3rd September 1947 was designed simply to set the HLMs back on their feet again after the interruptions of the war. It did so leaving the system as it had previously existed, entirely intact. The basic elements in the HLM system, which of course is parallel to the council house system in Britain, are that the authorities charged with the building of public housing for sale and to let are not the local authorities, as they are in Britain, but are organizations which are concerned only with housing and whose leading administrators are unpaid. The exact terms on which the state makes available financial assistance to the HLMs vary slightly from time to time but this aid has always been in the form of loans at an extremely low rate of interest, perhaps one or two per cent, which are repaid over a very long period of between forty and sixty years. These organizations enjoy a good deal of autonomy in the matter of the selection of tenants but they are closely controlled as to the minimum standards to which they must build, and also as to the costs of the operations which they mount. The fixing of HLM rents is not a matter which concerns only these organizations. Both government and the housing authorities have a part to play. But, naturally since the organization must balance its books, and since most of its borrowing is from the state on terms which the state defines, rents largely depend on the financial terms which are granted. The features of stability and continuity which we have already noted, with respect to the other sectors previously described, are found even more prominently in the HLM sector.

These three pieces of legislation, and the policies with which they are associated, have survived a number of major political changes in the past two decades. All three were enacted by Third Force governments, basically centre coalitions of the Socialist, MRP, and Radical Socialist parties but they survived the fall of the Fourth Republic in 1958 and have remained operative in the very different political circumstances of the 1960s and early 1970s.

## British post-war housing policy

One may now leave the description of the basic characteristics of the different sectors of French housing and contrast them with the arrangements and pattern of policy development in Britain. The method of exposition which has proved suitable for the French system and its development is not appropriate to the British case; one cannot describe the arrangements that were made in the early post-war years and then simply add that they have been maintained ever since. The British pattern has in fact been one of sharply contrasted policies that have been followed at different periods. Each period is separated from its predecessor by certain clear-cut political decisions which have brought about major changes in housing policy, usually changes that are not confined to one sector alone.

The first period covers the years in which the Attlee Labour Government was in office, from 1945 to 1951. During this period the system of rent control for the private sector was maintained without change as it had existed since its total reimposition in 1939. For some categories of dwelling the controls had continued without a break since 1914. A combination of political and economic circumstances had led to this result. Inflation was much less serious in Britain than it was in France and therefore rents did not decline so rapidly in real value, and the party in power was sympathetic to the tenant interest in both word and deed. With respect to new building, a high priority was given to council housing which was allotted at least eighty per cent of the new housing construction in any year. This was achieved by way of a system of building licences which allowed the government, through the local authorities, to control the size of the private programme for sale [3].

The years 1951 to 1955, which one may call the Macmillan period, were characterized by a rapid increase in the building programme, mainly in the council sector, so that the rate of building rose from a level of two hundred thousand per annum, which had been the rate towards the end of the Labour period in office, to one of three hundred thousand per year which was reached in 1954 [4]. Policy during this period in the privately rented sector was similar to that followed earlier by the Labour government. No measure of decontrol was introduced but the Housing Repairs and Rent Act (1954) allowed landlords to increase their rents, up to a certain limit, if they could show that they had spent a fixed amount recently on repairs [5]. This period also saw the beginnings of expansion of building for sale as the system of building licences was brought to an end and therefore builders began once again to build speculatively, that is to say that they returned to the normal practice of the inter-war period when one built without having any firm commitment from a future buyer in the assurance that buyers could be found when the houses were finished.

A third period begins in the autumn of 1955 and may be considered to have lasted at least six years. During this period, public building was reduced rapidly in importance, both absolutely and also as a share of new building, and the Rent Act of 1957 was introduced, bringing about a substantial decontrol of privately rented property. This period was also marked by a sharp fall in the element of subsidy in the financing of new council housing [6].

A fourth period began in 1961 and lasted until the Conservatives were removed from office in 1964. There was no change in policy towards the private sector of rented housing at this time although the process of decontrol was allowed to continue. The procedures placed at the disposal of the minister in the Rent Act for accelerating the process of decontrol were not used as had been previously expected. This period was characterized by the renewal of demands for a higher priority to be given to housing in public spending, and this produced some acceleration in the building programme in the private and public sectors. An element of subsidy was also returned to new council housing in general by Mr Brooke in 1961, which had only existed previously for housing designed for special purposes such as the housing of the elderly or displaced slum-dwellers [7].

A new period began with the success of the Labour Party in the 1964 elections, the adoption of the 1965 Rent Act and with legislation in 1967 to increase the subsidy for council housing, an increase which was backdated to the date of the 1964 election. There was no great increase in the size of the building programme during these years. The council sector tended to grow slightly and the private sector to stagnate or decline, but there was no extreme contrast here with the policy followed in the years immediately prior to Labour's victory. The period does however distinguish itself sufficiently from what came before and what was to come later by reason of the two pieces of legislation already mentioned.

A final period begins with the return of the Conservatives to power following the 1970 elections. The Heath Government's Housing (Finance) Act of 1972 completely remodelled the finance of council housing both past and future. This Act also contained important changes for the privately rented sector, which was in future to benefit from a housing allowance, and measures were also taken to raise the level of rents in both private and publicly owned property. The above description gives no idea of the significance of the Conservative legislation but, as has already been pointed out, what is said here is only intended to outline the pattern of policy development and in no way constitutes a description of policy.

## Conclusion

It is hoped that sufficient has been said in this chapter to give some idea of the contrast in policy development patterns that one may observe as between Britain and France. Emphasis has naturally been laid on the change from one period to another in the British case and the continuity in the French. In following this course it is not intended to suggest that there have not been some elements of stability in the British system and some innovations in France. Examples of both of these are not hard to find and ought to be mentioned here. In Britain, for example, the Building Societies continue to operate and to expand their activities on very much the same basis as they have always done. They continue to operate as non profit-making societies which collect liquid savings from a large number of individual savers which they channel into loans for the owner-occupier. The fortunes of the Societies have been hardly touched by the violent political storms which have swept through other areas of housing policy. Remarkably, the element of local discretion in the selection of tenants has also remained a constant feature of the council sector.

There are also some innovations which must be mentioned in order not to exaggerate the picture of continuity which has been given of French policy. There has been an attempt, for example, to develop in France a private system which will provide loans for the purchase of housing at market rates on the security of mortgages. It will be remembered that the bulk of French housing for sale relies for at least part of its financing on the *Crédit Foncier* which lends at below the market rate and therefore receives government assistance. These efforts have in recent years been crowned with at least partial success although the development of this activity has been difficult to bring about and the privately financed and totally unsubsidized sector of French housing still remains small in relation to that of Britain or other advanced industrial countries [8]. There have also been attempts in France to create a profit-making rental sector to supplement the HLMs but these have not been successful except on a very modest scale [9].

By way of conclusion, it is convenient to underline the contrast which has been described between the French and British patterns of policy development. In the first case it is possible to point to three seminal statutes, each associated with its sector of housing, which, taken together have formed the foundations for all post-war French housing policy. It may seem astonishing to those more familiar with British housing policy but it is no exaggeration to say that it is impossible to point to any legislation since 1950 which has fundamentally reoriented housing policy. Our account of British policy on the other hand, makes it clear that there are in this case many such examples. In Britain, when policy is changed, the change often extends to more than one sector. In France, the level of interaction between sectors is always low, and such incremental development as does take place is in line with the previously established pattern of development peculiar to each sector. But the contrast is not only one of gradual change as opposed to frequent oscillations. It is important also to remember that the oscillations in British policy are obviously linked to events and changes in the wider political arena. In France it is much more difficult to find such links even at times of great political upheavals. Perhaps one should not expect the transition from the Fourth to the Fifth Republic in 1958 to give rise to changes in housing policy, because these events turned mainly on colonial issues. But, in fact, from the start, there were important changes in the management of the economy, with a large devaluation and reductions in tariffs, but the new Gaullist broom left housing policy untouched. In raising the question of the relationship between political events and housing policy, however, we are moving from description to explanation, and we are not equipped to make this jump until we have examined policy, and its political convert, in greater detail.

*References*

1. A. Sauvy (ed.), *Histoire économique de la France entre les deux guerres* (Ed. Fayard, 1972), Vol. III, chapter IV.

2. *See* C. Alphandéry, *Les prêts hypothécaires* (P.U.F., collection 'Que sais-je?', No. 1326, 1968), chapter II, and Pierre Champion, *Le Crédit Foncier de France* (Editions de l'Epargne, 1966).

3. D.V. Donnison, *Housing policy since the war, Occasional papers on Social Administration*, No. 1 (Codicote Press, 1960), pp. 11–19.

4. *See* Table II.

5. H. Macmillan, *Tides of Fortune 1945–55* (Macmillan & Co., 1969), chapter XII, pp. 352–8.

6. M.J. Barnett, *The politics of legislation: The Rent Act of 1957* (Weidenfeld & Nicolson, 1969), chapter II, pp. 22–9.

7. *Housing in England and Wales*, Cmnd. 1290 (H.M.S.O., Feb. 1961).

8. *Le Financement du Logement en France et à l'Etranger* (P.U.F., Editions Centre d'Information et d'Etude du Crédit, 1966), p. 13; *Le Monde*, 20 March 1973.

9. *See* chapter IV.

# PART II

# The Privately Rented Sector

# Introduction

In accordance with the plan set out in chapter I, the aim here will be to examine the political characteristics which are proper to the privately rented sector. Such an examination is essential in order to render the later discussion of French and British policies intelligible and comparable.

Little needs to be said by way of explanation of the relation of landlord to tenant since this form of housing provision is a commonplace of life in all advanced industrial nations. The legal ownership of the property rests with the landlord but its use is the tenant's in exchange for regular payment. There are three areas of conflict inherent in this relation although the first two far outweigh the third in importance. Inevitably, the two matters of vital concern to both parties are the possible control of rent levels, as a result of government intervention, and the degree of security to which the tenant is entitled. The third matter of concern is the responsibility for repairs. But what gives this sector its peculiar political character is the sharpness and directness of conflict between two clearly defined groups, landlords and tenants. Although this chapter is concerned only with the privately rented sector, it is necessary, in order to understand what is meant by the directness and sharpness referred to, to draw some comparisons between sectors.

In the public sphere, there are inevitable conflicts between different groups with respect to the allocation of newly built housing. A further conflict turns around the proportion of new building to take place within the public sector. The latter conflict will bring into opposition those who believe their future accommodation will be as tenants of public housing and those who believe that their means allow them to rely for accommodation on the private market. In a sense, however, the conflicts just described are indirect as compared with those that arise between landlord and tenant, and it is necessary here to explain more fully what is meant by direct and indirect. The directness arises from the fact that the conflict expresses itself not only at the national level at which decisions are taken affecting landlords and tenants in Britain and France but also at the local personal level in day-to-day dealings between a landlord and his tenant. To put things at their most blunt, when the landlord demands and receives an increased rent, provided that the tenant's income remains constant, he will suffer a diminution of his real standard of living. The question of distribution of income between landlords and tenants is therefore directly posed. There will also probably be person-to-person conflicts over questions of repair. Since the landlord will normally be liable to pay for repairs, he will tend to minimize the necessity for carrying them out, and on the other hand, the tenant, who will benefit from the improved standard of accommodation provided by repair, will naturally tend to demand all that he feels he can obtain.

All that is said here is, of course, common sense, but it is well to bear in mind that this face-to-face confrontation between individuals who are clearly identified with different groups which themselves are in conflict at a higher level is not by any means always present in political conflict. It is not present, for example, in the case of the conflict between the tenant of publicly rented accommodation and the taxpayer, the size of whose contribution in the form of a housing subsidy, may partly determine the amount of rent which the tenant has to pay. The tenant of public housing and taxpayer may be more or less aware of the conflict existing between them in this matter, but they are not obliged to meet face to face. This peculiar quality of the conflict endemic to the privately rented sector should always be borne in mind when considering policy in this area. The existence of conflict between groups at the national level combined with conflict of the same sort between individuals at the local personal level gives rise to some parallel between the conflicts to be observed between landlord and tenant and those between employer and worker. In both cases one may observe conflict of an abstract nature at the level of government decision combined with conflict which may be more personal at the local level, either between individuals or at least between small groups who are personally well known to each other.

The parallel between employer/worker and landlord/tenant conflict is illuminating in other ways. If the government has no incomes policy and if there is also a general expectation that no such policy is likely to be adopted in the near future, worker/employer conflict at the national level will lose a great deal of its strictly political aspect. Conflict will take place either sector by sector or plant by plant and government will be less directly involved. Such was the case before government assumed the role of manager of the national economy, and such was the case to an even greater degree before government became involved in rent control. Before 1914 in Britain and France, there was no expectation that government might intervene in any way in the fixing of rents. This state of affairs came to an end with the 1914–18 war when national legislation was adopted in both countries to deal with the crisis thus created. Control has proved permanent in one form or another and in consequence so has the conflict at two levels just described.

In current French politics there is evidence in the area of rent control of the importance of the thesis just stated as to the personal and national character of conflict in this field. The French privately rented sector may be subdivided into two additional sectors, one in which rents are still nationally controlled and another in which rents are free. It is notable that political controversy rages very much more vigorously around the controlled sector despite the fact that it is less important numerically and continually decreasing in size. One naturally asks why conflict has been more acute and political where control of rent levels exists than in a free market. The explanation does not lie in the acuteness of the problem posed by rent to tenants in each sector. As one would expect, rents are much lower in the controlled sector. Nor does the explanation lie in the nature of tenants' organizations. One might suppose that since each sector has to some extent its own particular problems, there would be organizations specific to each sector. Such is not the case, for both the principal French tenants' organizations recruit their membership not only from the controlled and free private sectors but also from among tenants of publicly owned accommodation.

I would suggest that the explanation lies in the two-level nature of conflict which exists only in the controlled sector. Although both tenants' organizations demand the imposition of some form of control in the free sector, they understand that there is no chance whatsoever of the present Government agreeing to this. As far as the other sector is concerned, the Government has failed, despite considerable effort, to disentangle itself from the conflict and at present is obliged to fix the size and nature of increases in decrees which are published annually in June. The drafting of these decrees is a joint responsibility of the Minister of Finance and the Minister for Housing and Development, and the decision as to the size of the increases is discretionary. It is natural that a good deal of agitation should centre around these decisions since there are important short-term gains to be made from the tenants' point of view.

We have concentrated in our discussion of the political character of this housing sector so far entirely on the question of rent levels. This is normally the most important question at issue between landlord and tenant but should not be allowed to obscure the other vital matter of contention: security of tenure. When rent control was first imposed, the tenant was also necessarily accorded security of tenure. What is meant by this expression normally is that, provided the tenant pays his rent, the landlord cannot evict him. This situation contrasts strongly with the position at common law prior to the imposition of rent controls. In such a situation, unless the tenant has the benefit of a lease of a number of years, the landlord will normally be able to give notice to his tenant and evict him fairly rapidly at his own discretion. The acquisition of security of tenure therefore frees the tenant from subjection to the landlord's discretion. The description of the situation in legal terms does, however, exaggerate somewhat the precariousness of the tenant's position. A landlord will probably regard his property as an investment and will therefore normally have no reason to evict his tenant provided that the rent is paid.

One should understand why rent controls and the award of security of tenure of tenants are necessarily linked. If the discretion to evict tenants had been left with the landlord, it might have been used by him as a means of pressure to obtain a higher rent. If controls therefore are to be effective, security of tenure must be given as well as the right to a fixed rent and the decision on rent necessarily implies the decision on security of tenure.

The necessary link between these two tenant demands brings out once again the peculiar character of political conflict in this area. When governments were first obliged by circumstances to adopt policies more favourable to the tenant interest, they were not able to do so in an incremental fashion. The tenant demands for fixed rents and security of tenure had both to be granted at one stroke, and it seemed for the future that, if the government wished to restore the market processes in the fixing of rents, it would also be obliged to deprive the tenants of their acquired security of tenure. We see, therefore, in this sector, fundamental characteristics which tend to render extremely difficult the arrangement of any compromise and the balancing thereby of one interest against another.

In fact this seeming dilemma of government intervention is not quite as inescapable as it at first appears. One means of escape is the awarding of a limited degree of security of tenure, coupled with free negotiations of rent. One may envisage, for example, a provision requiring the landlord to grant a lease of a minimum of three years for all lettings. Such a situation is somewhat more favourable to the tenant than a condition of total lack of security, for once a rent has been agreed and the lease signed, he enjoys security of tenure and a fixed rent for at least three years.

We see here then a problem which has been posed historically in terms of the opposition of two extremes. On the one hand, there is the capitalist system in which rent is determined according to market conditions and the tenant has virtually no security of tenure at least at law, and on the other hand, the post–1914 situation of a total freeze on rents coupled with security of tenure. In Britain, at least until the Rent Act of 1965, it has appeared difficult to escape from the choice posed by the two extremes. In France the escape from this dilemma through the means of a limited security of tenure given to the tenant, coupled with rent freely negotiated, has been introduced more rapidly and has been more widely developed. Such a solution was envisaged as early as 1959 by M. Sudreau, General de Gaulle's first housing minister, in his discussions in that year with the Economic and Social Council [1].

When we come in this section to examine rent policies in our two countries, we shall observe that the compromise solution of limited security of tenure which appeared more rapidly in France is paralleled by a more flexible system of rent control which also sought to escape the dilemma of the two extremes from which the British Government found it so hard to escape. In both the matter of rent level and that of security of tenure, the French have reached this middle ground by a slow evolution from the situation of rent freeze and total security whereas the British have taken a more painful and oscillating route in order to arrive at somewhat similar final solutions. It will be noted that we have here in the field of rent control an example of the general contrast which was outlined in chapter II. The French have reached the existing position in this sector by way of a very slow incremental development of policy in one maintained direction. This pattern contrasts strongly with the lurches in first one and then the other direction which we observe in the British Rent Acts of 1957 and 1965.

Attention has so far been concentrated on the peculiar political features of this sector of housing policy. It is important however to supplement such a general discussion with a historical perspective, because although the sector gives rise naturally to acute conflict, such conflict varies in its sharpness according to circumstances. It is to this task, therefore, that we now turn.

## References

1. *Le Monde*, 16 and 22 December 1959.

# IV

# The Privately Rented Sector: France

## 1 *The 1948 Rent Act and its origins*

French policy in this sector is dominated by the Rent Act of 1948 which has remained in force ever since. It seems advisable therefore to familiarize the reader with the time-table of events surrounding the preparation and passage of this Act before examining this legislation in greater detail since this chapter will be dominated by it. The intention to promote important new legislation in this field was first made public as early as February 1947, during the Ramadier Ministry [1]. This, it will be noted, was just prior to the expulsion of the Communists from the then tripartite government. The responsibility for the early work on the preparation of the Bill seems to have been that of M. André Marie (Radical Socialist), *Garde des Sceaux*. In principle, the Bill was the joint concern of the Minister of Justice and the Minister for War Damage and Reconstruction, but since the latter was Charles Tillon (Communist), it seems probable that his department was not associated with drafting, at least not at this stage. In any case, the terms of the Bill, as later presented to the Assembly were in no way affected by the root and branch Communist opposition to the Bill.

There was some delay between the Government's first declaration of intention to legislate and the final examination of the Bill by the National Assembly and Economic Council [2]. The period between the Bill's publication and its parliamentary consideration saw the change from the tripartism of the immediate post-war years to a series of Third Force governments, but changes of government and of personnel do not seem to have had any serious effect either on the Bill or its passage. Delays resulted rather from pressure of other business and once serious consideration of the legislation began, the rate of progress was satisfactory. The Bill was discussed during the spring and summer of 1948, promulgated in September and henceforth referred to as the Act of the 1st of September 1948. The first decrees of application necessary for the working of the Act were published in December and the first rent increases consequent upon the legislation took place in January 1949. The preparation and passage of the legislation covered the periods of the Governments headed by Paul Ramadier (SFIO), Robert Schuman (MRP), and André Marie (Radical Socialist). The most important personalities involved with the legislation were M. H.L. Grimaud (MRP), deputy and *rapporteur* of the Committee on War Damage and Reconstruction, who stoutly defended the Bill throughout the Assembly discussions, and M. Eugène Claudius-Petit (UDSR), who became the Minister for Reconstruction and Town Planning in September 1948 and was responsible for the application of the Act. His influence on initial practice was vital since he continued to hold this post until January 1953.

There is no question that the problem of excessively low rents was one of the most thorny economic and social problems with which the early post-war governments were faced. One may give some idea of the state of affairs which had been produced by a rigid system of rent control and rapid inflation if one refers to a study carried out by the National Institute for Statistical and Economic Studies which found that, in January 1949, rent represented an average of 1.5 per cent of the family budget of a family of four living in the Paris region with one earner [3]. When the pre-1948 system is described as rigid, this term is used advisedly. Despite emergency legislation to apply across-the-board percentage increases between 1945 and 1948, it is clear that rent had fallen as a percentage of the family budget regularly since the imposition of control in 1914 [4]. The fact that it was necessary to have recourse to such exceptional procedures during this period is evidence of the gravity of the situation. The same point is underlined by the Government's assessment of the seriousness of the problem: 'Si l'on considère en effet le pourcentage modeste, ridicule parfois qu'occupe le loyer dans le budget familial, eu égard à la place qu'il tenait dans les budgets d'avantguerre ou qu'il tient encore aujourd'hui dans les budgets étrangers, la plus élémentaire justice exige que son montant en soit relevé' [5]. The appreciation of the exact character of the problems created by these low rents depends very much on the political view adopted. The level of rents was so widely recognized as exceptionally low that, in principle at least, all parties, from the Communists on the Left to the Independents on the

Right, were agreed that they must be raised. This did not mean however that there was any agreement on how this could be done. There are innumerable problems which are generally associated with very low rents. A political problem is first created by the claim in equity of the landlord who finds it unacceptable that the price which he is able by law to demand for the service he is providing is limited and therefore he is prevented from taking the action necessary to counteract the progress of inflation and maintain the real value of his rental income. A different problem is created by the inability of landlords to maintain their property satisfactorily. There may also be a tendency for mobility within the housing stock to decline and for a certain degree of maldistribution of available housing space to be created. Finally, as long as rents remain generally low, it will be difficult for investors in housing for rent to obtain a return which they consider satisfactory and any government which wishes to encourage such investment will be obliged to avoid excessively low rents [6].

All of these arguments were to be heard in France in the early post-war period but some were of greater importance than others. The claim of the landlord that he should be treated on a par with other sections of the community and allowed to charge the market price for his services remained a cry in the wilderness. It must be remembered that this was a time when the climate of political opinion was very unfavourable to any demand which might be associated with the Right. The general election of 1946 had produced a National Assembly, three quarters of whose members belonged either to the Socialist or Communist parties on the Left, or the Christian Democratic MRP of the Centre. All sections of political opinion recognized that the general decontrol of rents, which is what the landlords would have liked, was quite impossible in the prevailing conditions of extreme shortage. Decontrol would, it was thought, lead to violent social conflict and an unthinkable level of rents. The argument concerning the maldistribution of available space was somewhat academic since all observers recognized that however effectively available housing was distributed, the overall shortage would remain. As far as the argument concerning investment in housing was concerned, this was certainly a factor which proved decisive for many politicians of the Centre and Right. They saw no other means of providing the needed accommodation and were therefore convinced that a considerable rise in rent levels was necessary if a start was to be made on building the houses which the country so badly needed. As far as the Left of the political spectrum was concerned, the most important argument was that concerning repairs. It was generally admitted, at least by Socialist and MRP deputies, that rents had fallen to such a low level that landlords could not be reasonably expected to maintain a good level of repair.

But, as we have indicated, the real problem arose when one moved from the simple first step of recognizing that rents must be raised to the further stage of discussing how this was to be done. One may conveniently examine the political difficulties with which the governments of this period were confronted by describing political attitudes towards the rent problem, beginning with the extreme Left.

It has already been pointed out, and this is a fact which should not be lost sight of, that the Communist Party accepted the desirability in principle of higher rents. The Communist analysis of the rent problem was designed to show that the real conflict of interest existed between capitalist and worker rather than between landlord and tenant. In pursuit of this thesis they argued that, if the landlord was to receive the higher rent to which he was entitled, wages would have to be raised. The logical consequence of this analysis was that landlords and tenants should unite against the capitalists in order to obtain, on behalf of the workers, the wage increases necessary to permit the worker to pay a reasonable rent. The practical outcome of such an attitude was that, since the wage increases demanded by the Communists were not forthcoming, they opposed the rent increases which were a part of the suggested legislation [7]. In accordance with this attitude, they opposed the legislation throughout its passage and voted against its adoption in isolation from all other parties [8]. At no time in the post-war period has the French Communist Party advocated the nationalization of private residential property, and the party has always envisaged, even in the long term, the continuation of the system of landlord and tenant and that of owner-occupation [9]. At no time has any party on the French Left advocated a policy in any way comparable to the Labour Party policy of the municipalization of privately rented property [10].

In the nature of things the attitude of the Socialist Party was less clear-cut. The party were at one with the Communists in opposing any measures of nationalization but where they differed strongly from their colleagues on the Left was in their willingness to consider the housing problem in isolation from other economic and social questions. The consequence of this approach was that they were willing to accept rent increases that were not necessarily linked to wage increases. They stressed however that, though rents in general might need to rise substantially, the worker must be protected against a too rapid rise and that therefore some account should be taken of the possible hardship to individuals which would result from such rent increases. Like the Communists, and unlike those to their Right, the Socialists were agreed that security of tenure was a fundamental right which ought to be extended to all tenants throughout France without exception [11]. The Socialists could not agree with their MRP colleagues on the manner in which rent increases were to be calculated. The system suggested by the government when the bill first became public, and also embodied in the legislation as finally adopted, was known as the system of the *surface corrigée* (weighted surface area system). The technicalities of this system will be explained in greater detail later but the important aspect of it for the Socialists was that it imposed increases whose size varied considerably from dwelling to dwelling. This occurred simply because the new law aimed to remove existing anomalies and fix rents on the basis of totally new criteria, and expressly refused to take account of the rents previously demanded for particular dwellings. The Socialists found the differences in the size of the increases produced by the new system unacceptable and they therefore demanded that, if the weighted surface area system was to be adopted and an attempt made to wipe the slate clean and forget entirely previously charged rents, a ceiling should be imposed of a maximum increase of 33 per cent in any individual case. In asking for such a ceiling, they were attempting to deal with the problem of some families being asked to support much greater increases than others. In the process they were, however, inevitably perpetuating existing inequities and delaying the moment at which a totally new system of rent control could be established on a rational basis [12].

Coming to the discussion of the MRP, we arrive at the most important stage in our examination of political attitudes towards the problem of rent control since this party whole-heartedly supported the bill and was throughout its most devoted defender. With respect to political and economic policy this was a period in which the MRP emphasized its centre position. The party rejected with equal fervour the capitalist and socialist solutions to economic and social problems, finding the inequalities and inhumanity of capitalism as unacceptable as the loss of liberty which they regarded as inherent in the socialist approach [13]. These may seem extremely abstract conceptions by means of which to approach the very concrete problem of rent control but the position which the party adopted accurately reflected its unwillingness in principle to adopt either the capitalist or socialist solutions. The socialist solution which the MRP rejected (although, as we have seen, it was not advocated by either Socialist or Communist parties), was nationalization and the total dissociation of rent levels from the character of the service provided. Their rejection of the capitalist approach was more important since a system of freely negotiated rents had existed in France prior to 1914 and there were many landlords, and a few deputies among the parties of the Right, who saw the long-term objective as a return to such a situation. The MRP did not envisage such a final liberation of rent even in the long term. But when we have explained the solutions which the Christian Democrats rejected, it remains to describe the position which they actually took up.

In the party's view the rent demanded ought to represent the value of the service provided [14]. At first sight the enunciation of this principle does not seem to answer any of the important questions. How, for example, is the value of the service to be measured in the absence of any market considerations? But the principle of payment for the service provided does have certain important implications. It implies first of all that identical dwellings command the same rent, that is to say that rent depends upon the physical character of the dwelling in question and not upon conditions in the local housing market. The principle also implies that rent be fixed with reference to the dwelling rented and not with reference to the individual circumstances of the occupying family. As to the absolute level of rent to be permitted, this was to be calculated in order to allow the landlord to meet his repair and fiscal obligations and insurance, and to have over a small return on his initial investment. One may well ask in what way the small return which the landlord was to be permitted differed from profit. The answer would seem to be that the return would be fixed by the minister and would therefore not vary with local market conditions and also that it would be fixed at a modest level in relation to normal levels of profit. The minister's decrees of application established a theoretical return of one per cent on a landlord's investment although this figure bore no relation to any actual calculable return [15].

Outside the three major parties so far discussed there was no clearly defined view on social and economic questions, opinions varying from individual to individual rather than according to party affiliation. As already pointed out, there was no significant body of political opinion which demanded at this time a return to a free rent market.

But the views of many Radical Socialist, UDSR and other deputies to the right of the MRP are reflected in proposals for legislation tabled by Edgar Faure (Radical Socialist) and signed by several of his colleagues on the moderate Right [16]. What M. Faure demanded, and what the Government was unwilling to grant, was some guarantee to the landlord of the size of the immediate rent increase in the new legislation. The Government was unwilling to grant this demand because it preferred to leave the calculation of this increase to the decrees of application. M. Faure and his colleagues also demanded with respect to security of tenure, that some distinction be introduced into the legislation between town and country in order to allow the application of a more liberal regime for the rural communes. Whereas the Government made no concessions to its critics on the right with respect to rent levels, some modification in the legislation was permitted on the question of security of tenure so as not to grant such security to tenants in communes of fewer than four thousand inhabitants provided also that such communes had not experienced an increase in population of more than five per cent between the two most recent censuses. These rural areas were excluded from the operation of the Act because it was thought that there was a less acute shortage here, and that tenants were consequently in less danger of eviction.

The political difficulties with which the Government was confronted have now been described and we are in a position to examine the character of the legislation adopted and to come to some assessment as to the manner in which political problems were resolved. As indicated earlier, the essential feature of the Bill was the system of the *surface corrigée* (weighted surface system). The MRP remained throughout a partisan of this system of rent calculation, and it formed part of the original government draft and of the legislation as finally adopted. The object of the weighted surface area system was to assess on an objective basis the value of the service provided for the occupant of every dwelling in the country. For this purpose all dwellings were placed in categories which corresponded to the quality of the dwelling and hence of the service. There were four principal categories and an additional superior and exceptional category for buildings of special architectural or historic value. The most important of the categories, 2 and 3, were further subdivided in order to improve the precision of classification. The legislation provided that, by decree of application, the minister would fix the rent per square metre of floor area provided for each category. In order to calculate therefore the rent appropriate for a particular dwelling, it was simply necessary to ascertain the dwelling's category, measure its surface area, and then make the necessary multiplication. One element of refinement was added to the calculation in the form of what were termed the *équivalents superficiels* (surface area equivalents). These provided that certain facilities, such as a fixed bath or hot running water, might be considered as equivalent to, for example, two or three square metres of floor space. The surface area of a dwelling for the purposes of rent calculation might therefore be greater than its actual measured floor area. The essential feature of this system was that it wiped the slate clean of any reference to previously demanded rents and calculated the new rents on a universally applied formula. Rent regulation systems in general must choose between the alternatives of supervised negotiation and imposed calculated rents. The French system clearly opted for the latter of these two alternatives [17].

It becomes clear then that if one wishes to know the rent which a landlord might legally demand for a dwelling from 1st January 1949 onwards, the key element is the rent per square metre fixed by the minister in the decrees of application. Naturally the Act laid down principles of payment for service rendered, the minister was to enter into negotiation with the construction industry and the landlords, and arrive at estimates of repair costs, costs to landlords resulting from the taxation on the income from their rented property, and the cost of new construction. He was then to add the return of one per cent and fix the rent per square metre accordingly. But the figure thus arrived at for any particular dwelling, referred to as the *valeur locative* (rental value), was thought too high to be immediately applicable. Consequently the legislation also provided that an initial rent would be fixed by the minister and that twenty per cent increases would be operated at six-monthly intervals, beginning in 1949, until, after a period of six years, the *valeur locative* was reached.

An obvious danger to the scheme of rent increases envisaged in the legislation was that inflation would continue and that as a consequence the initially calculated *valeur locative* would soon be out of date and the twenty per cent six-monthly increases would lose much of their effect. Some attempts were consequently made during the Bill's passage to introduce into the calculation an element which would take account of increases in wages and therefore ability to pay. M. Claudius-Petit, later to become minister, was in fact personally responsible for one such attempt to amend the legislation in this direction [18]. The outcome of these efforts did not affect substantially the manner in which the legislation was applied since the minister was in no way obliged to apply the formulae of indexing which were suggested in the Act. As we shall see when we come to examine application, the element of indexing was never effective.

The essential provisions of the Act are the weighted surface area principle and the methods for calculating the *valeur locative*. The Act itself deals with a great many other matters but these comprise essentially a codification, with some modifications, of existing landlord and tenant law. This codification does not concern us here. But it should be borne in mind that, since a universal system of rent control had been adopted, all tenants of unfurnished properties were awarded total security of tenure. There was some provision in the Act for the minister to use his decree powers in order to take some communes out of the scope of the Act but at the time of the Act's passage no one envisaged the use of the powers in either the short or the medium term.

We are now in a position to ask ourselves how it was that the Fourth Republic was able to take such decisive and comprehensive action in tackling the problem of rent control. It should not be forgotten that at the time during which the Bill was being considered, 1947 and especially the spring and summer of 1948, the Third Force coalitions were being threatened from both sides. From the Left there was a threat from the Communist Party which was ready apparently to use the strike for revolutionary ends. On the Right the RPF Gaullist Party had been formed and was gaining large support in the country as the local election results of October 1947 witnessed. It was paradoxical that it was in fact the seriousness of the problem which assisted greatly in its resolution. The fact that rents had sunk to such a low level convinced everyone that some means had to be found for raising them. *Le Monde* commented in January 1947: 'De l'extrême droite à l'extrême gauche tous les députés qui ont tant soit peu étudié la question sont convaincus qu'il faudrait revaloriser les loyers' [19]. We have already discussed the limitations of this agreement but the fact that it was an agreement only in principle and did not cover either the means or the extent of permissible increases does not take away from its significance. The importance of even an agreement in principle is particularly well borne out if one makes the comparison between the French and British situations. In the immediate post-war period in Britain, where rents had been much less seriously eroded by inflation, there existed no agreement even in principle that they should be raised or freed in any way.

Another important element in the explanation of the successful passage of this legislation was certainly its essentially compromise and centrist character. In the debate which preceded the final vote, M. Dominjon, speaking on behalf of the MRP, defended the Act and explained how it had been necessary in order to obtain passage, to make concessions both to Right and Left [20]. In order to appease criticism from the Right, the concession already referred to, concerning the absence of security of tenure in the smaller rural communes, had been granted. With respect to criticisms coming from the Socialist Party, the sponsors of the Bill had agreed to amendments of articles 18, 19 and 20 which defined the exact limits of the landlord's right, in exceptional circumstances, to take back the property for his own use or for the use of members of his family. In order to save the Bill and gain Socialist abstention on the final vote, the MRP were willing to make some concessions on these articles and thus limit the freedom of the landlord more strictly than had been originally intended. In addition to these concessions, the basic principles of the Bill were such as to be at least acceptable to the Socialists and to offer those to the right of the MRP some possibility of immediate, and in the long run substantial rent increases.

But perhaps one of the most important elements which must be taken into account in explaining the successful passage of the legislation was that of delegation. As has already been explained, the precise rent increase which would be applicable in January 1949 could not be determined from an examination of the act which, on this subject, confined itself to principles. This meant that deputies were able to vote in support of the Bill knowing that the minister would have to bear the final responsibility for the size of the increases when they were actually applied and their unpopularity had made itself felt. This may seem a harsh criticism of the behaviour of deputies but in the light of the events of the spring of 1949, described later in this chapter, it seems justifiable. The Bill was finally adopted by the National Assembly on 25th June 1948 by a vote of 261 to 192. The only party to vote against the Bill was the Communist Party. The Socialists abstained and the MRP and the majority of deputies further to the Right supported the legislation [21].

Considerable attention has been paid to the explanation of the successful passage of the Rent Act of 1948, both because it is a keystone of the French housing system, and therefore its political origins are vital to this study, and also because it modifies considerably our estimate of the political system of the Fourth Republic and its capacity for dealing with serious economic and social problems. One is accustomed to accounts of this period which stress *immobilisme* and the inability of governments to take necessary but unpleasant decisions. It is also often alleged that the constantly changing coalitions of this period made continuity of policy extremely difficult to achieve and tended to encourage compromise short-term and palliative measures. Such was certainly the case with respect to the rent problem in 1946 and 1947 but long-term work on the preparation of the Rent Act was taking place during these years and the mechanisms of compromise, which in other circumstances might have stultified government action, succeeded on this occasion in producing a workable and reasonable system of flexible rent controls which balanced the interests of the tenants against those of the landlords and, whilst maintaining a system of controlled rents, permitted those rents to be raised gradually. Total hostility from the Communist Party, government instability, the vulnerability of ministers to pressures coming from the rank-and-file members of their own parties; all these were not sufficient either to obstruct the act's passage or to amend it so as to render it unworkable.

II *The application of the Rent Act 1948–58*

With the coming into force of this new legislation on 1st January 1949 we move into a new era in the politics of the privately rented sector. There is a clear division between the character of political problems as they presented themselves until this time and the character of the politics of rent control as they may be observed from 1949 onwards. The disagreement over fundamentals which we have just described was now at an end. A framework had been laid down and such was its solidity that no political party, the Communists excepted, called it into question at any time between 1949 and the present day. It is therefore legitimate, in what remains of this chapter, to abandon to some extent the chronological approach which has so far proved appropriate, and to look instead for the general characteristics of the politics of this whole period. Certainly there are changes and developments, particularly during the 1960s, but in my view these are not such as to prevent us from seeing the period as a whole.

From 1949 onwards, one observes clearly the slow and incremental pattern of policy development which was described in chapter II. The nature of conflict is also quite different. Whereas the important divisions had previously been vertical, between different political groups represented in the Assembly, the important cleavage now was to be horizontal, between the government on the one hand and the public on the other. This conflict between government and people was sometimes mirrored in the conflict between the responsible minister and the National Assembly. The basic factor was now the willingness and the capacity of the government to fly in the face of popular sentiment which naturally favoured continued security of tenure and minimum rents. It must be remembered that the Government was now, under the terms of the Act, engaged on a process of steadily raising rent levels. Every six months the public was forcefully reminded of this governmental responsibility when it was called upon to pay a considerably higher rent. In the early years of the Act's application, over six million dwellings fell within its scope and consequently a majority of the population was directly affected either as landlord or tenant [22]. Common sense suggests that the general public will normally be hostile to rent increases and even more to the relaxation of controls since there are bound to be very many more tenants than landlords in the population at large. This reasoning is supported by the findings of a public opinion poll of 1966 which suggested that 57 per cent of the public were willing to say that rent control was a good thing as against only 22 per cent who held the contrary view [23].

Public hostility to rent increases and popular support for the strict maintenance of rent control remained throughout the succeeding years the most important constant element in the politics of this sector. Much of the interest in policy development therefore lies in discovering to what extent different governments or ministers feel that they can challenge this popular sentiment. All the ministers who have held office and responsibility for this sector since 1949 have been favourable to the policy of higher rents in the controlled sector with, as a long-term aim, the raising of rents in the controlled sector up to the level pertaining in the free sector. The success of ministers in pursuit of this policy may be gauged in two ways. Firstly by the extent of the rise in rents which they were able to bring about and secondly, at least after August 1953, the extent to which they were able to reduce the scope of the 1948 Law so as thus to diminish the size of the controlled sector and increase the size of the free sector not subject to the Law. The fact that all ministers shared the aim of increased rents and that most of them who held office after August 1953 were also intent on reducing the extent of control as soon as practicable, again underlines the unity of the post-1949 period.

The minister responsible from September 1948 to January 1953 was M. Eugéne Claudius-Petit (UDSR). He stated his interpretation of the 1948 Rent Act and declared his strong support for the principles embodied in it in an important press conference in November 1948 [24]. In his view, low rents in France were a major cause of the housing problem, and he underlined this by pointing out that much higher rents were being paid in Britain and Holland. Only when this difference in rent levels was abolished by raising French rents, would there be any hope of improvement. Two months later a storm broke over him as the first rent increases were applied. These increases were dependent on the terms of the decrees of application which M. Claudius-Petit published in December 1948 [25]. It is not possible to give any indication of their size since, as already explained, the basis for fixing rents was totally changed and the amount of increase varied widely from case to case.

But before describing the storm of protest of January and February 1949, it is worth pausing to examine the way in which M. Claudius-Petit exercised the discretion which was granted him with respect to the fixing of initial rent levels. Rent levels per square metre were fixed by the Decrees of the 10th December 1948. The minister was faced with a real technical problem in that he was obliged, in consultation with the interests affected, to calculate construction and repair costs at a time when there was very little construction taking place and when therefore costs could not be regarded as typical of what might be expected when the construction industry had expanded to a more normal level of activity. In response to this technical difficulty, a decision was taken to assume that construction costs would fall substantially in the coming years and therefore costs for the purposes of the rent calculation were taken to be well below those which were regarded as current at the time of calculation. Needless to say, the expected fall in construction costs failed to materialize. Investigations carried out in 1951 and 1952 showed that the *valeurs locatives* fixed by the minister ought to have been multiplied by 2.5 if they were to be made more realistic [26].

But this forced optimism concerning construction costs was not the only way in which the minister gave evidence of the political pressures on him to produce the smallest possible rent increases. His technical advisers appear to have suggested to him that the *valeur locative* could be realistically fixed at a level of 6.25 per cent of construction costs. The minister found that the rents that would have been implied by this figure were unacceptable and he therefore fixed the *valeur locative* on the basis of a 4.25 gross return to the landlord [27]. Nor was any explicit provisions made in the 1948 Rent Act for revising the *valeur locative* upwards if construction costs should rise. The circumstances surrounding the drafting of the December Decrees give ample evidence that the minister already felt himself in some difficulty and the events of early 1949 were destined to confirm this impression.

The Communists were incensed that rent increases were taking place at a time when the Government was tightening its control over salaries and prices. The CGT, the Communist-dominated trade union federation, acting through their representatives in the Economic Council, voiced the Party's complaints as early as November 1948, that is to say, before the final text of the decrees of application was published [28]. By January 1949 agitation had become much more widespread and *Le Peuple* was calling for industrial action in order to obtain the wage increases necessary to pay the higher rents [29].

The Socialists also emphasized the relation between wages and rents but they were willing to allow for some rent increases without compensation in the form of higher wages. Their principal line of action during the agitation of January and February was to resurrect the demands which they had made, unsuccessfully, during the Act's passage for the imposition of a maximum percentage rent increase in any individual case. A Socialist proposal to this effect was discussed by the *Commission de la Justice* during January but the Committee rejected it [30]. The Communist deputies would not support the Socialist proposal because they were hostile to any increase in rents without proportionate wage rises. The MRP too would not vote with the Socialists. They tried to support the minister in his wish to maintain unchanged the increases resulting from the Decrees of December.

But even the MRP, who were most sympathetic to the minister's position, felt that some concessions would have to be granted in order to assuage the apparently widespread popular discontent. They felt that some modification in the detail of the calculation could be introduced so as to favour the lower categories of dwelling and also that the minister could widen the terms of eligibility for the housing allowance which had been created by the Act [31]. They asked that the allowance be available to all those earning up to 25% above the *salaire de base*.

What was notable in the agitation of January 1949, and also in the politics of the privately rented sector in France more generally, was that the criticism levelled at legislation raising rents came not only from those sections of political opinion that one would expect to be naturally sympathetic to the tenant interest, but from both Centre and Right as well, thus underlining what had already been said about the horizontal rather than vertical divisions separating the two opposed camps on this issue. For example, the Act was criticised during January and February in the conservative national daily *Le Figaro* and the PRL, a party of the traditional Right, tabled a proposal to amend the Act late in January [32]. It is true that the PRL's demands related to security of tenure rather than the size of rent increases. As a party of the Right, they were naturally inclined to accept the necessity for higher rents but such was the unpopularity of the Act that they appear to have felt that some show of activity on their part on behalf of tenants was necessary. For this purpose, they seized on a rather minor clause in the Act, which denied full security of tenure to those tenants who did not fully occupy the rented premises. This insecurity they found unjust and they demanded that the Act be amended so that tenants in this situation should be allowed to sublet, and thus more fully occupy the whole dwelling. No matter which political party is considered, one is inclined to sympathize with those who took a cynical view of the agitation of January and February. 'On peut regretter, . . . que les critiques formulées contre la loi n'aient pas été presentées lors du débat de l'année derniere' [33].

M. Claudius-Petit seems to have come to the conclusion during January that some modification of the December Decrees was politically necessary [34]. His natural sympathies would have led him to seek to appease the MRP rather than their rivals on the Left. He contemplated an extension of the housing allowance, which the MRP had asked for, but this seems to have been opposed by the Minister of Finance. Negotiations took place between M. Claudius-Petit and the *Commission de la Justice*, but these were complicated by the fact that the Committee could not always command the necessary support in the Assembly as a whole. A way out of these difficulties could only be found by a meeting of those principally concerned during February under the chairmanship of the Premier, M. Queuille [35]. The outcome of all this political activity, which was accompanied by mutual accusations of demagogy, was the publication of decrees on 17th March which amended the first decrees of application, which had appeared only three months earlier. The result of the amendments was to reduce the size of the initial increase for the vast majority of tenants by altering the rent per square metre originally fixed. All categories except 2(a) and above were affected by these changes (the heaviest concentration of dwellings was to be found in categories 3(a) and 3(b).

Several important conclusions may be drawn from these events which have significance for the whole of the post-1949 period. The basic lines of conflict to prevail in future years are clearly visible in early 1949 although the sharpness of conflict was much greater at this time than it was to be in later years, both because of approaching municipal elections, and because these were the first increases under the Act. Perhaps the most important outcome was that the Act remained unaffected in all essentials. Rents began to increase, and the six-monthly instalments were not postponed or interrupted. The weighted surface area mode of calculation was applied and was untouched by the amendments of March. From now on conflict was to be between the government on the one hand and the public, and to some extent the political parties, on the other. M. Claudius-Petit and his successors continued to push ahead with the policy of higher rents but within the established framework, and only to the extent which public hostility permitted.

As one traces the development of policy in this sector in succeeding years, one is struck by the tension between, on the one hand an extreme rationalism which attempted to define precise and quantitative goals, and, on the other, the facts of political life which constrained ministers to adopt all manner of subterfuges in an attempt to circumnavigate popular hostility. This conflict may be clarified by innumerable examples taken from the history of the later development of this legislation, and particularly by an examination of the unsuccessful attempts to relate rents to wage levels by means of an index. But the escape from politics did not prove as simple as had been thought. M. Houist, in a report prepared for the Economic Council in 1957, on the operation of the index, in the first years of its application, commented with some bitterness: 'Le gouvernment, par un certain nombre d'artifices, ne modifia pas le salaire de base servant au calcul des prestations familiales, de peur de contribuer à provoquer un processus inflationniste' [36]. Inflation was certainly one of the factors which encouraged the minister to resort to procedures in order to produce rents that would be lower than those which would have resulted from a more strict application of the spirit of the Act, but the events of January and February of 1949 suggest that more purely political, as well as economic considerations, also influenced his decisions.

Although it involves breaking away from a chronological account of the period, it is worth pursuing the question of indexing because of the light which it throws on the conflict which we have described between what politicians and administrators felt to be desirable and what they were in fact able to bring about. With the collapse of the Pinay Government in January 1953, M. Claudius-Petit ceased to have responsibility for housing and was replaced by Pierre Courant (Independent Republican) who remained in office for the duration of the Mayer Government (8.1.53–28.6.53). He was perhaps the most able Housing Minister of the Fourth Republic and immediately announced his intention of seeking a new form of index which would protect rent increases against erosion by inflation. The new system of indexing was adopted but was no more successful than its predecessor. Although rents were now supposed to be linked with the minimum wage, this link was broken as soon as it was necessary to raise the minimum wage. Not surprisingly, there now remained very little credibility in any further system of indexing although its desirability was still widely accepted. M. Chochoy (Socialist), the minister responsible for housing under both Guy Mollet and Bourgès-Maunoury, included in the Law of the 26th June 1957, not only the abandonment of the minimum wage index, but also a declaration of the intention to adopt yet another form of index, this time based on construction costs. But the Fourth Republic was not to last long enough for there to be any possibility of carrying out this intention. In the Decrees of 28th December 1958, M. Sudreau, the first Housing Minister of the Fifth Republic abandoned all attempts at indexing. The economic policy of the Fifth Republic has always condemned indexation as inflationary and this device has been out-lawed within the housing field, just as it has been for agricultural prices.

We must now return to a more strictly chronological approach to our subject and leave the question of indexing. The events of August 1953 and particularly the Law of the 9th of August are important in the history of the privately rented sector. We have already seen that the Act of the 1st of September 1948 made extensive use of delegation both for technical and for political reasons. When important changes were thought necessary in 1953 the same solution was tried. The Laniel Government (28.6.53–19.6.54) received from the Assembly the vote of the *pleins pouvoirs* which it demanded, and thus obtained the freedom to legislate in certain areas of social and economic policy without some of the restraints of parliamentary supervision. In political terms, delegation has always been viewed by those sympathetic to the tenant interest as a great danger. 'Les locataires courront de grands risques le jour où serait envisagée l'attribution de nouveaux pouvoirs spéciaux au gouvernement [37]'. These sentiments, expressed on a later occasion, were amply borne out by the contents of the legislation of the 9th August 1953 although the final outcome of this struggle was as usual indecisive. The most important change in the new Law was a government commitment to bring all control to an end on the 1st January 1958.

In the event, this expression of intent was not worth the paper it was written on, and, as we shall see later, encountered stiff political resistance and was not applied. The other provisions in the legislation were applied but they were of little importance as compared with the possibility of decontrol. If the government had felt able either to revise the *valeurs locatives* so as to bring them in line with current costs, or to apply correctly the indexing which the Law envisaged, then change would have been fundamental. But the Laniel Government and its successors were unable to do either of these things.

This incident in 1953 has some importance for our general theme of continuity and immunity from political pressure except of a negative and restraining character. Mention has already been made of the exceptional procedure used, and it should also be noted that August 1953 saw sharp social conflict over the retirement conditions of civil servants. Despite the fact that public attention was diverted away from the rent problem and despite the *pleins pouvoirs* which the Government had obtained, the system of rent control was only slightly modified, the six-monthly increases continuing as before. One may regard the events of August 1953 as demonstrating forcefully the unresponsiveness of housing policy to changes in the character of the governing coalition. The political centre of gravity had shifted to the right when the Socialists declined to participate in government when Pinay formed his ministry in March 1952. It is fair to say that the use which the Laniel Government made of the *pleins pouvoirs* was a direct consequence of the changed political complexion of the government. The modest results obtained are a direct measure of the significance for housing of wider political developments.

After the general election in January 1956 the Socialists, led by Guy Mollet, left the back benches to take part in government again. The Mollet Government took up the problem of rent in 1956 and

1957 when the responsible minister was M. Chochoy. Despite its size, the privately rented sector was not a priority for the Socialists. During his first year in office, M. Chochoy promoted an important *loi-cadre* to which we shall return in later chapters, but this ignored almost entirely the privately rented sector. One might have expected that when the time came to legislate, the Socialists would have taken some steps towards increasing the area of security of tenure, even if they allowed the rent increases to continue. Such was at least the intention expressed by them in a proposition which they had tabled two years earlier in 1954 [38]. In this proposal, the party made it clear that they were not only opposed to the suggested decontrol that was to take place on 1st January 1958, but also that they desired the extension of security of tenure to those rural communes that had been placed beyond the scope of the Rent Act from the outset. In taking up this stance, the party was acting consistently with the position they had taken up during the Bill's passage. The 1954 policy statement although referring to the hardship caused by rent increases, implicitly recognized that this process must continue. One is therefore more surprised to find that M. Chochoy took no action to extend security of tenure, than to observe that he allowed the six-monthly increases to continue as before. It may be that the Socialists were restrained by the make-up of the Assembly or the opinions of their coalition partners, but in any case, no attempt was made, for example, to restore security of tenure to those small rural communes to whom it had been denied in the Rent Act of 1948. The 1954 commitment to security of tenure as a general right remained, therefore, unfulfilled.

What then were the changes for which the Socialists can claim responsibility? They amounted simply to this: that an intention was expressed, in legal form, to allow rents to continue to rise further into the future for superior dwellings, whereas increases for more modest accommodation would stop at an earlier date. This was, of course, a gesture which had no effect on the current situation, and the insignificance of this reform is too evident for any commentary to be necessary.

III *Application of the Rent Act after 1958*

In December 1958, M. Pierre Sudreau, the minister with responsibility for housing from 1958 to 1962 in General de Gaulle's first ministry and in the Debré Government, had to make important decisions. After much discussion in both the Assembly and the Council of the Republic in December 1957, the inevitable conclusion had been reached that decontrol must be delayed, and thus the intentions of the Decree of 9th August 1953 were not respected. The newly substituted date was one year later, 1st January 1959, and therefore after coming into office, M. Sudreau had to decide whether to allow the process of decontrol to commence as had been intended. He decided to allow this, but only in those communes with a population of less than 10,000 which were still within the scope of the legislation. In so deciding, he naturally moderated drastically the more radical intentions of the Laniel Government.

This early decision of the minister showed clearly that there was to be no watershed dividing policies before and after 1958. If the Fifth Republic was to revolutionize social and economic policy, one would have expected a rapid move towards decontrol, and faster rises in controlled rents. Such was the demand made in the Rueff-Armand report [39]. M. Sudreau's early career suggested that he might prove less amenable to the constraints of politics. He was one of the technocrats whose presence in the early cabinets of the Fifth Republic attracted so much attention. As *Commissaire* for the Paris region, he had proved himself, even as a civil servant, capable of independent action. But the precedent set by his early decision relating to decontrol was followed in the matter of rent levels. No rapid acceleration was to be observed nor any intention displayed to amend the 1948 Act. The Fourth Plan envisaged a doubling of rents within the controlled sector in the period 1961 to 1965. M. Sudreau, however, more conscious of political restraints than the economist responsible for the preparation of the Plan, commented early in 1961 : 'En ce qui me concerne, je pense qu'une mesure gouvernementale de doublement serait excessive et dépasserait le but de notre politique, car les loyers de nombreux appartements ne sont plus très loin de représenter la valeur du service rendu' [40]. The last four words of this citation are particularly important because they signify Sudreau's acceptance of the principles underlying the 1948 Rent Act.

In our examination of the unsuccessful attempts at indexing rents between 1948 and 1958, we stressed that popular hostility to government policy was an important restraining influence. Successive ministers were unable to respect the spirit of the Act. In the new political conditions created by the establishment of the Fifth Republic, this hostility and its restraining effect were equally evident but there was a difference in ministerial response. Caution was still necessary but whereas before governments had sought to apply the legislation so as to limit increases, the object now was to produce maximum increases under an appearance of moderation, that is, to disguise the real extent of increases in controlled rents produced by ministerial decisions. The first change to take place was the substitution of percentage increases on a geometrical rather than an arithmetic basis. Another instrument for raising rents other than by the six-monthly increases was forged by M. Sudreau in the form of the maintenance coefficients. These permitted buildings whose state of repair reached a certain level to have their legal maximum rents multiplied by the maintenance coefficient. This system was devised not only to increase rents but also of course to provide landlords with an incentive to provide better standards of repair.

A second instrument was created by the possibility of altering the definition of the four categories in which dwellings were placed. For example if it is politically difficult to increase above a certain level the rents of category 3(a) dwellings, which are the most numerous in the stock, one may instead sidestep this difficulty by redefining category 3(a) so as to transfer a certain number of dwellings to category 2(c) in which a higher rent may be legally demanded.

Yet another means to the same end exists in the system of what are called the surface area equivalents.

These equivalents have been a part of the system of calculation of controlled rents from the outset but they have been modified during the sixties on a number of occasions so as to increase their weight and allow them to play the same role as the devices just mentioned. They are called the surface area equivalents because they permit a certain number of square metres of floor area to be added to the real measured area of the dwelling before the rent calculation is made. The quantity of surface area which may be added depends on the facilities provided in the dwelling. All these devices, the repair coefficients, the reclassification of buildings, and the surface area equivalents, are means to the same end. They serve to raise the rent which may legally be charged to a figure above that which would result from the simple application of the published percentage six-monthly, and later annual increases [41].

It should not be overlooked that, although the continued application of the Law of the 1st September 1948 shows a great deal of continuity as between the Fourth and Fifth Republics, there is a noticeable shift in the later period which brings policy slightly closer to the landlord point of view, as we shall see later when we deal with security of tenure. In the 1950s, as we have seen, ministers felt the need to try to apply strictly the principles of the Law but took every possible escape route that was open to them, which led to modifications in favour of the tenant, modifications which would produce lower rents. In the 1960s the ministerial approach to the principles of the Law was to try and find applications which would bring about higher rents than those that would have resulted from simply continuing the received practices. Continuity, though, is as important as contrast. In the first place both the earlier and the later ministers were content to work within the framework of the existing legislation and at no time was there any possibility of new legislation. In addition, the behaviour of politicians in the earlier as much as the later period was witness to the constant pressure from public opinion against any radical new departure.

These considerations lead us to ask whether the ministers of the Fifth Republic succeeded in raising rents more rapidly than their predecessors. The question is not easy to answer. By 1966 the controlled rent for a standard dwelling was seventeen times that charged when the 1948 legislation first began to be applied, that is seven times in real terms [42]. We may compare this with figures available for 1956 which indicate that the coefficient in real terms was then 3.3 [43]. These figures suggest that the percentage increases from year to year have been maintained and that there is little difference between the achievements in different periods. But a truer picture is obtained if we interpret the statistics politically. Since throughout the period controlled rent was increasing as a percentage of the family budget, the percentage increases under the Fifth Republic, which might be considered as comparable to those applied in the 1950s, were in reality more difficult to impose. In managing to maintain the rate of real increase in value, the ministers of the Fifth Republic were in fact doing better than their predecessors.

In discussing the approach of ministers under the Fifth Republic to rent levels in the controlled sector, it becomes more and more evident that the interaction between rent policy and general economic policy increases, particularly from 1963 onwards. Our account of the difficulties of ministers under the Fourth Republic laid most emphasis on the potential political opposition to rent increases coming from critics of the Government who felt that tenants were being asked to pay too much too quickly. In the 1960s this restraint certainly continued to influence policy but fears of inflation now tended to play a larger part in restraining the ambitions of ministers responsible for housing. This has been evident in the open disagreement between the minister responsible for rents on the one hand, and on the other, those members of the Government most responsible for economic policy, that is to say, the Minister of Finance and the Prime Minister. Such a conflict embarrassed the Pompidou ministry in May and June 1963. The Press carried reports during May, clearly based on information obtained from the Ministry for Housing and Development under M. Jacques Maziol, which suggested that the six-monthly increases would continue as usual despite economic difficulties [44]. But, on the 25th May *Agence France-Presse* issued a communiqué from the Hôtel Matignon which corrected previous reports and insisted that no final decision had yet been taken [45]. Inevitably, the view of the Prime Minister and the Minister of Finance prevailed, and increases were suspended for the first time since 1949 as part of the *plan de stabilisation* [46]. In June 1964, there was another conflict between M. Maziol and his colleagues. The Minister for Housing hoped that rent increases might now be resumed but he was forced to give way to his colleagues on two important points. Firstly, rent increases would be in future annual and discretionary in size. This was a considerable sacrifice since it was clear from the outset that such a discretion would normally be used to reduce rather than quicken the rate of rent increase. The second point on which M. Maziol was forced to give ground was the size of the increase to be imposed in July 1964. The caution of the President and the Prime Minister in a pre-electoral period, combined with the continued concern of M. Giscard d'Estaing about inflation, obliged him to accept increases for the most important categories, 3(a) and 3(b), of only 3% [47].

The differences which existed in 1963 and 1964 between M. Maziol and his colleagues proved to be the forerunners of parallel conflicts in later years. M. Maziol's successor at the Ministry for Housing and Development was M. Edgar Pisani. On more than one occasion in his period in office, it was quite clear that his ideas on rent levels, and also security of tenure were more radical than those of his colleagues [48]. During the preparation of the decisions concerning the annual discretionary increases in June 1971 the same disagreement was once again evident [49]. M. Vivien, Secretary of State for Housing, suggested to the Cabinet that the size of the increases should be 13% for category 3(a) and 7% for 3(b), with higher increases for superior categories. The final percentages were however only 8% for 3(a) and 6% for 3(b) [50].

There are a number of factors which need to be borne in mind in framing our conclusions as to the general character of the policy of the Fifth Republic with respect to the level of controlled rents. As we shall see later, when we come to consider security of tenure, the Government could well afford to show some moderation in this field, particularly towards the end of the period. The number of dwellings with controlled rents was constantly falling. This meant that investment could be attracted into housing because of the level of rents in the free sector. Tenant and landlord campaigning now tended to concentrate less exclusively on the controlled sector and turn instead to the free sector where there was particular dissatisfaction with the system of supplementary charges [51]. We have noted that rents continued to rise as rapidly as in the 1950s. As explained earlier, to be able to continue at the same rate was in fact to do much more than the ministers of the Fourth Republic had done. On the other hand, the familiar restraints on policy were still visible and were at times supplemented by fears of inflation. No breaks in the continuous development of policy can be identified but on the whole the stage showed itself marginally less subject to the pressure of public opinion.

We may now leave the question of rent levels and examine the Government's approach to the scope of the 1948 Rent Act, that is to say, security of tenure. In this area, as with the one just discussed, policy was developed progressively along well-established lines, using as far as possible discretionary powers and a flexible and undogmatic approach. We have already noted that a slow process of decontrol through change of tenants had been in operation since 1st January 1959 for the communes with a population of less than ten thousand. By 1970 the use of a variety of methods of decontrol had reduced the number of controlled dwellings to 1.4 million, one fifth of the rented stock. It will be our aim to describe, with particular regard to political factors, the way in which the Government was able to bring about this transformation.

The most obvious method, and one which most observers had envisaged from the outset was decontrol by category. By this is meant decontrol for sitting and new tenants, without geographical distinction, on the day on which the decree defining the categories to be liberated appears. It is a recognized phenomenon of the housing market that, as scarcity becomes less acute, demand for higher-quality accommodation will be satisfied first. The shortage of cheaper housing is almost certain to come to an end only at a later date. If, therefore, decontrol is justified by reference to the state of the housing market, it is logical that it should be operated by category, starting with the highest.

But despite these considerations, the Government did not use this method until the 1st January 1968. On this date all dwellings in categories (1) and 'exceptional' outside the Paris region were liberated [52]. This delay in dealing with the most expensive luxury accommodation is only explicable in political terms. There had been frequent attacks on the privileges of wealthy tenants occupying this class of controlled accommodation, and there was no conceivable justification for treating them advantageously. But the political necessity of advancing slowly and adapting methods of decontrol so as to minimize opposition was evident, not only in the delay in operating decontrol by category, but in all the methods of decontrol used by the Government in this period.

It is not difficult to show how political considerations entered into the choice of the method of decontrol by vacant possession (that is change of tenant), in the smallest rural communes which had been operating since 1st January 1959. This system of decontrol has considerable political advantages which have recommended it to governments in both Britain and France. The essence of this process is that it does not arouse the hostility of existing tenants because they intend, in the vast majority of cases, to remain where they are and therefore are not threatened by the possibility of decontrol. The burden of decontrol is instead borne by a less clearly defined and hence politically less significant group who are the new tenants. These may be either tenants who are obliged for one reason or another to change their place of abode or they are tenants who were not previously heads of independent households. The nature of this process is that the hardship of decontrol is borne individually by tenants in isolation rather than by all tenants collectively as a group. The process also has the appearance of being independent of Government action, which it is, except at the outset when the mechanism is set in motion.

Since 1959 the government has extended the area within which decontrol by vacant possession operates. This has been done not by simply raising the size of communes covered, but more cautiously, by publishing decrees which list towns in which this form of decontrol is to operate forthwith. This procedure was used particularly in the early 60s and by now all large towns including Paris, are covered by such decrees. Thus vacant possession releases a house from control. Despite the political attractions of this method, it must be remembered that it complicates the law very considerably. If one wishes to know whether a dwelling is or is not controlled, it is necessary, in some cases, to know when the last change of tenant took place and to compare this date with the date on which decontrol by vacant possession was introduced into the commune by decree.

There is a second method of decontrol by decree which is also gradual in the way in which it operates although it is not quite as mechanical as the one just described and therefore places the responsibility for decontrol somewhat more clearly on the government. This is the method which declares by decree that a particular town, or more probably list of towns, is, from the date of publication of the decree, decontrolled. This method, which must be clearly distinguished from that described in the last paragraph, affects all tenants whether there is a change of tenant or not, and therefore the impact is more sudden. This more radical approach has never been used by the government in large centres of population and would never be used for Paris where it would certainly raise tension between landlords and tenants dramatically.

But in choosing the two methods of decontrol described above, and in refusing to use until 1968 the more direct approach of decontrol of a category of dwellings, the Government has not exhausted its ingenuity in the devising of safeguards and protections against possible violent political reaction. When decontrol has been declared, by whatever means, it has only applied subject to certain conditions with respect to the physical condition of the dwelling, and also with respect to the granting of a lease for at least three years. In law, at least, this is a very important safeguard for the tenant who is going to experience decontrol, for he is at least given a guarantee that the dwelling must provide him with the basic facilities of bath, running water, etc. and also that he will have some security in the form of the three-year lease. Whether these legal provisions are in fact respected is unknown, since the necessary research has not been undertaken, but, in any case, the Government is still provided with a strong argument if it should be accused of advancing too rapidly on the road towards decontrol. It can always point to the gradual approach which has been adopted, to the guarantees which the tenant is provided with, and with the variation in speed according to local conditions.

Not content with the safeguards with which it had provided itself the Government, through M. Chalandon, the minister responsible, took further powers in legislation in 1970 which allowed additional nuances to be introduced into the process of decontrol. In future it would be possible not only to distinguish one commune from another but also to draw a distinction within an individual commune and free some categories of dwelling whilst continuing control for other, generally lower, categories [53].

Apart from the nature of decontrol itself, the Government has also sought protection against possibly adverse political reactions in the way in which it uses the local authorities. When the ministry feels that a particular commune might be taken outside the scope of the 1948 legislation, great care is taken to consult the local *conseil municipal* before anything is done and to obtain the consent of this body. Contact is made via the prefect concerned. If the council has reservations about the new step, then the ministry will allow a pause and take up the matter again at some later date when conditions may be more favourable. If, on the other hand, the consent of the council can be obtained, then the decree is published and if there should be any later repercussions, as there sometimes are, the minister may always say that he acted after consultation with those on the spot and was therefore careful to take account of both local opinion and local housing conditions.

Nor is the minister normally inflexible about the possibility of a return to control if this seems necessary. Such was the case at Belley in the winter of 1970 where decontrol had taken place in the way just described [54]. In this case, such was the force of local protest at the hardship that was being caused by the new higher rents, that the local authority decided to go back on its previous acceptance of the decontrol decision. This has always been possible and the minister is normally willing to accommodate a local authority in such cases, and withdraw the earlier decree of decontrol and hence return the commune in question to the status of a controlled commune within the scope of the 1948 act. The same thing has happened even more recently in the case of Fos-Sur-Mer where decontrol coupled with rapid economic development had produced alarming rent increases [55].

This account has quite intentionally concentrated on the history of the application of the Rent Act of 1948. Such a course is justified by the political importance accorded to the process surrounding decontrol. But it must be remembered that the rented accommodation still under control in 1973 is now very much reduced and in fact only constitutes nationally one fifth of the stock of rented housing [56]. It is therefore necessary to ask whether new issues have not begun to come to the fore which relate to the quantitatively more important free sector.

The answer to this question would appear to be that certain new issues associated principally with the free sector have appeared, but that as yet, despite the size of this sector, they are politically relatively unimportant. During 1971, there were a number of locally organized rent strikes which centred on the issue of the size and composition of service charges. Three political parties tabled bills in Parliament designed to deal with this problem. The Government showed sufficient sympathy with these complaints to negotiate an agreement with the Union Nationale de la Propriété Immobilière (UNPI) on the subject, but this is only morally binding on individual landlords who are members of the UNPI, and deals with the services which may be provided rather than their cost. Since the Government has successfully conveyed the impression that there is no chance of its acceding to tenant demands for reimposed controls, it would appear that the policy of administrative and political disengagement which has been followed so far is likely to continue without serious difficulty and that political conflict concerning the decontrolled sector will continue to concentrate on side issues, such as service charges.

Table IV.1 provides useful statistical evidence of the cautious and gradual process of disengagement in which governments have been involved. Two points particularly need stressing. In the first place, the table shows clearly how government policy has distinguished between large and small towns, holding back the process of decontrol in the former. Secondly, the table brings out the contrast between those areas with the greatest housing shortage, in central districts, and areas further out where decontrol has been allowed to proceed more rapidly.

The impression that an observer derives from an examination of this area of policy is that of an administration which feels itself very vulnerable but which, with great hesitation and apparent weakness, nevertheless succeeds in advancing very gradually along the path which it has chosen for itself. Initially about six million dwellings fell within the scope of the 1948 Rent Act. This figure had fallen to 3.3 million by 1966 [58], 1.4 million by 1970 [59] and to 1.1 million by 1975 [60]. The most recent official assessment of problems published in 1975 and therefore prepared entirely since the election of Giscard d'Estaing as President of the Republic, only reinforces the observations already made about the character of policy in this sector. Although Messrs Nora and Eveno see rent control as an important cause of poor maintenance and low housing standards in general, they do not envisage decontrol along British lines as a practical

## Table IV.1

*Distribution of unfurnished rented dwellings according to their*
*legal status, in percentages of total housing stock\**

| Type of Commune | | Rents controlled under 1948 *Rent Act* | HLM | Other Dwellings | Total |
|---|---|---|---|---|---|
| Urban area with population between 10,000 and 100,000. | | | | | |
| | Centre | 20·8 | 11·3 | 67·9 | 100 |
| | Whole Area | 13·5 | 30·9 | 55·6 | 100 |
| Urban area with population of 100,000 and over | | | | | |
| | Centre | 40·1 | 10·0 | 49·9 | 100 |
| | Whole Area | 24·0 | 25·1 | 50·9 | 100 |
| Paris and its suburbs | | | | | |
| | Centre | 68·3 | 10·9 | 20·8 | 100 |
| | Whole Area | 40·0 | 27·4 | 32·6 | 100 |

\* M.E. Hans, 'Les conditions de logement au centre des agglomérations',
*Economie et Statistique*, 55, April 1974, Table 5.

policy. Instead, they add to the variety of tools employed by the
government in the process of disengagement. They suggest that
remaining controlled dwellings should be progressively taken outside
the scope of the Rent Act, but that rent increases be limited by the
terms of contracts to be negotiated between local representatives of
the administration and associations of landlords.

It would appear, then, that after almost thirty years of rent control,
certain constants in the character of policy persist: the refusal to see
the problem in terms of a choice between free market and controlled
rents, the acceptance of only gradual change, the willingness to
adapt policy to local conditions, and the flexibility which makes a
backward step possible when required. Why have the French been

able to achieve this relative success whilst British policy has oscillated wildly and only reached generally acceptable solutions and more effective policy in the late sixties? This is a tantalizing question but we must unfortunately delay answering it until we know more about the policies of rent control in Britain.

## References

1. *Annexe au Procès-Verbal de l'Assemblée Nationale, Journal Officiel (J.O.),* 28 February 1947.

2. *Le Monde,* 28 March 1947 and 29 July 1947. *Le Bulletin Economique,* 19 December 1947.

3. *Le Monde,* 4 February 1949.

4. Claude Alphandéry, *Pour une politique du logement* (Ed. du Seuil, 1965), p. 32.

5. *Projet de loi, Annexe au Procès-Verbal de l'Assemblée Nationale, J.O.,* 28 February 1947, p. 2.

6. A. Lindbeck, 'Rents control and housing policy', and G.H. Gelting, 'Economic effects of rent control in Denmark', in A.A. Nevitt (ed.), *The Economic Problems of Housing* (Macmillan, 1966); D.V. Donnison *et al., Essays on Housing* (The Codicote Press, 1964), pp. 19–23.

7. See speech by Gabriel Citerne, Debate of 25 June 1948, *J.O., Débats,* pp. 3921–3.

8. ibid., p. 3928.

9. *Proposition de loi déposée par les membres du groupe Communiste, Annexe au Procès-Verbal de l'Assemblée Nationale, J.O.,* 10 June 1948.

10. See chapter XI.

11. *Le Populaire,* 22 November 1948; speech by M. Minjoz, Debate of 25 June 1948, *J.O., Débats,* pp. 3925–7.

12. *Le Monde,* 26 June 1948 and 6 August 1948.

13. P. Williams *Crisis and Compromise* (Longmans, Green and Co. Ltd., 1964), pp. 103–15.

14. The principle of payment according to the value of the service provided and the whole of the Act is well described by the MRP deputy, M. H.L. Grimaud in the *Rapport fait au nom de la Commission de la Justice et de la Législation sur le projet gouvernemental, Annexe au Procès-Verbal de l'Assemblée Nationale, J.O.,* 11 July 1947.

15. Guy Houist, *Rapport présenté au nom du Conseil Economique (Avis et Rapports du Conseil Economique,* 23 and 24 July 1957) chapter III.

16. *Propositions de loi déposées par M. Edgar Faure et al. Annexe au Procès-Verbal de l'Assemblée Nationale, J.O.,* 30 May and 25 June 1947.

17. *Rapport Grimaud,* op. cit.

18. *Le Monde,* 27–28 June 1948.

19. *Le Monde,* 4 January 1947.

20. See the speech of M. Dominjon, Debate of the 25 June 1948, *J.O., Débats,* pp. 3923–4.

21. ibid., p. 3928.

22. Guy Houist, *Rapport présenté au nom du Conseil Economique* (*Avis et Rapports du Conseil Economique*, 23 and 24 July 1957) pp. 620–1.
23. *Le Monde*, 24 August 1966.
24. *La Documentation Française*, 3 December 1948.
25. Decrees of 10 December 1948.
26. G. Houist, *Rapport présenté au nom du Conseil Economique* (*Avis et Rapports du Conseil Economique*, 23 and 24 July 1957) chapter I.
27. ibid.
28. *Le Monde*, 18 November 1948.
29. *Le Peuple*, 6 February 1949 and 13 January 1949.
30. *Le Monde*, 23 January 1949.
31. *L'Aube*, 29 and 30 January 1949.
32. *Le Figaro*, 8 January 1949.
33. *Le Monde*, 30–31 January 1949.
34. *Le Monde*, 29 January 1949.
35. *Le Populaire*, 18 February 1949.
36. Guy Houist, *Rapport présenté au nom du Conseil Economique* (*Avis et Rapports du Conseil Economique*, 4 January 1957) p. 3.
37. *Combat*, 10 July 1955.
38. *Annexe au Procès-Verbal de l'Assemblée Nationale*, *J.O.*, 4 March 1954. Proposition 7948.
39. *Le Monde*, 27 August 1960.
40. *Le Monde*, 8 February 1961.
41. G. Mathieu, 'L'anarchie des loyers', in *Le Monde*, 4, 5, 6 and 7 May 1966.
42. *Le Monde*, 5 May 1966.
43. Guy Houist, *Rapport présenté au nom du Conseil Economique* (*Avis et Rapports du Conseil Economique*, 23 and 24 July 1957) p. 627.
44. *Le Monde*, 25 May 1963.
45. ibid; *La Vie Française*, 31 May 1963.
46. Decree of 13 September 1963.
47. *La Croix*, 28, 29 June 1964. *Combat*, 29 June 1964.
48. *Le Monde*, 19 November 1966.
49. *Le Monde*, 19 June 1971.
50. *Le Monde*, 23 June 1971 and 26th June 1971.
51. For further details, *see* chapter IV.
52. *Paris-Presse l'Intransigeant*, 16 January 1968.
53. Law of the 9th July 1970.
54. *Le Monde*, 3 Nobember 1970.
55. *Le Monde*, 8 March 1972.
56. *Le Monde*, 24 April 1973.
57. *Proposition de loi 2037*, *U.D.R.*, *Annexe au Procès-Verbal de l'Assemblée Nationale*, *J.O.*, 3 November 1971; *Proposition de loi 2278*, *P.S.U.*, *J.O.*, 26 April 1972; *Proposition de loi 2270*, *P.C.F.*, *J.O.*, 26 April 1972.
58. *Le Monde*, 4 May 1966.
59. *Le Monde*, 24 April 1973.
60. S. Nora and B. Eveno, 'L'amélioration de l'habitat ancien', *La Documentation Française*, 1975, p. 24.

# V
# The Privately Rented Sector: Britain

## 1 *The continuation of control: 1945–56*

We may now for a time turn away from French problems and deal with those with which the British Government was faced in the area of rent control beginning with the Labour Government of 1945. Labour made no important changes in the system of rent control and it is not difficult to see why. The inheritance, both economic and political, was very different in the English case. As we have seen, very rapid inflation in France had reduced rents to an abnormally low level. This was not the case in Britain where inflation had been much less rapid. Evidence from the early 50s in Britain suggests that rent and rate levels for tenants of privately owned property were approaching 10 per cent of the average weekly wage [1]. Expressed as a proportion of the family's weekly budget this was a figure to which the French were only able to aspire in the long term and which, as we have seen, they had not reached even by the mid-50s and after eight years of government policy designed to raise rents.

In addition to the lack of any obvious economic constraints, the government was not under any political pressure to make changes in the privately rented sector. The Ridley Report of 1945 recommended that wartime controls continue for the time being, and this is clearly what Labour intended anyway. At this time the Conservatives also accepted that any decontrol was out of the question.

As we leave the immediate post-war situation of acute shortage and the Conservative Government takes power with a small parliamentary majority at the election of 1951, the principal question of political interest in this sector is that of deciding when the Conservatives are going to tackle the thorny problem of rent control. Early signs were that they would do so quickly. In referring to the problem of rent control, it was stated in the 1950 Conservative Manifesto

'The Right Road for Britain': 'Owing to the changes in the housing situation and in building costs which have taken place since that time [1945], a Conservative Government will appoint a new Committee to review the whole subject again as a matter of urgency' [2]. It would appear that this position was found politically dangerous after the near victory of the party in 1950. Whatever the explanation, no commitment was to be found on the question of rent control in the 1951 Manifesto. We may suppose that after this date the narrowness of the Government's majority in the Commons tended to encourage postponement of any important legislation on the rent problem. Other factors may also have helped to divert the Conservatives from their originally declared intention of tackling the problem rapidly. Between the 1950 and 1951 elections, the party had given housing a higher priority because of the adoption of the target of 300,000 houses per annum which was pressed upon a reluctant leadership at the Blackpool Conference of 1950. The adoption of such an ambitious target implied that the party considered the housing shortage to be still acute and not capable of resolution within less than two or three years, the time necessary to expand the building programme to the new target. In such circumstances, it would have been difficult for Conservatives to argue that the housing shortage would be coming to an end within a short time and that therefore the moment had been reached to consider the possibility of even a limited degree of rent decontrol. Nor can the appointment of Mr Harold Macmillan as Minister for Housing and Local Government in the autumn of 1951 be neglected in the explanation of this slight change of course. It should be remembered that at this time Mr Macmillan was clearly identified as a Conservative of a more leftish and moderate hue because of his differences with Conservative leaders over economic and social policy in the 1930s. Mr Macmillan continued to occupy this post from 1951 to 1955.

II *The Rent Act and its aftermath: 1956–65*

'Rent control in the words of a minister whom it would not be fair to name, has been regarded as a nettle to be seized only by a government with a large majority in its first year of office or by a doomed government in its last' [3]. This comment, made in November 1953, proved prophetic for, in the autumn of 1956, eighteen months after the Conservative victory at the polls, Mr Sandys, Mr Macmillan's successor, announced that the Government was undertaking a review of rent control legislation [4]. This review was in fact to lead to the famous Rent Act of 1957. In view of some of the controversy which raged around this Act in later years, it is well to attend closely to the initial justification which Mr Sandys offered at the time when the review was first announced. Considerable stress was laid on the provision which was envisaged in future legislation, which would enable owner-occupiers to let parts of their own houses without being subject to the rent control legislation. This provision proved to be uncontroversial and of little importance and was presumably given prominence in the minister's speech because it tended to give the impression that the new legislation was undertaken in favour of the owner-occupier rather than for the benefit of landlords.

A further point stressed in Mr Sandys' speech was that existing arrangements were unjust to all the parties concerned. This aspect of the Conservative Party's justification of change deserves elaboration for the argument is not simply that there is injustice to the landlord. It is argued that if the tenant is unable to pay the market rent for the property which he is obliged to occupy, then he should be helped to do so normally by some form of financial assistance. This means that the cost of social assistance of the sort thought necessary for tenants should be borne by the nation as a whole rather than by one section of the community, but it is not simply the landlord who is considered to have suffered injustic according to the Tory view of rent control. It is also the owner-occupier who has to pay the full cost of his housing and who may not be any wealthier than the tenant who obtains his accommodation at below market price. I do not intend here to examine the merits of these arguments; attention has only been drawn to them because they occupied a prominent place in Mr Sandys' announcement.

One further point should be noted from the speech. Mr Sandys made it clear from the outset that he intended to introduce in the legislation two forms of decontrol: by vacant possession, and by rateable value. That is to say, after the date on which the Act came into force, there would be decontrol when a new tenant came to occupy premises which had previously been controlled, and all houses above a fixed level of rateable value would be decontrolled immediately on the date of the Act coming into force.

Before examining the political conflict which surrounded the passage of the Bill which was to become the Rent Act, it is necessary to describe the contents of this legislation. This account is essentially concerned with politics, and therefore no attempt will be made to provide an exposition of the entire Act, but it is felt that the following account will at least serve the purposes of this study. It was considered that the most important part of the Bill was that which provided for decontrol by rateable value. According to this provision, all dwellings with rateable value of about £30, or £40 in London and Scotland, were to be decontrolled. The Bill also provided, as Mr Sandys had envisaged in his announcement, for decontrol by vacant possession. This proved to apply to all dwellings regardless of rateable value. This needs to be emphasized for it is theoretically quite possible to combine the two approaches and to allow, for example, vacant possession to give decontrol only to houses of above a certain rateable value. Such was the approach which had been used during the 1930s. A third feature of the Bill concerned those dwellings whose rateable value was below the ceiling fixed for decontrol. The landlords of these dwellings were entitled to demand increased rents up to a limit of twice the gross rateable value. This meant, naturally, that security of tenure was maintained for this sector of the housing stock whereas tenants who were decontrolled either by vacant possession or by reason of rateable value lost their security of tenure. The Bill also gave the minister power to lower the rateable value limits in order to permit him to accelerate decontrol in the future if he so wished. In the use of this power, he was permitted to distinguish between one area and another.

The first point to be noted about the Rent Act from the political point of view is that it went far beyond what one might normally have expected from a Conservative Government. The Act is sometimes described as if it were nothing more nor less than a simple application of Tory philosophy. I shall seek to show that it was considerably more than this and in fact was a very radical measure. It is certainly true that some legislation bringing about decontrol was inevitable, given that the Conservative Government, because of its success in increasing the rate of construction, was convinced that the housing shortage was almost at an end. The party was also undoubtedly sympathetic to the argument that a restriction on the normal operation of the market could only be justified as a temporary and exceptional measure and must come to an end at some point in time. However, the orthodox approach to the problem, if one is to judge by the precedents of the 1920s and 1930s, would have been to establish some form of enquiry which would then have made recommendations, after examining in detail the situation with regard to the supply of houses of different types. As we have seen, no such enquiry took place, and the minister committed himself from the outset, and before the Bill had even been drafted, to the process of decontrol by vacant possession. The radical nature of this step is borne out by the following remark which was made by the Ridley Committee in examining this very question at the close of the war. 'We are emphatically of the opinion that . . . the principle of decontrol on vacant possession should not be revived since the evidence shows that in the past this principle has been responsible for many of the hardships which have arisen' [5]. In addition to rejecting decontrol by vacant possession for the future, the Ridley Committee also envisaged that, when the time came to legislate, there would be an independent inquiry. We have already noted that initially the Conservative Party, in its 1950 manifesto, was also in favour of a review prior to legislation.

In order to understand the political significance of the use of decontrol by vacant possession, it is necessary to take account of the arguments used against it. Many of these were based on inter-war experience and no doubt weighed heavily against the method in 1945. Decontrol by vacant possession is something of a blunt instrument as compared with its alternative. If one uses the method of decontrol by value, one can, at least in principle, find a point in the scale of value at which the supply and demand of houses for rent is approximately in balance. One will normally find that there is a sufficient supply of the more expensive accommodation, but that in descending the value scale, a shortage begins to appear at some point. In theory, therefore, one may discover this point and use it as the limit below which decontrol will not operate. Vacant possession, on the other hand, presumes that there is already or soon will be a sufficient supply of all classes of accommodation for rent since a house of any value will be affected as soon as there is a change of tenant. It was precisely this difference between the two methods which had led to modifications of inter-war decontrol policy. The Marley Committee of 1931 found that the vacant possession method had decontrolled houses in Class C and that in many areas of the country, there was still a great shortage of this class of accommodation. Because of this shortage, landlords were able to demand rents which were considered exorbitant for the class of accommodation in question [6]. The bluntness of the vacant possession approach may be somewhat modified if a geographical distinction is introduced into the legislation, such as has always been the case in France. But

Mr Sandys did not contemplate any such modifications.

The radical nature of the act is further emphasized when one considers the transition from total security of tenure, which had previously existed for all unfurnished tenants, to the insecurity which was the result of decontrol. In English common law, the security to which a tenant is entitled, that is to say the notice which he is permitted to demand from his landlord, depends on the period of the tenancy and is therefore one week in a weekly tenancy. The Act did modify this common law rule in allowing one month's notice, but this fell far short of what might have been desirable from the point of view of a tenant, particularly bearing in mind that tenants had become accustomed to a degree of security almost comparable to that of the owner-occupier. This was also a point which had been stressed in earlier official discussions of the question. The Marley Committee had emphasized that on humane grounds it was impossible to return to the insecurity which had prevailed before 1914, even when it was felt necessary to decontrol rents [7].

The radical nature of the provisions regarding security of tenure is clearly seen if one compares the situation of a tenant of residential premises with that of a tenant of commercial premises. The position in English law at the time of the passing of the Rent Act was that a commercial tenant, if he disagreed with his landlord over the rent to be fixed in a new lease, could demand the arbitration of the Court who would fix a reasonable rent. There was therefore no strict rent control in the sense in which we use this term when speaking of residential accommodation, but security of tenure was given the tenant of commercial premises in the sense that the landlord could only evict him if he could show the Court that certain specified conditions were satisfied, for example, that the premises were needed for redevelopment. The tenant of residential premises who occupied decontrolled property after the passing of the 1957 Rent Act had no such security of tenure, and a landlord could remove him for no other reason than that he wished to install a different tenant in the same premises.

As already indicated, one of the more radical features of the legislation and its political background was the absence of any preliminary enquiry, the object of which would have been to examine the housing situation and make recommendations as to the appropriate form and extent of decontrol. If we examine the exact reasons for the use of this approach to legislation on previous occasions, we may see more clearly the radical character of Mr Sandys's initiative.

Every major inter-war piece of legislation on rent control had been preceded by an interdepartmental enquiry, and the repeated use of this procedure suggests that it was not a mere accident of circumstances but that there was some characteristic of this particular sphere of legislation which suggested the use of some extraordinary process. In my estimation, the object of the procedure was to have a policy determined outside the arena of controversy between the two major parties. The Conservative and coalition governments of the inter-war period clearly felt uneasy about decontrol unless they could obtain some kind of sanction other than that normally provided for in the procedure of election and ministerial and Cabinet decisions. They knew that decontrol was extremely unpopular and that any non-Labour government, in these circumstances, was vulnerable to accusations of dogmatism and class legislation. If, however, it could be shown that the necessity for some measure of decontrol was recognized by non-political opinion, then the hand of the Government would be greatly strengthened. Such a procedure inevitably involved certain risks for it was always possible that impartial examination might recommend unpalatable measures. But the governments of the inter-war period were apparently willing to run this risk in order to strengthen their hand, and they were also willing to play the game respecting the view of the experts consulted, even when their opinion did not entirely coincide with that of the party in power. Hence the National Government of 1932 was ready to accept the recommendations of the Marley Committee whose report constituted an indictment of the process of decontrol as it had been operated under Conservative legislation during the 1920s. They made the modifications to the legislation suggested by the report and in doing so slowed down considerably the process of decontrol.

In the light of these precedents and of the recommendation of the Ridley Committee, it seems reasonable to suppose that Mr Sandys' decision not to use the enquiry procedure prior to legislation was deliberate. His reason for declining to do so was probably that he believed it necessary to follow a radical path and that he was not certain that such a course would necessarily be recommended by a committee of enquiry. The absence of any preliminary enquiry went entirely unnoticed in 1956 and 1957 and was not a point on which the Opposition laid emphasis, but it seems a reasonable conjecture that the rejection of any preliminary enquiry was one more sign that the minister was intent on unusually radical decontrol. It should not be thought that in abandoning the enquiry procedure

Mr Sandys was simply ignoring rather ancient pre-war precedents. A discussion of the rent control problem in the early 1950s which took place in the House of Lords, although not otherwise significant, did serve to demonstrate that leading spokesmen on both sides of the House considered the non-political preliminary enquiry the normal method of approach to the problem of decontrol [8]. The advocacy of this method which we find here on both sides of the House serves to emphasize that it was not only the Tories who feared the political weight of tenant opinion. Those on the right of the Labour Party such as Lord Morrison clearly felt that decontrol would be necessary at some point and that the only way in which it could be obtained in a moderate form under either Labour or Conservative governments was to introduce a non-political element into the procedure of decision-making.

The radical character of the new rent policy is further underlined if we bear in mind the political character of the two men most closely connected with its preparation. These were Mr Sandys, the Minister of Housing and Local Government from 1955 to 1957, and his Parliamentary Private Secretary, Mr Powell. Both are associated with the right of the Conservative Party and the coming together of these two men at a crucial turning point in the development of post-war housing policy was clearly of great significance. Had Mr Macmillan continued to exercise responsibility in the area of housing, it is clear that there would have been some measure of decontrol but it is doubtful whether it would have been as radical.

The unusually radical nature of the 1957 Rent Bill is also brought out if we consider it in the context of housing policy as a whole, rather than simply with respect to the privately rented sector. Mr Sandys, the minister responsible for the Rent Act, had, exactly one year earlier, promoted important legislation reducing the element of subsidy for new local authority housing. In fact the whole aim of the public housing sector had been changed from supplying general needs to providing accommodation for particular groups such as the elderly or slum dwellers. This is not the place to examine in detail the legislation of 1956 which brought about these changes in the public sector, but it is important to bear in mind that the two changes were closely connected and that, taken together, they formed a watershed in housing policy, the like of which is not seen again until the Labour Party's return to power in 1964. In chapter II, when an outline of policy development in Britain was sketched, emphasis was laid on the link between politics and policy and a large number of successive periods were distinguished from one another. On closer inspection, one finds that some of the lines of division between these periods are more important than others and the boundary between the Macmillan period and its successor which we suggested would stretch from 1955 to 1961 is of much greater significance than, for example, the 1951 or 1961 turning points.

It has been suggested in the foregoing passage that the Rent Bill was something more than the anticipated measure of decontrol which was to be naturally expected some years after the war when the housing shortage had lost some of its acuteness. The exceptional character of the legislation may be seen not only in its conception and preparation but also in the politics surrounding its passage and enactment. A feature of the Bill's passage through Parliament was that responsibility for this legislation (which had been prepared by Mr Sandys and which bore his personal imprint) was transferred to Mr Henry Brooke when he became minister in January 1957. The Bill had still to pass its report stage, committee proceedings and third reading. It was in fact during this period that opposition to the Bill from both the Labour Party and some Tory back-benchers was most apparent. Labour Party opposition to the Bill was fundamental and extremely virulent. Labour members on both second and third readings evoked class loyalties and concentrated particularly on the transfer of wealth from the poor to the wealthier landlords which would be brought about by the Act [9]. Opposition was particularly forthright from some trade union M.P.s and there was talk, although not at the national level, of token strikes against the Bill [10]. Labour also organized a petition and their opposition during the committee stage was sufficiently robust to oblige the minister to introduce the guillotine [11].

One may presume that this opposition was expected but the minister had to contend with other criticism as well. This came from some back-benchers on his own side of the house, and was sufficient to carry a minor amendment against him in committee, which was later removed on report [12], and to force him to accept another, delaying the date at which decontrol would start. Conservative opposition concentrated on those parts of the Bill which were likely to affect wealthier tenants, expecially those in the London area.

What emerges from this survey of the Act's passage is stiff opposition from a number of quarters which succeeds in producing only minor modifications in the Act. This outcome is important for our general conclusion relating to the contrast between Britain and

France in this area of policy. Had the opposition been more successful, it might have been able to moderate the Bill and in so doing bring the British pattern of policy development closer to the French. As it was, the ineffectiveness of criticism and the imperviousness of the official view to outside pressure are shown to be important elements which maintain the contrasted British and French patterns.

The Rent Act is clearly a crucial case in the illustration of the pattern of policy development in Britain. In describing the preparation of the Act, I have underlined its radical character. This proved important for the future and served to perpetuate the pendulum-like oscillations of British housing policy. Had the Act been more moderate in its aims, if, for example, decontrol by vacant possession had not been used in London, it is possible that there would never have been such a violent reaction to Conservative policy in the early 1960s and that the Act would have survived the return of the Labour Party to power. As well as the rapid decontrol which the Act produced, it is important to consider this legislation from an ideological point of view. Here the Act made few concessions. It was hoped to create private investment in housing to let, something which had virtually come to an end in 1914, to encourage a better standard of repair, and to increase mobility within the privately rented sector. It was argued, particularly by Mr Powell, that the market would do all of these things [13]. Since the Act was justified in these terms, it naturally provoked criticism along the same lines. Labour continued to defend municipalization as the only way to solve the problems of the sector, and was not concerned to find any common ground with Conservative back-bench critics of the Act. In this way, the politically motivated and oscillating pattern of policy development was perpetuated.

Students of politics are only too familiar with the Act whose passage is strongly opposed but which ceases slowly to be a matter of controversy and slips into the background as new controversies arise with the passing of time. Such was not to be the case with the Rent Act for it was to remain a subject of dispute between the parties until it was repealed by the Labour Government in 1965 when passing their own Rent Act.

Hostility to the Act seemed to be having some effect when Mr Brooke, in the run-up to the 1959 Election, gave a pledge that the Conservatives would not undertake any further decontrol if returned to power [14]. Mr Brooke was clearly responding to Labour allegations that a Tory victory would mean higher rents and even more drastic measures of decontrol. These gestures were of considerable political importance and interest, particularly the undertaking given prior to the election, but they were of limited importance at the grass roots level where decontrol was proceeding rapidly as a consequence of tenant mobility, especially in London. Mr Sandys' decision to rely mainly on decontrol by vacant possession made it quite impossible for the Government to arrest the process once it had been set in motion, even had they wished to do so.

Only one year after the election, rents were once again a subject of controversy. Referring to the undertaking to carry out no further decontrol, *The Financial Times* in August 1960 said: 'It was understandable that, having somewhat to its surprise emerged unscathed from the storms that raged around the original Act of 1957, the Government had decided not to try its luck too far. But by last year the rent front was so quiet that the Conservative decision seemed to some an unnecessary piece of caution. The anxiety and agitation which have arisen over London rents within the last week or so is proof that the decision was a prudent one and evidence that housing is still the most tricky and potentially explosive domestic issue with which the Government has to deal' [15]. The Government was apparently disturbed by the agitation referred to in this comment. The minister issued a circular shortly afterwards in which he suggested to local authorities that they might use their powers of compulsory purchase to acquire buildings where they found that exorbitant rents were being charged [16]. This was a clear recognition that decontrol was already leading to abuses and also that the Government had no effective means at its disposal with which to combat these abuses. The procedure of compulsory purchase is naturally a slow one since it contains safeguards which are appropriate to an administrative act of such importance. It may take many months before acquisition is final and compulsory purchase is therefore not an effective instrument to use in cases where tenants' security is threatened or where it is felt that exorbitant rents are being charged. The circular also contained no definition of what constituted an exorbitant rent, and furthermore compensation based on the excessive rent would have been payable to the landlord under this procedure. Cost would therefore have severely limited the scope of enforcement. This circular is interesting because it shows that rents were still a live political issue on which the Government felt obliged to take some action, but it is of less importance with respect to results achieved.

The Rent Act created problems for the Government because of the decontrol to which it gave rise. But these difficulties were to some extent anticipated. It had been argued, for example, that some hardship was inevitable but that, in the long run, private investment in housing to let would begin and that the situation would in this way right itself. Unhappily for the Government this investment did not appear and so in 1961 Mr Brooke decided that he would have to show the way. In February of that year he announced that the Government would be making £25m available for aid to voluntary housing associations who would provide unsubsidized accommodation to let [17]. The development of this sector was regarded as desirable in itself but it was principally argued by the Minister that the Government's actions would show that there was a market for unsubsidized rented accommodation and in this way bring about the investment which the Rent Act had been supposed to encourage [18]. Despite the example which the Government thus set, investment was not forthcoming. When the Conservatives returned to power in 1970 it rapidly became clear that they had abandoned hope of reviving the privately rented sector. When asked by the Francis Committee to remove controls on the rents of new buildings imposed by the Labour Party, they declined. But we shall return later to the changed Conservative attitude to the sector and the political consequences of this change.

In 1961 and 1962 there were indications that the Government was encountering increasing difficulties in London as a consequence of the continued operation of the decontrol legislation. The L.C.C. was alarmed at the increase in homelessness, some of which they ascribed to the provisions of the Rent Act [19]. This tendency was alleged to have been strengthened by the decision not to extend the 1958 Temporary Provisions Act when it expired in 1961. In 1962 the Department set up its own enquiry into rents in the London area and possible abuse by landlords and, according to Sir Keith Joseph, the findings were inconclusive [20]. Agitation continued, with criticism coming particularly from Labour M.P.s, such as Ben Parkin, who represented Central London constituencies. In the White Paper published in February 1963, the Minister announced his intention of setting up an enquiry into housing in Greater London [21]. Some of the details of the activities of Mr Peter Rachman were now beginning to come to public notice, and the Government was further embarrassed by the connection which was established in the public mind between the activities of Rachman and the Profumo affair. The abuses which were associated with the name of Rachman were important because they symbolized in a most dramatic way the tyranny of the landlord over his tenant in a situation of chronic housing shortage and absence of security of tenure. The Conservatives naturally argued that his activities dated from well before the coming into force of the Rent Act and that in any case he was not typical of the landlords. Both these points were true statements of fact, but rachmanism had become a common term in the political debate of 1963 and 1964, and the Milner Holland Report, when it was finally published in 1965, did reveal that intimidation was widespread in London and that it was caused, in part, by the process of decontrol by vacant possession (started by the Rent Act) and the insecurity to which this process gave rise [22].

The issue of rachmanism was explosive enough but it weighed even more heavily when it could be linked with other criticisms of Conservative housing policy. In this period there was much discussion of speculation in land, and Labour propaganda was able to associate speculation and intimidation. The 1964 election was, of all British post-war elections, the one in which housing in a variety of forms played the most important part. Many politicians were convinced that the miscalculations of the Government in this area and their effective exploitation by the Labour Party were an important contributory cause of Conservative defeat. *The Times* political correspondent wrote two years after the election: 'If there was one over-riding point in domestic policy for Mr Wilson before he took office in October 1964, and for several months afterwards, it consisted in this: Labour must make the housing of the people an absolute priority. As Mr Wilson saw the prospect, here was the main social good on which the Labour Government he led must concentrate. Other good things could come later but first the houses [23].' The Conservative Rent Act and other housing policies associated with it played an important part in Conservative defeat. The 1964 election proved to be an important turning point because it led directly to the Labour Government's Rent Act of 1965 which repealed the 1957 Act and replaced it by a totally new approach. But before considering this legislation, it is necessary to assess the political importance of the Milner Holland report which was published early in 1965 [24].

Although this report is concerned only with problems in London, it in fact contributes more than any other document which has appeared since the war to our understanding of housing problems and particularly of the problem posed by the shortage of accommodation to rent. The general theoretical interest of the findings of this report will be treated later in this study, but there were several conclusions which had particular importance for the privately rented sector. It was first established beyond doubt that in London (and the presumption was that similar findings would appear in other major conurbations), there was a considerable shortage of accommodation to rent and that this shortage was certain to continue for many years to come. This finding must be set against the optimism of the mid-50s, during which period it was the official view that, although local difficulties might persist, the shortage of accommodation to rent was in the process of being overcome, and that the removal of controls on rent levels would assist in satisfying demand. It was also established that rents had been rising very rapidly where decontrol had taken place but that the real problem of the rented sector was not so much the level of rent as the lack of security. Intimidation was investigated and it appeared to be not a case of a few isolated incidents, but a widespread practice in those inner central areas where the shortage was most apparent. It was also concluded that the removal of limitation on rent levels had not produced any significant quantity of private building for rent and that under existing tax arrangements this was unlikely to take place. It was pointed out that whereas the council sector benefited from a subsidy and the advantage of pooled rents, and the owner-occupied sector benefited from very considerable tax concessions in the form of relief from income tax on interest paid, the privately rented sector had no equivalent advantage, and therefore was extremely uncompetitive except for types of accommodation which the other two sectors were unable to provide, such as, for example, luxury accommodation to rent. The report also concluded that shortage was not simply a question of a lack of accommodation and could not therefore be overcome simply by a larger council building programme. The London shortage was partly the result of the population structure of a central city area in which were concentrated many small households competing for space with low-income families. In such a situation the absence of a sufficient number of small dwellings for the single person or couple without a child meant that there was direct competition between the poor family and the small wealthier household, and in such circumstances, new building was unlikely to be a sufficient answer. The report therefore suggested that increased control over sales and lettings in central areas was necessary and that a special authority for this purpose ought to be set up. Such an authority would protect the privately rented sector by preventing sales to owner-occupiers and by bringing to a halt conversions which raised rents beyond the means of poorer families.

The report was also of great political importance for housing at least in the short term. Its scholarly impartiality and freedom from ideological preconceptions and the weight of the evidence which it produced through its own research had the effect, at least for the time being, of creating a new consensus of the problems of the privately rented sector. There was evidence of this when the Conservative Party did not divide the House on the second reading of Mr Crossman's Rent Act. The Conservatives now accepted, at least for London, the necessity of the reimposition of rent control in some form and the restoration of security of tenure. The committee was not empowered to make suggestions as to future policy as they were simply a committee of enquiry. But nevertheless it was reasonable to argue that when the Rent Act did restore control and a measure of security, it was in fact following the line of argument developed in the report. Had the Conservatives won the 1964 election, the weight of evidence contained in the report would have been even more important politically since it would then almost certainly have been instrumental in bringing about a reversal or at least a substantial modification of Tory policy. With Labour in power, the effect of the report was less since the party was already committed to a restoration of control and security not only for London, but for the whole country. There were, however, at least two implied recommendations in the report which, for political reasons, the Labour Party did not feel itself able to implement. Most importantly no steps were taken to set up the special authority which was considered by Milner Holland necessary to deal with the particular problems of central London. Evidently the implications of such an initiative for the structure of local government were sufficient to block this proposal. The discussion of tax problems in the report had also suggested that a depreciation allowance ought to be awarded to the private landlord if it was felt that this source of accommodation was to be developed for the future. The Labour Party, however, has always been hostile not only to the landlord but also to the system of privately owned property to rent and the depreciation allowance was not introduced despite Conservative pressure. The strength of the party's objections to relying on this sector may be judged from the fact that they also declined during their period in office to introduce a housing allowance whose object would have been to aid private tenants paying a high rent and living on a low income. Such an allowance was advocated during this period by some of the most authoritative housing experts, but was never adopted as official Labour policy [25]. The Government's unwillingness to assist the privately rented sector contrasted with its expansion of aid to the council and owner-occupied sectors.

III *The 1965 Rent Act*

We are now in a position to examine the Rent Act of 1965. The Minister responsible for the preparation of this legislation was Mr Crossman who was appointed as Minister for Housing and Local Government after the Labour election victory of 1964. Labour had been firmly and consistently opposed to the Rent Act of 1957 from as early as Mr Sandys' announcement in 1956 and formally committed to its repeal since the annual conference of 1957 [26]. There had never been any wavering on this point and the leadership's commitment was as unconditional as that of the back-bencher or party militant. Political undertakings in this area had, however, remained almost entirely negative, for little indication had been given of Labour's programme for the privately rented sector. At the 1957 conference, it was made clear that it would be administratively impossible to return to the pre-1957 rents for decontrolled houses. Such had always been the demand of the left-wing of the party. There had also been some talk of 'fair' or 'reasonable' rents and the extension of the use of tribunals, but no indication had been given of the way in which such tribunals might work, nor had the terms 'fair' or 'reasonable' received any precise definition. The view, therefore, which was most commonly held on Labour's accession was that security would be restored generally and that some form of control would be reintroduced, perhaps with the use of tribunals, but that it remained for Parliament to define the principles upon which the tribunals would base their rent assessments.

The most important decision which had to be taken in the framing of the Rent Act was finally embodied in Section 27 which contained the definition of what came to be called a fair rent. Labour had often proposed fair or sometimes reasonable rents but of course in all discussions after 1965 the term becomes a term of art. The following definition was finally adopted:- 'In determining... a fair rent..., regard shall be had... to all the circumstances (other than personal circumstances), and in particular to the age, character and locality of the dwelling-house and to its state of repair. . . . For the purpose of the determination it shall be assumed that the number of persons seeking to become tenants of similar dwelling-houses in the locality on the terms (other than those relating to rent) of the regulated tenancy is not substantially greater than the number of such dwelling-houses in the locality which are available for letting on such terms' [27]. The formula is clearly extremely vague and leaves a good deal of discretion in the hands of the rent officer who is the official created by the Act with the task of fixing rents after application to him by either landlord, or tenant or both of them jointly. The only guidance which he may draw from the above definition is that the rent must be related to the physical condition of the accommodation and also that any scarcity value represented in the previous rent should be fully discounted. It appears from the wording of the Act that the starting point for the calculations is either a market rent where such exists free of scarcity or the officer's estimate of what the market rent would be free of scarcity. Later enquiries have tended to suggest that the vagueness of the formula has led to a variety of approaches being used and rents being fixed at varying percentages below the market value, perhaps 10 or 20 per cent in typical cases but higher percentages when the poorer quality of property was in question. The Act established as the most important elements in the rent-fixing machinery the rent officer who in most cases was to attempt to bring about agreement between landlord and tenant and, failing this, to fix a rent on the basis of the principles contained in section 27. Appeal was permitted from his decision to the Rent Assessment Committee. The task of the R.A.C. was to ensure uniformity within its area of jurisdiction. The Act also imposed a freeze on all existing rents and restored security of tenure to the unfurnished sector throughout the country. The old controlled rents which were still at twice the gross rateable value were left untouched for the time being although the minister indicated that at some later date the Act would be used to assimilate the controlled in the regulated sector and hence to fix rents for old controlled accommodation by the new machinery. The rent freeze covered all existing accommodation of a rateable value of up to £200, and £400 in London. The machinery of the Act and rent control was also to apply to new building.

The interest of this study lies not so much in the intricacies of the new machinery for fixing regulated rents as rather in the political justification which was provided for the Act and the reflection of these political considerations in the legislation. In both the White

Paper which set out the details of the new system and in Mr Crossman's speech on second reading considerable emphasis was laid on the justification of the Act as a piece of moderate legislation which was taking the sensible road between two unjustifiable extremes. Rent control as it had existed prior to 1957 was not seen by Mr Crossman as an absolute good and a necessary protection for the tenant. His White Paper justified it instead in the following terms: 'Full-scale rent control was reimposed on the outbreak of war and continued in the post-war years along with other forms of rationing as the only means of preventing exploitation of an essential commodity in short supply' [28]. Such an approach was in Mr Crossman's view therefore inappropriate twenty years after the war since, although shortage was still admittedly present, it was not the same universal and chronic shortage which had characterized the late 1940s.

The minister also rejected the Conservative approach, but his criticism of it concentrated more on the evils of insecurity and intimidation than on the problem of high rents. The middle way was not to apply in the case of security of tenure which the Minister regarded as a basic human right, hence its restoration in full in the Act. The middle way was seen more in the machinery and principles for the fixing of rent levels. There was, of course, a universal freeze on all rent increases, but either tenant or landlord could escape from this freeze by making an application to the rent officer. One justification of strict rent control is based on the hardship experienced by poor tenants. This had certainly been the justification supported by Labour before 1957, but Mr Crossman's Act made quite explicit the point that no reference was to be made to the personal circumstances of the tenant in fixing the rent. The information on which the rent officer was to base his decision was to be based only on two elements, local housing conditions, and the physical condition of the house in question. Certainly scarcity value was no longer to be allowed to push up rents but the market was retained as guide for rent officers, and landlords could ask for a regulated rent to be revised upward after three years. In his speech, the Minister stressed that the task of the rent officer was analogous to those of arbitration in industrial disputes, that is, the object of the procedure was to reach agreement between the two parties. What was considered unsatisfactory was not so much any state of affairs defined in economic terms of rent levels, as the disagreement existing between landlord and tenant. The Minister was quite insistent on the lay functions of the rent officer and the fact that he need not have any professional qualifications or experience in the sphere of valuation. He in fact rejected a Conservative amendment designed to institute such a professional qualification for all rent officers [29]. The rent officer was to be a man of common sense, possessing knowledge of local conditions whose aim it would be to bring the parties together in agreement. This aspect of the rent-fixing machinery, with its reliance on agreement between landlord and tenant, combined with the vagueness of the fair rent formula and its reference to market conditions, set the new system of regulation apart from any earlier system of control.

The political significance of the Rent Act is further illuminated if we examine it not only in the light of the justifications which the Minister used but also in relation to the case made against it by critics, either from the left of the Labour Party or from the Conservative benches. Most discussion of the Bill before its final form was made public assumed that the professional element would play a large part in the reconciliation machinery [30]. As we have seen the Minister did not follow this path. The Conservatives and the landlord organizations continued to prefer a more professional form of assessment of rents and the Labour formula was attacked as unnecessarily vague. The landlords clearly felt that rents would be fixed at a higher level if the professional valuer played a more important part in the process of rent fixing. Such a belief appears to have been borne out by the evidence contained in the Francis Committee's report of 1970, from which we gather that the Rent Assessment Committee, which contains a more professional element than is generally represented among rent officers, has tended to fix higher rents when it has been called upon to judge the decision of rent officers on appeal [31]. As well as demanding that professionals play an important part in the fixing of rents, the landlords would also have preferred a formula which was based on gross rateable value. Mr Crossman, however, followed the recommendation of the Ridley Committee in not applying this method which he considered would create anomalies and injustice as between one part of the country and another.

The left-wing of the Labour Party was also dissatisfied with the more flexible and vague formulas contained in the Rent Act and would have preferred a formula based on gross rateable value, although naturally one resulting in much lower rents than those desired by the landlords. There were some elements in the legislation, however, which were more acceptable to the Left-wing. The ceilings above which control would not exist were fixed at a very high level so as to include almost all but the most expensive luxury rented property. The Conservatives naturally found this extension of control excessive and passed amendments in the House of Lords designed to lower these ceilings, amendments which, however, were naturally later removed when the Bill returned to the Commons [32]. There was also some disagreement about the geographical extent of the scope of the law. The Left wished to have the law applied throughout the country without possibility of geographical distinction and the Conservatives stressed that the Milner Holland Report had referred only to London, and hence there was no justification for any nation-wide application of control. Mr Crossman continued consistently in his middle way, applying the law initially throughout the country, but inserting into the legislation powers which enabled him, should he wish, to release from the scope of this law areas to be defined in statutory instruments.

But the moderate character of the Rent Act should not be stressed to the exclusion of all other elements. In many ways this Act was one of the most successful and most innovatory pieces of Labour reforming legislation. It began the process of dispensing entirely with the old dichotomy of control versus the market. Its central position in the political spectrum naturally exposed it in later years to criticism from both Left and Right, but as we shall see, this criticism was less funda-mental than that which had raged around earlier Rent Acts, and the Rent Act of 1965 gives every impression of having now become one of the foundation-stones of British housing administration. Its strength certainly lies in the fact that security of tenure is to some extent separated from the control of rent. Whereas previously a fixed rent meant security of tenure and the absence of such security meant a market rent, the system of regulation now established combined security with a flexible form of rent determination. Such in fact has long been the essence of the settlement reached in the sphere of the commercial lease, but it has taken much longer to find this central ground in the naturally more emotional area of home and hearth.

The new Rent Act fundamentally altered the legal framework of rent control but it also restructured political controversy in this sector. Because the Act occupies the middle ground politically, it has been largely accepted by majorities in both parties. It is true that the Conservatives criticized the Act at the outset for applying to the whole country solutions that were appropriate to London. But, this objection found no echo in Conservative policy between

1970 – 1974. In fact, the fair rent system so appealed to the Conservative party that it decided to extend it to the public sector [33]. Although the furnished sector may seem to provide evidence that traditional disagreement persists, this is not so. Although Labour extended control to the furnished sector in 1974 against Tory opposition, disagreements between the parties on this subject are not as significant as they seem. Neither party likes to stress it but both are agreed that security of tenure cannot be extended to the tenants of landlords sharing the house with them, and Francis found that 40 per cent of furnished tenants in stress areas were in this position [34]. In addition, whatever the extent of real disagreement over the furnished sector, it is less significant than the differences which existed between the parties before 1965, which concerned the whole of the privately rented stock.

There is additional evidence for an emerging consensus in the privately rented sector. Although the Francis Committee, set up by Mr Greenwood to look into the operation of rent control, reported in 1971 in favour of lowering the ceilings above which the market would be allowed to fix rents, Conservative ministers did not take up this suggestion, and in fact only two years later, in response to pressure from back-bench Conservatives with constituents living in expensive rented property, the Government agreed to raise these ceilings. The sight of a Conservative government thus extending rent control is ample evidence of the widespread support which the system of flexible control, coupled with security of tenure, embodied in the 1965 Rent Act, has now secured. Whereas Tory ministers like Mr Sandys and Sir Henry Brooke believed that it was possible to encourage private investment in rented housing, clearly their successors, Mr Peter Walker and Mr Paul Channon, do not think so, and prefer to rely instead on the Housing Association movement.

In assessing the Rent Act and its political impact, I have been obliged to describe some of the conflict of later years. This in itself is a sign that the Act has provided a new framework for political discussion. In my estimation, the changes which the Act has produced will prove of long standing. The radical transformation of the Conservative attitude towards the privately rented sector and to the idea of security of tenure and rent control, is evidence of this. In this sector at least, the oscillation of policy seems to have come to an end. At this point, many questions naturally present themselves; notably, are the French and British situations now much closer to one another than they were? Both have, after all, finally reflected compromise of a sort. But these are questions which need to be discussed in comparative terms and they are therefore best left to be dealt with in the next chapter.

## References

1. A survey by the Oxford Institute of Statistics is summarized in *The Financial Times*, 12 July 1954.
2. *The Times*, 3 March 1952.
3. *The Manchester Guardian*, 4 November 1953.
4. *The Times*, 12 October 1956.
5. *Report of the Interdepartmental Committee on Rent Control*, Cmd. 6621 (H.M.S.O., 1945), p. 9.
6. *Report of the Interdepartmental Committee on the Rent Restriction Acts*, Cmd. 3911 (H.M.S.O., July 1931).
7. ibid., p. 112.
8. *The Financial Times*, 11 December 1952.
9. *H.C. Deb.*, Vol. 560, *see* especially G.R. Mitchison, cols. 1777–96, J. Silverman, cols. 1812–17 and G. Lindgren, cols. 1856–68; 21 November 1956; M.J. Barnett, *The Politics of Legislation* (London: Weidenfeld and Nicolson, 1969), pp. 211–31.
10. *The Times*, 18 February 1957.
11. *The Times*, 1 and 21 February 1957; M.J. Barnett, pp. 180–3.
12. *The Times*, 21 February and 27 March 1957.
13. *H.C. Deb.*, Vol. 560, cols. 1759–77, 21 November 1956.
14. *The Times*, 10 October 1959.
15. *The Financial Times*, 5 August 1960.
16. *The Times*, 20 August 1960.
17. *Housing in England and Wales*, Cmnd. 1290 (H.M.S.O., February 1961); *The Times*, 15 February 1961.
18. *H.C. Deb.*, Vol. 637, cols. 969–70, 27 March 1961.
19. J. Greve, *London's Homeless*, Occasional Papers on Social Administration, No. 10 (G. Bell and Sons, 1964).
20. *The Times*, 23 July 1963.
21. *London – Employment, Housing, Land*, Cmnd. 1952 (H.M.S.O., February 1963).
22. *Report of the Committee on Housing in Greater London*, Cmnd. 2605 (H.M.S.O., March 1965).
23. *The Times*, 2 December 1966.
24. *Report of the Committee on Housing in Greater London*, Cmnd. 2605 (H.M.S.O., March 1965).
25. D.V. Donnison, *The Government of Housing* (Penguin Books, 1967), pp. 262–9; A.A. Nevitt, *Housing Fixation and Subsidies, A Study of Housing in the United Kingdom* (T. Nelson and Sons Ltd., 1966), pp. 146–72.
26. *The Times*, 10 October 1957.
27. *Rent Act, 1965*, Section 27, (1) and (2).
28. *Rents and Security of Tenure*, Cmnd. 2622 (H.M.S.O., March 1965), p. 2.
29. *The Times*, 1 July 1965.

30.  *New Society*, No. 122, 28 January 1965.

31.  *Report of the Committee on the Rent Acts*, Cmnd. 4609 (H.M.S.O., March 1971), Table 25, p. 43.

32.  *The Times*, 23 July 1965; 27 July 1965; 30 July 1965; 27 October 1965; 2 November 1965.

33.  *Fair Deal for Housing*, Cmnd. 4728 (H.M.S.O., July 1971).

34.  *The Times*, 3 August 1974.

35.  *The Times*, 28 February, 1973, 9 March 1973.

# VI

# Conclusions

The object of this chapter will be to define as clearly as possible the contrasting patterns of policy development already described and to attempt to explain this difference. As the account has made clear, the dominant contrast is between a pattern of continuity and continuous linear development on the one hand, and one of oscillation finally settling down on a compromise policy on the other. One may express the same contrast differently. In France an early settlement was reached, which was sufficiently well founded to withstand attack of a radical character from whatever quarter. In Britain, an equivalent settlement, with an equally firm foundation, was not achieved until much later. In speaking of a settlement in these two cases, it is as well to make clear exactly what is meant. The 1948 French Rent Act and the British Rent Act of 1965 seem to me to constitute settlements. In both cases a solution was reached, after considerable deliberation, which appeared to command sufficiently strong political support to weather criticism for some time. In the French case, the Act is still in force after twenty-five years although, by the use of decree powers and occasional amendment, its substance has been slowly eroded during the 1960s. In the British case the Act has seemed to grow in strength and importance with the years as its principles have been extended to cover areas not originally within its scope.

Since we have described both the French and British Rent Acts as constituting settlements, a good deal of parallelism between the two cases is clearly implied. I believe that, speaking in political not technical terms, the achievements of the two Acts are comparable. But this does not mean that these achievements were obtained in the same way. The most striking contrast appears in the different manner in which acceptance was gained. The principal factors at work in Britain were the legitimacy which attaches to a party fulfilling its electoral pledges, impartial review of policy by a body without political affiliations, and with time, the conversion of other organizations and parties to support of an Act to which, at the outset, they had been hostile.

In France, acceptance had to be gained in a quite different manner. The compromise worked out during the Act's preparation and passage was certainly important but probably even more so was the ability of the Government, more by persistence than courage, to overcome popular hostility and its reflection in the Assembly. One might fairly claim that in Britain the formal machinery of democracy proved useful in gaining acceptance whereas in France, less orthodox means proved necessary. Whatever the means used, the result obtained was the same: the establishment of a permanent settlement which took the issues of rent and security out of open politics.

But if the French and British situations are politically similar in that a settlement of some permanence has now emerged, it must be remembered that in legal not political terms the French landlord is in a much stronger position and can generally fix a market rent and evict his tenant freely.

It is worth pausing in order to explain this difference in the existing situation. One might suggest that the stronger legal position of the French landlord, and the more liberal rent regime which he enjoys, taken overall, are a simple consequence of recent French political history. After all, the Right or moderate Right has been in power now for almost fourteen years, and even under the Fourth Republic, the Left always governed with the necessary cooperation of the Centre. In my view this is not the most important reason for the difference. As this study proceeds, we shall tend to find more and more examples of the weakness of the French State when faced with the opposition of certain groups, particularly when they are defending established privileges, and I suggest that the constant presence of Right-wing forces in power would not have been sufficient to establish a system for new building to rent, which is extremely unfavourable to the tenant, had not other factors played an important part.

In saying this I do not wish to overstate my case. All the governments formed since the establishment of the Fifth Republic have followed conservative economic and social policies. This has been an important precondition of the development of policy more favourable to the landlord interest. All I wish to suggest is that the political complexion of the majority in recent years is not the most important explanatory factor.

The most important of these factors is the different character of the publicly rented sectors in Britain and France. The weakness of the French HLM system means that the government has had to rely on private capital for the building of a certain number of dwellings to rent in any year's production. It is not so much that the HLMs are not capable of the same output as the British public sector but more that they have only been building on a substantial scale since the mid-fifties whereas the public sector in Britain was well established in the 1920s. There was also a much more chronic absolute shortage of accommodation in France until recently and this obliged the government to use all the means at its disposal, particularly since, for financial reasons, it is not willing to expand the public sector much beyond its present size. The government in France is therefore obliged to regard the privately rented sector not merely from the static point of view as part of the housing stock, but also from the dynamic viewpoint as a contributor each year to the new building programme.

In Britain the situation is quite different because of the long-standing policy of building publicly for rent which has created a large stock of publicly owned accommodation for renting which is constantly in process of enlargement. In any one year the need for new accommodation may be met, with regard to the rented sector, not only from newly built council housing, but also from re-lets of council houses that have become vacant for one reason or another. This factor almost doubles the number of council houses which are effectively made available each year for prospective new tenants. The advantages of this stock do not exist in France.

It is not then so much a question of political inclination as of inherited practices combined with immediate needs. The French Government cannot create the houses which ought to have been built in the 1920s and, since almost any means of housing construction is welcome, it must accommodate itself to the needs and demands of investors in new private rented accommodation. The British landlord is an owner and renter of existing property but he has no sway with the Government when current construction is being considered, since he has failed to contribute to new building, with very few exceptions, for the last fifty years. The explanation of the existence in France of a free market in the rents of new housing, and in the rents of a great deal of gradually decontrolled property is not so much a matter of politics in the traditional sense of organization or lobbying, nor is the explanation found in the political complexion of the government concerned. It lies instead in the availability in Britain to a government of whatever political complexion, of means of satisfying the demand for rented accommodation in the form of new and vacated council houses. With this source of housing provision at hand, the government is freed from dependence on those who might be induced to invest in housing for rent.

If evidence of this conclusion is required, it exists in several different forms. There is firstly the fact that the construction of new buildings for rent, without subsidy and for profit, is carried on in France whereas it is not in Britain. There is also evidence from government policy that the authorities in Britain, whether Conservative or Labour, have come to accept this handicap whereas the French Government continues to believe in the usefulness of commercial operations of this sort. In addition to this factor of building expressly for rent, it should be noted that the French market for all types of housing depends greatly on the investing landlord and not, as in Britain, solely on the owner-occupier [1]. In order to bolster up the explanation which has been given of the more favourable regime for the landlord in France, one may briefly examine recent French and British political initiatives in the field of new unsubsidized constructions for rent.

In 1958 the first Gaullist initiative in this sphere was the establishment of what were called the *Sociétés Conventionnées* (contract companies) [2]. These were companies which were given extensive tax concessions and entered into an agreement with the Government in exchange for these concessions to build new accommodation to rent to a high standard. The agreement also contained a guarantee for such companies which protected them against any future imposition of rent control. The impetus to this initiative was provided by a situation of chronic housing shortage coupled with a determination to limit public expenditure as part of the financial and economic reforms of 1958. The *Sociétés Conventionnées* had their status revised in 1964 and were renamed the *Sociétés Immobillières d'Investissement* (property investment companies). Neither of these two institutions had as much success as expected. In 1964 they provided 3% of all finance in the housing field but this had fallen to only 1.5% by 1969 [3]. Nevertheless their creation did demonstrate on two separate occasions that the government was willing to attempt to animate the private commercial rented sector of construction. This is particularly important, bearing in mind that the government invested a great deal of its prestige in these two ventures which it still defends as worthwhile. There are further examples of the government's determination to perpetuate and re-animate the private construction of accommodation to rent in the provision which it allows the *Crédit Foncier* to make for rented accommodation. The contrast with the British case is clear. The Conservative Party is much more interested, first of all, in owner-occupation and appears to lack enthusiasm for the task of attempting to recreate profitable building for rent. The view taken in Britain is generally that the wealthier section of the community will naturally prefer to own their own accommodation and the credit facilities available from either Building Societies or insurance companies make this a much more feasible proposition than is the case in France. The only government initiatives which have attempted to revive a non-subsidized rental sector have been those of 1961 and 1964 respectively. In 1961 Mr Brooke announced that he was making £25,000,000 available to housing associations who would be able to use this money to provide new rented accommodation at cost [4]. The same basic principles were to apply when Sir Keith Joseph established the Housing Corporation in 1964. In the latter case, finance was to be for both cost rents and co-ownership and was to come from the government and the Building Societies. The initial justification of Mr Brooke's initiative was that it would show that it was still possible to find tenants for rented accommodation outside the council sector [5]. It was hoped that those with available capital would be persuaded by this example to follow in the footsteps of the Government and invest in new construction for rent. This did not happen and the idea of pump-priming had given way by 1964 to the alternative rationale of establishing a cost rent rather than a profitable rental sector. In short, the political and economic strength of home ownership as an ideal in Britain has rendered impractical and to some extent unnecessary the development of a profitable rental sector comparable to that which exists in France.

In conclusion, it may be pointed out that, if the Conservative Government in Britain had any intention of attempting to emulate the French Government's initiatives in the field of profitable building for rent, it would surely have accepted with more enthusiasm the recommendations of the Francis Report. Notably, it would have abandoned rent control for new building. In fact, although the report advised this, Mr Amery did not accept this advice [6]. There is much evidence that the legal regime, more favourable to the landlord, which exists in France, has been necessary in order to provide a favourable economic environment within which renting for profit can develop. We have already referred to this evidence. Whereas support for this sector from the Right in France has been persistent and effective, in Britain it has been neither of these. Even at times of more doctrinaire Conservative policies and safe Conservative parliamentary majorities, nothing has been done to revive the profitable rented sector.

But our basic concern in this chapter is not the explanation of current differences in the housing regimes as between Britain and France. The problem which principally concerns us is rather the explanation of the varying patterns of policy development observable in the past twenty-five years. We must therefore now move from description to explanation. One possible explanation of the extremely gradual way in which policy develops would rely on an examination of interests and the way in which they are represented in the political process at the national level. On this view it would be argued that French political conditions favour articulation of a wide variety of interests, but render very difficult the aggregation of these different points of view into new government politics. Little has been said in the account of British and French policy of the organized groups which play a part in the political debate, and it is intended to examine their role briefly at this point in order to discover whether they play an important part in the maintenance of the stable French pattern and whether they contribute to the oscillating pattern of British policy.

Landlords in Britain are organized at the national level in the National Association of Property Owners, whereas tenant organization is only significant at the local level, and even here, it is more often found in the public than the private sector. These facts alone are enough, at least in the case of tenants, to rule out the possibility of organized groups playing an important part in policy formation. As we have seen, the British political debate about policy in this sector has been open, public, and usually conducted with reference to general principles. It is easy to understand that this does not provide a suitable environment within which pressure groups might have an important role to play. It seems to me that the history of government intervention in this sector in the 1950s and 1960s shows clearly the importance of traditional party ideologies and policies. If this is so, then I think we must conclude that the landlords are also without influence as an organization. Finally, despite the recommendation of the Milner Holland report in favour of improving the tax position of landlords, the Conservative Government in its most radical phase immediately after the election of 1970 did nothing to implement this recommendation.

In the French situation it is not quite so easy to dismiss an explanation which relies on interests and the way in which they are able to participate in national political life. One is obliged to consider the potential role of interest groups in French politics more seriously because observers in France and abroad have concentrated considerably on this aspect of French political life [7], whereas in Britain the national political scene is dominated by well-organized and disciplined parties which are normally considered an unfavourable breeding ground for effective interest group representation. The Gaullists, for example, frequently castigate the Fourth Republic for its weakness in face of particular interests and we shall see later that in the field of the HLMs there is plenty of evidence that this criticism of the Fourth Republic was well founded. Any examination of French fiscal arrangements in the Fourth and Fifth Republics will soon make clear the importance which interest groups have in certain areas of French policy-making at least. It is also inherently feasible to suggest that the influence of interest groups in the field of privately rented accommodation would tend towards inertia rather than to any decisive development in policy. The two interests concerned would naturally be the landlords and tenants and, one balancing the other, their influence would tend to inhibit the Government in taking any initiative. It is after all almost impossible to act in any way with respect to the privately rented sector without favouring either landlords or tenants in the process.

There are other reasons which tend to suggest that pressure groups might be more important in France. We have already noted that rent issues are much less often the subject of national debate in France. In such circumstances, where the role of the party is less important, it would seem natural for working relations to grow up between the government and those interests affected, and for a government anxious to keep issues out of the public arena to seek to accommodate interests as far as possible. It also seems inherently likely that pressure groups would have a greater part to play where policy development was incremental and where basic principles had been settled beforehand. Some observers of the Fifth Republic have noted that, as part of a reaction against the all-powerful Assembly of the Fourth Republic, Gaullist policy has often sought to develop direct links with interests affected by new policies [8]. Let us therefore examine the plausibility of the interest group thesis as a possible explanation of the French pattern of policy development in this area.

There are two main tenant organizations in France, and the most important of these is the *Confédération Nationale des Locataires* (CNL [9]. This is a Communist-dominated organization which dates back to the First World War and which was reorganized after the Liberation and has continued since then to play an active part in the debate on housing questions. Of the organizations in the field, it is generally regarded as having the widest support and it has recently been officially recognized by the government and taken part in official discussions at the national level in connection both with the privately rented sector and in more general discussion of housing questions [10]. The CNL, for example, has participated in the preparation of the Sixth Plan and was invited by the minister, M. Albin Chalandon, to take part in a round-table discussion in 1969 on the problem of rents, security and repairs in the privately rented sector [11].

Less important but still worthy of attention is the *Confédération Générale du Logement* (CGL). The CGL is an organization of much more recent date and only became firmly established in the mid-50s as a consequence of the national campaign of Abbé Pierre. The organization is not specifically Catholic but its view of the housing question is extremely close to that of the more progressive elements in what was the MRP. This organization is particularly loyal to the Law of 1948 which, as we have seen, was principally the responsibility of the MRP.

If one expects to find that tenant organizations have had a direct influence on policy, an examination of the activities of the CNL and CGL will prove disappointing. In my estimation, however, these organizations have some importance in rendering public opinion on housing questions somewhat more volatile than it would otherwise be. They have at least the standing which enables them to gain some publicity for their criticisms of government policy initiatives, at any rate in those sections of the press which are more or less sympathetic to the tenant interest.

It would be fair to say that, like most areas of housing policy, those issues of disagreement which naturally arise between tenant and landlord have only occasionally become the subject of national political debate in France. One of these periods of debate was in the early 1950s and culminated in the passage of the Law of the 4th March, 1953 [12]. At first sight, this might seem an instance of tenant organizations gaining concessions from the government, because this Law was mainly concerned with limiting the number of occasions on which a landlord might rightfully regain possession of his property. In fact, however, although the CNL was active at this time, it is difficult to believe that the politicians of the Left and Centre who voted for this Law were susceptible to influence from Communist quarters, especially at a time when the Communist Party was totally isolated politically. More important, perhaps, is the point that it is difficult to find any evidence of tenant influence in a policy which has evolved steadily, if always slowly, in the direction desired by landlords. In saying this, I am thinking particularly of the obvious slowness with which governments were able to raise rents in the 1950s, and of the subterfuges that have had to be used in doing this in the 1960s. But the constraints on government, visible throughout this period, seem more probably related to unorganized public opinion than to anything which the unimpressive tenants' organizations might be able to do. An examination of some events in the early 1950s will serve to bear out the view of the role of tenant organizations adopted here.

These events appear to me to contain the essential elements which we shall find again and again in the examination of both interest groups in general and also of the role of the landlord and tenant interests in this sector. One has a degree of organization and militancy far greater than may be observed in the British situation. But sensitivity to interests, where it exists, does not appear to depend upon this organization but rather on more general aspects of the political system, in this case the sensitivity of Fourth Republic deputies to all manner of popular agitation. In any case, the basic decisions with regard to the privately rented sector had been taken when the 1948 Rent Act was adopted and a start made on its application. This being so, the government had very little leeway in its dealings with tenants and landlords at this time. Landlords clearly felt that rents were totally inadequate and ought to rise immediately to much higher levels. Tenants felt that rents were already excessive and that increases were almost always unjustified. The government had adopted inevitably a middle course and was unable to deviate from this path given the long-term objectives which had been adopted. It should be remembered also that the basic settlement achieved in this sector in 1948 and 1949 was worked out between different political parties, and, later, between the Government and a volatile public opinion favourable to the tenant interest. Organized interest group activity played no significant part either in the working out of the 1948–49 compromise or even in the passage of the additional protective measures provided for tenants in 1951 and 1953.

When discussing the difference in policies towards the privately rented sector that had been adopted by the Fourth and then the Fifth Republic, it was observed that continuity in policy was maintained despite a change in constitutional arrangements. Very much the same observation may be applied to the activities of the tenants' interest groups except that there was one important change resulting from the diminished role of the National Assembly. Activities on behalf of the tenants in the early 1950s are not paralleled in the Fifth Republic. The only example of legislation affecting this sector which has originated during the last fourteen years, not from the government but from activity of deputies, is what is known as the *Loi Krieg*, which is a minor measure of decontrol voted by the majority in 1969 concerning only the *chambres de bonnes* in Paris [13]. But we have already concluded that the two Laws of the early fifties were of fairly peripheral concern to the privately rented sector and were essentially simply evidence of the ability of the tenant interest to arouse sympathy among a wide range of deputies. The importance of the volatility of opinion remained as great in the 1960s as it had been in the 1950s but neither the CNL nor the CGL can claim any particular credit for this state of affairs. There has been some development in the character of tenants' activism, however. The CNL has recently attempted to broaden both its appeal and the scope of its activities, and this has been symbolized by the change in the name of its monthly journal from *Réveil des Locataires* to *Logement et Famille*. The emphasis now is not strictly confined to the privately rented sector, and the CNL campaigns on all matters connected with housing including the problem, for example, of land speculation. The CGL, on the other hand, plays a much less important part in political life now than it did at the time of its creation in the mid-fifties, when it was sufficiently militant to indulge in squatting and other forms of direct action.

Both organizations have participated in the preparation of that part of the Sixth Plan which is concerned with housing and both were invited in 1969 to take part in the round-table discussions on rents, security and repairs [14]. This discussion will be treated in more detail when we come to consider the problem of repair and improvements, but with respect to rents and security of tenure, the dialogue between the Government, the tenants and the landlords, which took place in 1969, serves well to illustrate the imperviousness of the Government to influence on most points. The landlords demanded 15 per cent across-the-board annual increases whereas the tenant organizations preferred the policy of increases graduated according to the category of accommodation in question. The Government decided to continue to increase rents annually at a rate of well below 15 per cent and also to continue modulating the increases, so as to move forward more slowly for the lower categories. The importance of the round-table lay not so much in its conclusions as in its taking place. The Government clearly feels that it will profit from a climate of opinion in which hostilities between landlord and tenant are reduced, and hence its attempt to draw the two sides together with itself in tripartite discussions. 'Pour éviter le recours abusif au congé, plus facile à l'avenir si l'on aboutit au marché libre des logements, à la suppresion corrélative du droit, au maintien dans les lieux, il est utile de chercher une amélioration des rapports locataires-propriétaires, en particulier par l'institution de mécanismes nouveaux et souples de règlement du petit contentieux locatif' [15]. Both tenant organizations also made it clear during the round-table that they disapproved of the anomaly created by the division of tenants into two classes, those in accommodation still covered by the 1948 Law and those living in uncontrolled or decontrolled accommodation. The Government was naturally unwilling to accept the tenants' solution to this problem of bringing in some form of flexible control over all rents whether in old or new accommodation.

The French landlords are organized into two groups: the *Union Nationale de la Propriété Immobilière*, the UNPI, and the *Chambre Syndicale des Propriétaires de Paris*. Once again, the ineffectiveness of particular organizations in influencing policy development is testified to by the description of this development already given in chapter IV. As we have seen, the process of satisfying landlords' demands has been an extremely gradual one and the State has always shown itself sensitive to possible discontent and unpopularity which might arise from too rapid an increase in rents, at least in the controlled sector where it is held directly responsible. The French landlords also have a militant tradition which has not been forgotten. Memories of the inter-war repair strikes were revived when a similar threat was made in November 1963, shortly after the Government's anti-inflation plan had brought regular controlled rent increases temporarily to a halt [16]. Such threats have never materialized and the Government did not lift the ban on rent increases until it felt that inflationary dangers had subsided. The reason for the lack of any direct influence of landlords or their organizations on government policy is very much the same as that already outlined in the case of tenants. What the landlords want is so far from what the government feels itself capable of delivering, that no sort of deal or compromise is possible or even advantageous to the government [17]. But if the organized interests are insignificant in Britain as influences on policy, and if French gradualness cannot be explained by a deadlock of opposed interests, one is obliged to look elsewhere for explanations of the contrast in pattern of policy development. One possible approach would be to concentrate attention on the relations between the political and administrative spheres in the two countries. It is often said of France that governmental or ministerial instability is counterbalanced by a strong administration which regards itself as responsible for the maintenance of continuity. This explanation might be complemented in the British case by suggesting that the British politician, supported by a more developed level of Cabinet solidarity, and with a united party behind him, and without the inconvenience of coalition government, is better able to master his department and impose politically oriented policies which, in a two-party system, are bound to produce some variations according to the political complexion of the party in power. This is certainly so in the British case.

There is a particularly striking example in the Crossman Diaries of the way in which sharp changes in the direction of policy are not modified, at least in the area of housing, by the opinion of experienced officials [18]. Crossman relates how he received a deputation of his civil servants, including the Permanent Secretary, who forcibly argued the need for inserting a provision in the Rent Act, the effect of which would have been to facilitate private redevelopment by denying security of tenure to some unfurnished tenants. Despite the arguments put to him about the way in which security of tenure would hamper redevelopment, Crossman insisted that party policy would not permit any derogation from the principle of security of tenure for all unfurnished tenants. One would not expect the convictions of civil servants to affect manifesto commitments such as the Labour Commitment in 1964 to repeal the Tory Rent Act and restore security of tenure. The above incident is therefore all the more significant since what the Department was seeking was not a reversal of policy but a modification of it on a point which some observers might have considered technical. It is therefore clear that in Britain the Civil Service does not significantly affect the pattern of policy development in housing, but at first sight it seems more plausible to suggest that the continuity of French policy derives in some degree from the influence of administrators.

In fact the situation is not one of a cautious compromising middle-of-the-road administration which follows its own course regardless of the more ideological preferences of its political masters. It seems almost certain that the administrators and politicians, at least in the sector which concerns us here, are agreed that more radical policies ought ideally to be followed and that rents ought to be raised much more rapidly and decontrol pushed ahead also at an increasing rate. The experts of the Fourth Plan, for example, suggested in the early sixties that some decontrol by category should be possible before 1965 [19]. Yet, as we know, the first decontrol of this type applied only on 1st January 1968 and then only to the two infinitely small categories 'exceptional' and '1'. In fact it is the specialists and the administrators who would like to go more rapidly and the politicians who are holding them back for political reasons. This has been obvious on at least two occasions in the Fifth Republic. The first was in June 1964 when there was a difference of view between M. Maziol, minister responsible for housing, and the Prime Minister, M. Pompidou, who, careful not to incur too much unpopularity on the eve of the 1965 presidential election, and more concerned with inflation and general economic policy, obliged his Cabinet colleagues to accept increases very much smaller than the housing experts considered necessary. The same thing was apparent in 1971 when M. Vivien's proposals, which clearly reflected the views of the Ministry of Housing and Development, and which were considerably more radical than those of the Government as a whole, were pushed aside and more moderate proposals were adopted instead for political reasons [20].

It will have become clear from our accounts of national policies that an important stabilizing element in France after 1948 has been the ability of the Government to keep housing out of the realm of open politics. There are exceptions but it is undoubtedly the case that housing in France is only intermittently a subject for political debate at the national level, whereas in Britain it receives constant attention from both political parties and political commentators. There are many reasons for this but one which is particularly important when dealing with the rental sector is the compartmentalization of housing policy. It has invariably been the case in post-war France that each sector of housing provision has been treated by the government separately. To maintain this separation between sectors clearly aids the government in keeping controversy to a minimum and avoiding political confrontation. For example, when M. Courant, Minister in 1953, introduced important changes in the system by which loans were made available to promote construction in the owner-occupied sector, he did not accompany these changes by any reduction in the public building programme, or change in the system of rent increases under the 1948 Act. The same is true of the Decrees of December 1963, which again affected the owner-occupied sector. These Decrees were not regarded by the Government as part of a general reorientation of policy.

It is clear that these French practices contrast sharply with the British style of debate and policy-making. In chapter V we stressed that Mr Sandys' Rent Act was clearly seen by him as part of a general reorientation of policy which included also the Housing (Subsidies) Act of 1956. The Conservative Housing (Finance) Act of 1972, although primarily concerned with the public sector, also makes important changes in the privately rented sector by making provision for the scheduled transfer of all dwellings from the controlled to the regulated sector. Whereas in France successful compartmentalization aids in establishing an administrative approach to housing problems, in Britain there is a constant attempt to apply general principles which span all the housing sectors. In Britain there is a constant comparison of one sector with another and these comparisons are an important moving force behind many changes in housing policy.

The question is frequently asked: is the advantage which sector A is receiving justified when one considers that sector B does not receive this particular advantage? Prior to 1957 the position was that the council and privately rented sectors were regarded as privileged since the former enjoyed a subsidy and the latter achieved approximately comparable rents by means of rent control. The assumption was very approximately that, if one could afford to buy one's own house, one did so and that if one could not, one would be catered for by either of the two sectors where some form of financial aid was provided. But this justification was somewhat precarious because the housing subsidy did not aim to and could not produce stable council rents. The element of cost was important in these rents and hence, even if the general needs subsidy had not been abolished in 1956, council rents would have risen constantly. There was therefore bound to come a point at which the argument of parallel advantages as between council and privately rented sectors became untenable.

This occurred with the Rent Act of 1957 but the problem of comparability as between the different sectors of housing provision still remained. According to the Conservative view, the decontrolled tenant was now justly placed on a par with the owner-occupier since both were paying the market price for the accommodation which they were occupying. In this view the council tenant was still receiving a subsidy because he was in need, the assumption being that the tenant of privately rented accommodation who had not received the allocation of a council house was not in such need. As the Milner Holland Report pointed out, these arguments concerning comparability contained several weaknesses. Firstly, the owner-occupier was paying the market price but he was receiving tax concessions on his borrowing and the private tenant was receiving no such advantage either personally or by way of tax concessions to his landlord. It was also pointed out that tenants in the private sector were often as poor if not poorer than council tenants and were also more often in acute need of housing. Comparability and rationality of allocation as between the different sectors therefore appeared to have broken down entirely.

When Mr Crossman introduced his Rent Act, it was partly justified as an attempt to rectify the imbalance just described. The measure was regarded as one designed to redress the balance in favour of private tenant. At the same time, the level of subsidy for the Council sector was also substantially increased. But in fact, as time passed, it had become more and more apparent that it was difficult to justify rationally the different principles which operated in the two sectors. In the aftermath of the Rachman affair and the exposure of intimidation of tenants prior to the 1964 election, there was a tendency to regard the restoration of security of tenure and some form of rent control as a solution of all problems in this sector. It is now increasingly realized that the 1965 Rent Act is not so much a welfare measure designed to aid tenants who are in need but more a measure of simple regulation designed to avoid abuse. The problem of the tenant in need as distinct from the problem of the tenant subject to extortionate rent or intimidation therefore remains unsolved by the Rent Act whose rents, as we have already pointed out, were not fixed with any reference to the tenant's income. The outcome of this criticism was the introduction of the Housing Allowance available for private tenants in the Conservatives' Housing Finance Act of 1972. This provides private tenants with advantages comparable to those received by council tenants who benefit from the

National Rent Rebate scheme. Once again the arguments of comparability are seen to play an important part in innovation. The constant attempts to rationalize the various forms of aid to the different sectors of housing provision, and the comparisons which are consequently made between one sector and another, are not a feature of French discussion or policy-making. In France, expert assessment of housing policy may at times seek to point to anomalies and wastage [21], but less specialized discussion and political controversy do not reflect these concerns. As already pointed out, when reform does take place, it is piecemeal and operates within and not across sectors. The compartmentalization of discussion and policy-making in France is clearly associated with a lower political saliency of housing issues.

It would seem that an additional and important element in our explanation can be found if we examine the different roles played by political parties in Britian and France. The French political system suffers from a wide gap between the government and the society to be governed. The inability of the government and the governed to accommodate one another has been demonstrated too many times in French history for it to be necessary to underline the point once again here, but the unfortunate consequences of this distance between the rulers and the ruled are not felt only in the instability of political regimes and recurrent constitutional crises. They make themselves felt also in the mundane field of policy formation which is the subject of this study. This is apparent in the inability of the government to impose its own view of the situation on the public, and the result is the extreme hesitancy and consequent gradual character of policy development which has been observed in France. In Britain it would appear that this difficulty is surmounted to a large extent by the importance of the political party. The party is not simply an instrument for the obtaining of power but is also a means by which the government and the public are brought into line on particular policy matters, at least in those areas of policy, such as housing, where both parties have well-established distinct and traditional points of view. In a recent survey of research bearing on the relations between the attitudes of voters and the policies of their party, it emerges that housing is one of those issues which succeed in uniting the voters for each party with their elected representatives, and dividing the major parties from one another [22]. In the 1970 election campaign housing was the only issue to which both Labour and Conservative spokesmen referred frequently [23].

Typically, each party cultivated a policy area which it regarded as favourable to its own electoral success. Housing is therefore exceptional as an issue, and would seem to be one in which both parties are confident of substantial support for partisan policies. Because the Conservative and Labour parties are more deeply implanted in British society than any French political party, they can be sure, when in power, of bulk support from many sections of the community and hence do not hesitate under normal conditions to impose their own view on problems and their necessary solutions. This factor is particularly important when one is dealing with an area where interests are sharply opposed. There is evidence of the importance of the party and its electoral victory in the timing of both the principal pieces of post-war legislation on rents and security in Britain. The first was clearly associated with the increased Conservative majority obtained in the 1955 General Election and the second was drafted and passed into law within one year of the Labour Party coming to power in 1964. In sharp contrast to this, one finds that in France housing plays a minor role in election campaigns and there is not one piece of post-war French housing legislation which derives even remotely from an electoral commitment. In any democratic system the increased authority which a government obtains from a recent demonstration of majority support is extremely important when it has to deal with controversial and divisive matters.

Such a strengthening of government authority is impossible in France for a number of reasons. There is first and foremost the more artificial character of French political parties. This is just as much a feature of political life today as it was under the Fourth Republic, as any examination of the groups lying between the UDR and the Socialist Party in the centre of the political spectrum will make clear. By artificiality, I mean that many groups or political parties owe their existence simply to recent events and are in some cases only identifiable to the public by reference to one prominent personality who is associated with the group. Even if one takes as an example the most powerful current French political party, the UDR, and if one is willing to gloss over its frequent change of names in the last fourteen years, one is still obliged to remark that the party was designed purely with regard to constitutional questions and loyalty to the person of de Gaulle, and that in such circumstances a high degree of cohesion on economic and social policy cannot be expected either amongst its militants or amongst supporters within the general public. However vague may be the ideological assumptions of Conservatives and their supporters, they are a real factor and they do assure the Conservative Party of a certain broad acceptance within the public when it is enacting policies which can be seen to coincide clearly with what are called Conservative principles. The same is even more true of the Labour Party.

Against what has been said about the weakness of French political parties, it may be argued that, despite its youth, and the peculiar circumstances of its birth, the UDR has grown in authority and become more comparable to the British Conservative Party. My argument presumes that the UDR suffers from many of the traditional weaknesses of French political parties and that it cannot yet play a role parallel to that of the Conservative Party. It must be remembered that I am judging the UDR, not on its electoral support, or its ability to establish a party-machine for winning elections. I am judging it rather on its ability to command the popular following which is necessary to put through unpopular legislation in the social and economic field.

On more than one occasion since 1958, it has been clear that the desirability of decontrol has been strongly felt but that the accompanying political capacity has been lacking. For example, soon after taking up his responsibilities in 1962, M. Maziol was at pains to deny unofficial rumours of a plan to achieve total decontrol in stages over a six-year period [24]. Such a target was clearly desirable in the Government's view but politically too risky. Only shortly after this, in January 1963, the same minister was implying that at least the two highest categories of dwelling, 'exceptional' and '1', would be decontrolled soon [25]. In fact this was not carried out until 1968.

In 1966, the then minister, Edgar Pisani, spoke quite openly of his desire to see all dwellings decontrolled by 1970 but, as we have seen, there were still, in 1970, an estimated 1.4 million dwellings whose rents remain controlled [26]. We have also already referred to M. Vivien's inability to obtain the rent increases which he desired when he was minister. This last example is probably the most significant since M. Vivien is not simply a minister chosen by the President or the Prime Minister for his talent but an important figure carrying considerable weight within the UDR.

These hesitations should be contrasted with the behaviour of the Conservative Party in the late fifties and early sixties. At times during this period, the Government incurred the displeasure, not only of the public, but also of some of its own back-benchers, and yet it felt able to carry through its decontrol legislation, legislation of a more radical character than anything which the Gaullists have ever considered. It should not be forgotten that the decontrol operated in France in the 1960s has always been subject to minimum standards and that in most cases decontrol can only be obtained by the landlord in exchange for a lease of three years granted to the tenant. No such limiting conditions were specified in the Rent Act of 1957.

I have felt it necessary to emphasize my view of the importance of the role of the political party because what I have said, especially with reference to the UDR, runs counter to a good deal of authoritative writing on this subject [27]. In my view, the assessment made here is unorthodox only because evidence of a new type has been taken into account. Writers on political parties usually pay most attention to membership, structure, voting support, and leadership. I have adopted quite a different perspective and concentrated on performance.

One does not have far to seek in order to find examples, in British policy-making, of the importance of the continuity of a political party and its clear identification in social and economic terms. We have referred to the Conservatives' commitment in the 1950 Manifesto to review rent legislation, and all observers are agreed that when the Conservatives came to power in 1951, regardless of the lack of any precise commitments, the time would come when the Party would necessarily bring about substantial modifications of the system of rent control. The same sharing of expectations by ruled and rulers was apparent in 1964 at the time of the Labour victory. In this case there was even a precise commitment to repeal the Rent Act which had been maintained consistently by the Party for at least seven years.

In my conclusion to this chapter, I have concentrated for explanatory purposes on the differing roles and character of the political parties in the British and French systems, and on the way in which debate about housing in France is limited and compartmentalized, thus restricting the scope of reform when it comes. These factors seem to me to be of crucial importance when one is dealing with the privately rented sector. When we come to examine other areas of housing policy, where we shall find the same general contrasts between the British and French patterns repeated, we shall find that this explanation is supplemented in other ways. In many other sectors, however, we shall again find in France the same resistance to innovation, the same yawning gulf between government and society, and the same continuity of policy problems and government response.

## References

1. Estate agents in the Paris region reported that, in the last quarter of 1972 and the first quarter of 1973, sales to investing landlords, as distinct from owner-occupiers, made up between one third and one fifth of their total business (*Le Monde*, 22 June 1973).

2. *Combat*, 17 September 1958.

3. P. Consigny, *Rapport sur l'Aide Publique au Logement* (Groupe de Travail sur l'Aide Publique au Logement, 1969) p. 11.

4. *Housing in England and Wales*, Cmnd. 1290 (H.M.S.O., February 1961); *The Times*, 15 February 1961.

5. *H.C. Deb.*, Vol. 637, col. 970, 27 March 1961.

6. *The Times*, 11 February 1971.

7. P. Williams, *Crisis and Compromise* (3rd ed; Longmans, 1964), pp. 352–85.

8. Y. Tavernier, 'Le syndicalisme paysan et la politique agricole du gouvernement de Juin 1958 à Avril 1962', *Revue Française de Science Politique*, Vol. XII, No. 3, pp. 621–2.

9. *Pour que le droit au logement devienne une réalité* (Confédération Nationale des Locataires).

10. *Le Figaro*, 22 October 1069.

11. *Rapport des Commissions du VIème Plan, 1971–75, Rapport de la Commission de l'Habitation*, Vol. I, pp. 106–11.

12. J. Minjoz, *Rapport au nom de la Commission de la Justice et de la Législation, Annexe au Procès-Verbal de l'Assemblée Nationale, J.O.*, 12 June 1952; *Combat*, 25 May 1950 and 12 October 1952; *Le Monde*, 22 January 1953; *La Croix*, 22 April 1953.

13. *Le Monde*, 9 January 1969.

14. *Livre Blanc, Politique de l'Habitat Existant, Table Ronde du 25-9-1969. Rapport des Commissions du VIème Plan 1971–75. Rapport de la Commission de l'Habitation*, Vol. I, pp. 106–11.

15. *Livre Blanc, Politique de l'Habitat Existant*, Table Ronde du *25-9-1969*, p. 13.

16. *Combat*, 11 November 1963.

17. On the general question of pressure groups *see* J. Meynaud and A. Lancelot, 'Groupes de pression et politique du logement', *Revue Française de Science Politique*, Vol. VIII, No. 4, p. 821. Meynaud and Lancelot's study does not attempt to deal with housing policy but concentrates instead on a description of the relevant pressure groups. They are extremely cautious, for methodological reasons, about reaching any conclusions on the influence of pressure groups but on the whole they seem to feel that they are not very influential, particularly in the case of the CNL and the CGL. This negative conclusion accords with my own view and is all the more significant since tenant militancy was at a peak at the time that they wrote and has fallen off sharply since.

18. R.H.S. Crossman, *Diary of a Cabinet Minister* (Hamish Hamilton & Jonathan Cape, 1975), pp. 162 ff.
19. *Rapport de la Commission de l'Habitation du Quatrième Plan* (1962–65), p. 86.
20. *Le Monde*, 19, 23 and 26 June 1971.
21. P. Consigny, *Rapport sur l'Aide Publique au Logement* (Groupe de Travail sur l'Aide Publique au Logement, 1969).
22. R. Rose, *The Problem of Party Government* (Macmillon 1974).
23. ibid., p. 309.
24. *L'Aurore*, 12 and 13 May 1962.
25. *L'Aurore*, 12 and 13 January 1963.
26. *Le Monde*, 19 November 1966 and 24 April 1973.
27. J. Charlot, *The Gaullist phenomenon. The Gaullist Movement in the Fifth Republic* (Allen and Unwin, 1971); P. Williams and M. Harrison, *Politics and Society in de Gaulle's Republic* (Longmans, 1971), pp. 86–102.

# PART III

# The Public Sector

# VII

# Introduction

In the privately rented sector, which has just been discussed, we have observed that political controversy is almost always present, although its importance may vary from year to year and as between countries. It would appear, however, that the extent of controversy in this sector is on the decline, at least in the long run, if only because this form of housing provision is of declining importance in both Britain and France. As we have already pointed out, disputes in this area have concentrated principally on the manner in which the existing stock of privately rented houses is to be used. This is natural, since in Britain, new private building for rent is almost non-existent, and in France it is very much less important than either building for sale for the owner-occupied sector or building for the public sector.

The situation in the public sector is quite different. Political conflict and direct government involvement in the public sector are inevitable here, unlike the other sectors. Since public agencies of one form or another are involved in the building and renting processes, it is impossible for the government to escape responsibility by invoking the desirability of allowing economic forces to govern the extent and nature of activity. Such an argument clearly makes no sense when one is dealing with activities under government control. The sector is also clearly contrasted with the one described in the preceding part in that it is of growing importance in Britain and France if one judges this importance by the share of the existing housing stock which is in public ownership. If one speaks in round figures, the present British percentage would be approximately 35 per cent of the housing stock as against 15 per cent in France. Whereas therefore the privately rented sector may be declining in importance and political interest, the reverse is true of the public sector which is expanding continuously in both countries. The political importance of the public sector is guaranteed by its own nature. When there is a demand for housing, as there always is, it is inevitable that the government, as a provider of the substantial share of new housing, should bear the weight of some of this demand.

But if the government decides that it should bear directly some share of responsibility for the provision of new housing, which all governments in developed countries do, the vital question remains as to the exact rationale which is to determine the extent of this provision. Considerable thought has been given to this question, particularly in France, since it is there that the forms of state intervention in housing are seen in the greatest variety [1]. The most frequent justification of public building and letting is that this process is necessary in order to provide accommodation of a reasonable minimum standard and that if public intervention were not undertaken, the market would not be capable of providing a range of housing, the cost of which would make it accessible to all sections of the community. One might grant quite readily in theory that there are types of housing provision which might not be available on the market but which the State could provide at cost without subsidy, but in fact it soon becomes clear, both in principle and in practice, that the major difficulty is one of cost and that if the State is to enlarge significantly the clientele for new housing, it will be obliged to introduce some element of subsidy. It is at this point that we encounter the central political problem posed by the existence of a public housing sector. Subsidy to particular individuals to whom the new housing is allotted seems necessarily to provide the accommodation in question. Yet, what is to be the justification of the subsidy in question? Normally it is argued that a subsidy is justified by the income of the recipient: he is too poor to be able to afford the market price of the accommodation which is considered necessary for him and his family and a subsidy is therefore needed. But the argument is not as simple in the case of housing subsidy as it would be for an income support in cash. What is then the difference between a subsidy or some form of personal financial assistance justified by poverty and a housing subsidy the benefit of which goes to the tenant of public housing because he is considered to be too poor to pay a cost or market rent?

The main difference is that, in order to be eligible to benefit from the housing subsidy, it is not necessary that a tenant be poor in the sense that his standard of living falls below a nationally accepted minimum. He may, and quite probably will be, employed, and will therefore not be receiving Supplementary Benefit or its equivalent. His receipt of a subsidy must therefore be justified not on the grounds of general poverty but on the grounds of what we might call housing poverty. This expression may need a little explanation. Let us suppose, for the purposes of an example, someone earning £3,000 per annum. He is not poor in any normally accepted sense of this term, but he may well be unable to buy a house of his own at the market price, given the prevailing limitations on the size of the mortgage debt which he may contract. A house in the area in which he lives may well cost more than £10,000, and in such circumstances, the only possible form of accommodation for his family will be publicly owned and subsidized, presuming that no privately rented accommodation is available. The fundamental observation to which this example is intended to draw attention is that the income level at which it is necessary to introduce a housing subsidy will almost always be different from and higher than the nationally defined poverty level. Even if this fact is accepted by those professionally connected with housing provision, it is bound, nevertheless, to raise certain political problems since the community will be supporting the income, even if indirectly, of someone who is not below the nationally defined poverty line. Therefore there will always be conflict over the exact definition of those who are entitled to such a subsidy with those on the Left suggesting a more extensive use of the subsidy, or perhaps its application to all forms of housing provision, and those on the Right suggesting that, although an element of subsidy is necessarily involved in public housing provision, it should be confined as narrowly as possible so as to assist only those in need. This word 'need' contains an important ambiguity, for it may refer to poverty or near-poverty, or, alternatively, to what we have described above as housing poverty, that is, an inability to pay the market price given local conditions in the housing market. The conflict over the exact definition of 'need' will naturally oppose tax-payers on the one hand and tenants or potential tenants of public housing on the other. This conflict is endemic to the field of public housing, although, as we shall see, its importance varies very much according to cultural assumptions. To anticipate the conclusions of later chapters, whereas in Britain the conflict over the extent of subsidy in public housing is constant and always important, in France the subsidy gives rise to much less controversy.

As has been indicated, this conflict is endemic to public housing, but its importance may vary notably according to economic conditions. Particular problems for those who try to defend housing subsidies are posed by the phenomenon of inflation. Although some costs in a public housing programme, such as management and repair, will be related to current cost levels, the most important cost is the initial capital outlay and the loan charges on this capital. If, in later years, nominal incomes rise and the value of money declines, the debt incurred at the time of construction will diminish in real value and the rent required from the house to balance the loan charges will diminish as a proportion of the income of the tenant. If no other factors intervene to counterbalance this advantage, inflation will therefore tend, in the eyes of the authorities, to reduce the need for subsidy, even if its necessity was accepted at the outset.

A further and similar difficulty posed in the justification of a housing subsidy, not so much by inflation but by increased real prosperity, is that there is a widely held assumption that, as real living standards increase, forms of assistance which involve the transfer of income from one section of the community to another will become less and less necessary and will be justified only in the case of an individual income falling below some defined minimum level. Expressed in terms of the housing sector, there is an assumption that as real incomes rise, more people will be able to afford, without assistance, the price of new housing, whether for sale or to let, and that therefore, if a subsidy is still necessary, it will be so for a diminishing proportion of the population [2]. The fallacy in this argument lies in the assumption that rising living standards mean a more favourable ratio of annual earnings to house prices. The evidence seems to indicate, in Britain at least, that this does not occur.

Nor does this exhaust the political difficulties which arise as a consequence of housing subsidy. Particular problems are posed when one begins to compare one sector of housing provision with another. The point may first be illustrated by comparing the public and privately rented sectors. If a system of rent control of some kind is in force in the private sector, tenants of such housing are receiving a benefit, even if its cost is borne by one section of the community rather than by the community as a whole. In such circumstances, it will be difficult, on grounds of equity as between private and public tenants, to deny the justice of some form of subsidy for the latter. If, on the other hand, rent control is in the process of being dismantled, there will be a natural tendency, again on the grounds of equity as between private and public tenants, to reduce or abolish the housing subsidy. The task of achieving some rationality with regard to the advantages accorded to private and public tenants is in fact even more complicated than the foregoing summary of the situation has suggested. Even if one presumes, for example, that the majority of tenants in both sectors can afford the market price of their accommodation, and one consequently decides to remove all rent control for the private sector, it is still difficult to justify the charging of a market rent in the public sector. To do so would logically involve profitable public housing with government deriving income from the rent paid by its tenants. To follow this policy in the public sector is to uproot the conceptions which the general public holds with regard to this sector and also to modify substantially the role of the professional working in this field. The public has always considered publicly provided housing as being available for those in need, and it naturally comes as something of a shock if it is suggested that some profit should be drawn from this sector. In both Britain and France there are also strong traditions of social service in the field of public housing and these traditions are naturally hostile to any suggestion of profit or surplus in the public sector.

Difficulties in connection with the housing subsidy also arise if one compares the public and the owner-occupied sectors. In most developed countries, it is customary to award substantial tax advantages to those who borrow in order to buy their own housing. Such has long been the position in Britain and France. This form of aid may also in some cases be supplemented by especially advantageous forms of saving which may be provided by the government for those who use their savings to buy their own house. It is only understandable if the supporters of a housing subsidy for the public sector demand that this sector receives some form of quid pro quo for the benefits which are awarded to the owner-occupier sector. A dynamic comparison of these two sectors reveals further difficulties. The tenant of publicly rented housing will almost certainly experience periodic increases in rent. This is not because the cost of his own house has changed over the years, but rather because his rent is almost certainly pooled with that of other tenants of public housing. Therefore, as costs rise, pressing particularly hard on the current housing programme and new tenants, he will be called upon to pay an increased rent and share some of the burden which would otherwise fall more heavily on new arrivals. The newly arrived tenant of public housing is often charged less rent than would be necessary if the only aid he received was the current subsidy. His rent is further reduced by raising the rents of older tenants of the same authority. The occupier of his own house, on the other hand, is not normally faced with this mounting obligation, although he may have to pay an increased monthly charge if the contract which he has signed with his loan institution allows that institution to alter the interest charged on the debt during the period of repayment. Generally speaking, however, the charge to the owner-occupier is stabilized as compared with the constantly rising rent of a tenant of public housing.

The political difficulties posed by a demand for equity as between these two sections of the community are once again aggravated greatly by the process of inflation. In the case of the public tenant, the position is somewhat equivocal. On the one hand, inflation will reduce the real value of the debt which has been incurred in the construction of his housing, but, on the other, he will be called upon to shoulder some share of the burden of the cost of new housing which will be affected by inflation, and the government of the day may also argue, in attempting to lighten its financial burden, that, as prices generally rise, it is only normal and just that the rents of public housing should rise also. The position of the owner-occupier in process of repaying a debt is, however, unequivocally advantageous in an inflationary situation. Not only will the value of his debt be decreased by this process, but his nominal income will almost certainly rise, and therefore the share of his income which he must devote to repayment will certainly fall with the passing of the years. In addition he profits from the increase in value of the asset which he has acquired. The foregoing should make it quite clear that any attempt to achieve equity as between the owner-occupier and the tenant of public housing faces innumerable complications. It is a gross oversimplification, for example, to suggest that both are treated alike if the subsidy for public housing is withdrawn.

It may be seen from the examples which have been given that the division of housing provision into a number of clearly defined sectors is a considerable inconvenience for government. Spokesmen for any particular sector may point to the advantages which are accorded to other sectors and demand that these be extended. If the Government is unable to resist this type of demand, its freedom of action is extremely reduced. A change in housing conditions or in the political assessment of the situation may suggest changes in one sector, but to bring about these changes will almost certainly spark off demands for adjustments elsewhere [3]. Numerous examples of this process will be found when we come to examine the course of policy development in both Britain and France. The strategy of any government, whether consciously adopted or not, will tend toward dealing with sectors individually. The government will attempt to argue that each sector has its peculiar characteristics and that advantages accorded to one sector are justified per se. For example, it may be argued that a savings incentive is desirable in order to encourage saving and investment and reduce the pressure of demand. In this way the authorities will be able to resist the demand from other housing sectors for some form of financial benefit which may be said to correspond to the advantages accorded the owner-occupied sector by way of a savings incentive scheme.

An example of this strategy applied to the tax advantages accorded the owner-occupied sector may be found in a Conservative publication, one of the authors of which was at the time the Party's Opposition spokesman on housing matters [4]. In this pamphlet, which argues for the abolition of the general means subsidy for public housing, the tax advantages accorded the owner-occupied sector are not treated as an instrument of housing policy. An analogy is instead developed between the purchase of a house and the purchase of future pension rights. In both cases it is suggested that net rather than gross income ought to be subject to taxation and in this way a distinction is established between the expense of the owner-occupier in repaying his debt and the expense of the council tenant in paying rent which is used to pay off the housing authorities' debt. On occasions the government may not attempt to deny the validity of parallels between different housing sectors. Such a strategy involves radical politics. The occasions on which this strategy may be observed are therefore comparatively rare under normal conditions and are best observed in the initiative of 1955–6 in British housing policy when the Government readily accepted the parallel between privately and publicly owned accommodation to rent and followed deliberately a policy of withdrawal of special advantages from both sectors simultaneously. The same process, although on a more limited scale, may be seen in the Housing Finance Act promoted in 1971 and 1972 by the Conservative Government. In accordance with the general observations which have already been made as to the pattern of policy development in France, it is natural to find that on no occasion in post-war history has this radical strategy been adopted. The government resists attempts to treat sectors jointly, and policy for each sector develops without reference to what is done in other sectors. This accords with the incremental pattern of French policy development which has already been observed.

To some extent, the political questions which must be decided with respect to the fixing of rent levels in the public sector are simply a reflection in a different form of the difficulties already described, but there are other rent questions. Principally, there is the issue of differential rents. The principles which underlie a policy of differential rent are simple. The total rental income required from public housing may be fixed by the financial conditions determined centrally for the financing of public construction but such determinations on financial and other grounds do not necessarily imply the fixing of a particular rent for a particular tenant. Since public housing is bound to vary in quality and cost, it would seem natural to vary the rent demanded so as to allow it to correspond to the quality of service provided. If this is not done, it will be objected that some tenants are receiving much more for their money than others. In such circumstances, it will inevitably arise that some tenants are in very much greater difficulty than others. One way of dealing with the problem posed by this situation is not to adjust rent to the physical condition of the dwelling or its situation, but rather to take some account of the income of the tenant, fixing a lower rent for the poorer tenant or, alternatively, awarding him an allowance which reduces the rent which he effectively pays. Before any attention is given to the form which a differential rent scheme might take, one may encounter opposition even to the principle of such an approach. Housing authorities may argue, and have argued, that their task is essentially one of town planning and of providing a public service and it is no business of theirs to deal with what they regard as a social problem of poverty [5]. Objections of this sort are likely to be all the more forcibly expressed since experience shows that differential rent schemes in whatever form are rarely popular with tenants and they are always more complicated to administer than forms of rent determination which do not take into account the personal circumstances of the tenant. There are also objections to the principle of the differential rent which are more fundamental. The basic problem is that of the poor tenant who is considered unfairly penalized if called upon to pay the rent which other tenants pay and which is determined by the conditions of the financing of public housing. One answer to this problem is to refuse to consider the distribution of the burden as between tenants as a question separate from the conditions of financing as a whole. Such has sometimes been the position of left-wing critics of differential rent systems who have argued that rents ought to be fixed so as to be acceptable to the poorest tenant and the terms on which public housing is financed adjusted in order to make this possible [6].

Other difficulties will arise when the principle is accepted but the form of its adoption remains undecided. The most radical form of differential rent scheme involves the examination of the income of all tenants periodically. This approach is unpopular with tenants and for this reason a system of rent rebates may be used instead. Under a rent rebate scheme, the basic rent is fixed but may be reduced if the tenant makes an application and provides the necessary evidence that his income entitles him to a lower rent or an allowance. Inevitably the wealthier tenant will object to this scheme, if the loss of revenue from the lower rents is in fact to be made up not out of central funds, but out of the total rent collected. Such is often the case with differential rent schemes since the government may decide what level of subsidy it considers appropriate and then allow the distribution of the consequent rent burden to be determined by income. In such circumstances, the wealthier tenant may naturally argue that if there was no differential rent scheme, it would be possible to fix a lower across-the-board standard rent. Chapters VIII and IX will show how different solutions to this problem have been adopted in Britain and France, and how such solutions are politically determined.

The examination of any programme of publicly provided housing will soon reveal conflicts between the centre and the locality, that is to say between central government whose principal task is the provision of finance, and those organizations whose responsibility it is to conduct the detailed operation of housing construction and management. Some of these problems are of a purely administrative character and therefore do not interest us in this study, but housing invariably provides examples of more political conflicts between the centre and the localities. Disputes over the distribution of functions between centre and localities are often strongly politicized because substantive policy issues are involved. Arguments about the extent of local autonomy are almost always connected, not only with disagreements between locality and centre over the correct distribution of responsibilities, but with opposed views on questions such as the policy to be followed in the allocation of new housing or the type of rent structure which is desirable. There are a number of reasons why housing particularly exhibits this type of mixed conflict. If one is engaged in building between one and two hundred thousand houses per year, detailed matters such as the size of projects, their location, the allocation to them of new tenants and many other problems, are much too complicated for decision at the centre. On the other hand, the enormous capital expenditure involved in a programme of this size makes central government control in some areas inevitable. This is particularly so because the central government is not only interested in the budgetary charge which will result from the elements of subsidy involved in new housing, but also has responsibility for managing the total level of demand and for sharing out the available capital among public investments of different sorts. Local authorities endowed with housing responsibilities or those professionally involved in housing cannot be expected to share the government's economic perspective and this adds an extra element to local-central conflicts. But if, on the one hand, the executing and local authority is unsympathetic towards the government's economic priorities, the central authority on the other hand will itself be less sensitive than the local to tenant feelings and hostilities which may affect the course to be followed in some areas of housing policy. Central authorities, for example, will always exhibit this more detached attitude with regard to allocation policies and rent structures.

The existence of a public housing programme gives rise to various conflicts because of the interaction which inevitably exists between this and other forms of housing provision. The most obvious of these, which hardly needs to be discussed at length because of its familiarity, is that of the balance to be struck between public and private provision in a given year. There are other interactions which give rise to conflicts of a less obvious character. For example, the levels of rent in public housing are generally considered to have an important impact on the level of demand for privately provided houses. If the conditions of financing make low rents in public housing possible, then the demand in the private sector may well be reduced. If rents are high, however, the advantages of the public sector are proportionally decreased and potential tenants may decide instead on the balance of advantages that they should attempt to purchase in the private market. Whether the facts of the housing situation in fact support the analysis just described may be a matter for dispute. Some observers would argue that the group of those who may fall into either one or other sector of housing provision is either non-existent or very small. Whatever the situation may be, there is no doubt that many of those involved recognize a link between rent levels and the demand for private housing, and in such a situation this conflict acquires political importance. Because of the interconnection between the levels of public rent and demand for privately provided housing, those on the Right may often argue that public rents are too low, and that, consequently public money is being wasted in providing housing for those who might very well purchase their own accommodation if rents were raised. From the other end of the political spectrum the argument will normally be that rents are too high or rising too rapidly and that, as a consequence, some needy tenants are being obliged to seek less satisfactory forms of housing provision and existing tenants are being unjustly penalized in relation to those who have had the advantage of purchasing their own homes. This conflict has an eternal and insoluble character because the position of the protagonists is based partly on conceptions as to the amount that an individual or family in given circumstances should normally pay for housing. No agreement on questions of fact can ever resolve differences of view on such a question.

On general grounds it might be thought that the question of allocating newly available public houses would be a subject of considerable political dispute. After all, one is inclined to presume that one of the basic issues in any political situation is that of who gets what. In my view, allocation policy in the public sector will not normally be a subject of great national political conflict, regardless of the general considerations just referred to, and despite the enormous importance of this area of housing policy. The reasons for this important matter not becoming one of political controversy seem to relate to the characteristics of housing and housing allocation as a sector of policy-making. We find here once again an example of the way in which generally sound observations as to the nature of the political process must be modified when one focuses on a particular area of policy-making. When the questions of rent and security of tenure in the private sector were examined, it was observed that one of the important features of that area of policy was the degree of clarity of definition of the groups involved as distinct from the effectiveness of their organization. The question of group definition is of prime importance in allocation policy. The first point to note is that whereas in the privately rented sector one has two clearly defined and inevitably opposed groups, allocation policy concerns a wide variety of groups, each of which appears to have an equal claim on the available housing. There are the newly married couples, the low-paid worker and his family, the elderly, the large family, and those whose rehousing is made necessary by slum clearance or other forms of redevelopment. By their nature, these groups are less clearly defined than, for example, landlords and tenants. They are rather categories which are defined by those whose business it is to allocate new housing or to discuss allocation policy. In addition to what one might call the artificial character of these groups, there is the difficulty of linking their claims to any view of a desirable state of society. It would be difficult, for example, to find a political philosophy or ideology which would recommend giving a priority to the old rather than to the overcrowded or the slum-dweller. These characteristics of the groups involved seem to explain the normally non-political character of conflicts over allocation, although, as we shall see when we come to examine this question with respect to France, it is still possible that particular circumstances give the allocation question political significance [7].

A further issue in the public sector is that of sale to sitting tenants. This is a question which is bound to be posed with increasing insistence as time passes and the size of the stock of publicly rented houses increases. At the outset, public housing will be in principle allocated to those who cannot afford to buy, but, with the passage of time, tenant income may increase or the relation of wages to house prices may alter so as to enable new strata of the population to buy their new housing. In favour of permitting sales, it may be argued that the housing authority will receive useful income from such sales and that to sell is likely to be popular with those tenants who can afford to buy. Against it, those on the Left argue that a house sold today is a loss of the possibility of allocating this house in future to a family in need. The merits of the arguments on each side would seem to depend very much on local housing conditions. The issue is not likely to have the weight and political importance of some of the more fundamental questions which have been discussed earlier in this chapter because it mainly concerns the interests of those tenants of public housing who wish and are able to buy. But what the issue lacks in the numbers of those directly interested, it often gains in terms of ideological overtones. This element in the controversy may increase in importance, particularly if opponents of sale introduce into the argument the possibility of tenants later selling their acquired houses at a profit. A cry may then be raised of private speculation with public assets.

This survey of the politics which surround any public housing programme has concentrated on those political issues which are endemic to the sector. When we come to place public housing in the context of a particular political and administrative system, the picture becomes more complicated and at the same time more interesting. Some issues lie dormant whilst others assume considerable and constant importance. The point has now been reached when we may abandon the general discussion and proceed to the examination of policy development in each of the two nations which concern us.

## References

1. M. Salaun, *Réflexion sur les aides à la construction* in *Rapports des Commissions du Sixième Plan : Rapport de la Commission de l' Habitation*, Vol. II.

2. *Rapports des Commissions du Sixième Plan : Rapport de la Commission de l' Habitation*, pp. 163–66.

3. *See* chapter VI.

4. V.F. Corfield and G. Rippon, *Target for Homes* (Conservative Political Centre, July 1965).

5. Memorandum from Lichfield Rural District Authority and Memorandum from Bath Borough Council, *Fourth Report from the Estimates Committee : Housing Subsidies* (Session 1968–69), Vol. II, pp. 328–34 and Vol. III, pp. 773–96.

6. Memorandum from Bedwellty Urban District Council, *ibid.*, pp. 461–82; *Le Nouvel Observateur*, 1 December 1965.

7. Although allocation policy is usually non-political in the sense that it is not the subject of open political debate and conflict, this does not mean of course that policy in this field is without political significance in a broader sense.

# VIII

# The Public Sector: France

## 1 *1945–53*

In the early post-war years none of the problems which are ordinarily associated with public housing were of any great political importance in France. There is no mystery as to the explanation of this absence of the HLM movement from the political scene at this time. Governments of all political complexions gave an overriding priority to the re-establishment of oridinary economic life and the recovery of inter-war levels of production. This meant that a priority in public investment was given to what were regarded as productive investments and housing did not figure under this heading. One is startled to learn that up until the end of June 1952 only 10 per cent of an extremely low level of housing production was within the HLM rental sector [1]. Whilst the public housing programme remained insignificant both in total size and as a proportion of the year's housing production, most of the political issues which might have caused conflict were necessarily of little importance. The rent levels to be fixed, the means of finance, and the selection of HLM tenants, could hardly arouse political passions when so little was being done and so few individuals were involved. One might have expected, however, that the low priority which was given both to public housing and to housing in general would have created political difficulties, for a low level of inter-war construction and a total absence of construction during and immediately after the war, coupled with the rapid increase in population from the war years onward, were already aggravating the existing housing shortage.

As I have already made clear, these were years in which there was little public discussion of housing. This phenomenon can be readily understood so far as officials and politicians are concerned, but it is difficult to understand why there was not more popular demand for houses. Even the briefest description of the housing situation will indicate the gravity of the situation. The 1954 census revealed that 22 per cent of the population were living in acutely overcrowded conditions [2]. The standard used in the determination of this figure was not a generous one. In order for a three-roomed dwelling to be classified as acutely overcrowded, it had to contain six or more persons. If one compares the ratio of persons to rooms in Britain and France, as measured in the 1951 and 1954 censuses, one finds that in Great Britain there were 0.78 persons per room as against 1.01 in France [3]. Whereas in France 41.6 per cent of all dwellings were without an internal supply of running water, the British figure was only 18.6 per cent [4]. Looking back with the benefit of hindsight in 1963, M. Dumont was obliged to conclude that the situation was deteriorating in the late forties and early fifties and that a building rate of 250,000 per annum, maintained between 1954 and 1962, only just succeeded in preventing further deterioration [5]. These years saw no substantial improvement as measured in terms of overcrowding. Nor were these conditions accepted by the population as natural and unavoidable. A survey carried out in the summer of 1953 disclosed that 33 per cent of the adult population were generally dissatisfied with their own housing conditions, mainly because of a lack of space [6]. This figure rose to 38 per cent for tenants and even higher in the larger cities and Paris. The fact that these conditions and the attitudes to which they gave rise did not pose political problems in the early post-war years is remarkable testimony to the low saliency in France of the housing question.

One may readily comprehend the priority given by officials, politicians and leaders of industry to the re-establishment of the mechanism of production but it is more difficult to understand why the absence of new housing at a time of chronic shortage did not create more popular discontent and demand for government action and investment. That this was not so is demonstrated by an interview given in 1947 by the then Minister of Housing, M. Jean Letourneau, MRP, at a time when housing construction was almost entirely non-existent [7]. The minister referred to the *Plan Monnet* which represented official government policy at that time on new investment and referred to the absence of housing among the priorities in this Plan. He accepted this position, entirely comforting himself with the thought that two out of the six priority categories of investment designated in the plan, steel and cement, did have some connection with housing construction. His emphasis was, however, entirely on the establishment of order in the housing field and little hope was held out that there would be much new housing in the near future.

One finds the same acceptance of a low priority and non-controversial attitude towards public housing in the circumstances surrounding the passage of the basic Law of the 3rd September 1947 which re-established the HLM organizations very much on the same basis as they had existed before the war. The Bill passed through Parliament almost without discussion, debate or amendment [8]. Housing did not figure prominently in any of the elections of the immediate post-war period although soon after the election of 1951 there were some signs that deputies were beginning to harry ministers over the slow progress in the housing field. A cartel of deputies from a variety of groups was formed to press for the spending of one thousand million new francs on the HLM programme during the financial year of 1952 [9]. This demand was not met and in fact investment only totalled just under a half of this figure [10]. But the deputies' disappointment at this failure does not appear to have been very great because little was heard of the cartel in subsequent years and one is left with the impression that there was at this time very little political significance attached to housing either by the responsible minister or by the ordinary deputy.

This is not the place in which to enter into the contrast between the British and French situations, but it should be remarked that the absence of public housing from the list of government investment priorities and its equal absence from the sphere of public political debate was a fact of life in France but certainly not in Great Britain or Germany, in both of which housing was considered an important economic and political problem. In both cases substantial effort was put into the housing programme and into the building of publicly owned houses for rent.

Another factor deserves our attention if we are to understand the absence of controversy over public housing between 1945 and 1953. The minister responsible for housing was not regarded as having this as his main function. His proper title was *Ministre de la Reconstruction et de L'Urbanisme*. His title reflected current political preoccupations in that he was regarded well into the 1950s as primarily responsible for the reconstruction, and particularly the restitution programmes which were to compensate war sufferers for their losses and to give them back the houses which had been partially or totally destroyed by military operations. Unlike the national housing problem as a whole, the programme of reconstruction and compensation for war victims aroused considerable political heat and controversy and remained a major preoccupation of all those interested in housing for at least ten years after the cessation of hostilities. The programme had a very harmful effect on the progress of new housing as it was financed out of the budget and took the greater part of the funds available to the minister leaving very little for the general housing programme. The awarding of funds and housing under this programme was an extremely complicated bureaucratic process since it involved investigations into the circumstances of war damage and the classification of war victims in order to make available reconstructed housing in accordance with the terms of the legislation. This reconstruction programme therefore not only took much of the financial support away from the building of new housing for those in need generally but also diverted much bureaucratic and political effort into a field which was only indirectly connected with the housing problem and which, judged quantitatively, produced very little return for the effort involved [11].

## 11 Rent levels

But, as the public housing programme slowly began to increase in importance during the 1950s, those questions, which we have described in chapter VII as endemic to the public housing sector, were bound at one point or another to come to the fore. The first question to raise political difficulties was that of the fixing of HLM rents. The Law of the 3rd September 1947 had given the minister the power to fix these but his use of this authority until 1953 gave rise to little controversy as anyone who was fortunate enough to succeed in obtaining a newly built HLM was in an extremely privileged position with regard to the rest of the population and could hardly complain at whatever rent he was asked to pay. In fact, the regime which was established in 1949 was largely inspired by the principles underlying the Law of the 1st September 1948 which was of course intended to deal with the private sector. The criterion for HLM rents was therefore the physical nature of the buildings, and the exact rent to be charged was calculated by the *surface corrigée* formula combined with a rent per square metre for nine categories of HLM which was fixed by the minister in 1949 and raised at six-monthly intervals by percentages. The similarity of this approach to that adopted for privately rented housing needs no underlining.

Although the system was not politically controversial, it caused considerable administrative inconvenience. Most notably, it failed to take account of the varying financial circumstances of each HLM authority. In some areas construction costs might be higher than the national average but this could not be reflected in the rents charged which were fixed with reference to what was provided in terms of surface area, number of rooms and facilities, etc. There might and certainly would normally be differences in the type of loan contracted by the HLM organization in order to finance its building. Government finance would be available to all organizations at equivalent rates but this would always need to be supplemented by borrowing elsewhere at higher rates of interest. If these expenses were not to be taken account of in the rents charged, then such organizations would in the long term incur deficits.

The principles governing HLM rents were substantially modified by the Decree of 9th August 1953 made by the Laniel Government. As already noted in chapter IV, this Decree also marked an important stage in the development of policy in the privately rented sector. The principle embodied in this Decree is termed the *loyer d'équilibre*. The application of this principle meant that one calculated the total cost and loan charge due on each building and, from this, one deduced directly the rent which was to be demanded in order to balance the charges incurred. This did not mean of course that a cost rent would be charged as the bulk of the finance in question would have been obtained from the Government at extremely low rates of interest, equivalent to the subsidy system in Great Britain. Nevertheless, the system was designed to produce higher rents because it defined the limit of the government assistance to the HLMs in the terms of finance which was granted to them. Previously HLMs might have incurred deficits for which the government would ultimately be responsible. The response from the UNFO–HLM (*Union Nationale des Fédérations d'Organismes d'HLM*) was immediate and outspoken. M. Langlet, Secretary General of UNFO–HLM, said before the relevant Commission of the Economic Council: 'La notion de rentabilité est contraire au principe même du fonctionnement des HLMs. Vouloir que les HLMs aient une rentabilité absolue, c'est nier que nous devons avoir des préoccupations sociales' [12]. In fact, of course, although the objection to the new scheme was expressed in terms of absolute principle, of opposition between social objectives and profitability, the real dispute was much more technical and concerned alterations in rent levels rather than in the fundamental aims of the HLM movement. When M. Langlet referred to *rentabilité*, he was in fact only referring to the necessity imposed in the Decree of 9th August 1953 for each organization to balance charges by income from rent. He was not referring to profitability in any capitalist sense, nor even to the possibility of a cost rent, because the loans which the Government made available to the HLM organizations were of course to continue to be at well below the market rate of interest. Discontent with the new system was not limited to those directly involved in its application but was voiced also by deputies of a variety of groups in March of the following year [13].

The minister, M.G. Lemaire, was not slow to respond to the protests coming from the HLM movement, and in the Decree of 28th December 1953, he modified the new rental structure which had been set up only four months earlier. According to the terms of the new Decree, the *loyer d'équilibre* would not have to be calculated for each building but instead for all the housing owned by each individual HLM organization. This relaxed the rigidity and to some extent the centralization to which the HLMs had taken so much objection because it allowed them to distribute the rent burden between one group of buildings and another as they saw fit, provided that the total rent income was sufficient to cover their costs. If it had been strictly applied, the Decree of 9th August would have deprived them of any discretion in the area of rent levels. In this episode one should note particularly the outspokenness of the HLM movement, the rapid success which they achieved in obtaining important concessions from the minister, and the sympathetic aid which their complaints received from the National Assembly.

But now that the rent question was open to political discussion, it was felt that a more permanent solution ought to be sought, and this was successfully achieved during the Edgar Faure ministry in the Act of 18th April 1955. This measure was adopted without difficulty, the only party opposed to the Act on principle being the PCF. Strange as it may seem, the principles embodied in the new Act were not very different from those which had inspired the Decree of 9th August 1953 which had apparently aroused such discontent. The principle that costs must be balanced by rents at each site was, however, still absent from the new Law, but the general principle of *loyer d'équilibre* was present in this legislation as it had been in the Decree of 28 December 1953. In addition, however, to the principle of *loyer d'équilibre*, the new Act awarded the minister an increased responsibility in the area of rent fixing, for he was to fix both a maximum and a minimum rent for each defined category of HLM. Within the bounds fixed by the minister's definitions of minimum and maximum rents, the HLM organization was to be free to fix its own rents provided that it respected the principle of *loyer d'équilibre* and also provided that it respected the system of weighted surface area. As we shall see when we continue the discussion of rent levels later in this chapter, the continuance of the legislation of 1955 does not mean that the disagreement between the Government and the HLM authorities on rent questions has come to an end. In fact the pattern which one can observe developing in the years 1953–55 has persisted since that date. This pattern is one of constant but rather hesitant pressure which continues to come from the central authorities and which attempts to impose higher rent levels on the HLM organizations, and a constant and largely successful resistance which these organizations carry on.

The terms of the debate have shifted slightly since 1955. Before this date, conflict concerned the rules governing rent fixing and it was presumed that loans would continue to be made available on the same basis as previously. Since 1955, the minister having acquired the discretion to fix minimum and maximum rents per square metre, there has been more disagreement with regard to the terms of central financial assistance. These have been altered on a number of occasions since 1955, and always in favour of the central authorities and against the wishes of the HLMs. The slightly higher interest rate and shorter term for repayment of loans which have been embodied in new arrangements since 1955 have tended to raise the rents in the public sector. What has been said about the general pattern of conflict holds both for the mid-fifties and for later periods, whether the subject of conflict has been rent levels themselves or the financial arrangements which largely determine those levels.

III  *Tenant selection*

Tension existed and came to a head between the minister and the HLM organizations over another question at about the same time as over rent levels. This was the question of the selection of tenants for HLM new housing. From the foundations of the HLM movement until the present day, the following formula has been accepted by both the leaders of the movement and the political authorities as a correct description of those for whom HLM housing should be provided: 'des personnes peu fortunées et notamment les travailleurs vivant principalement de leurs salaires'. This formula is found, reaffirmed, without alteration, in the Statue of 3rd September 1947, and has continually been referred to in disputes over the problems of selection in the post-war era. It is of course only the vaguest indication of the category of persons for whom the HLMs are intended, although one is entitled to conclude from this formula that the movement ought to find the bulk of its clientele amongst the poorer sections of the community. The formula loses any small degree of precision which it might otherwise have possessed as a consequence of the inclusion of the words *'principalement'* and *'notamment'*. The vagueness of the formula corresponds exactly to the expression 'working class' which is to be found in comparable British legislation prior to 1949.

It was suggested in chapter VII that the question of tenant selection was inherently one which was unlikely to arouse political conflicts as important as those concerning some of the other issues which arise in connection with public housing. It was argued that the importance of this question in France arose from particular French circumstances. It is the relation between central and local housing authorities, between the government and the HLM organizations upon which it must rely, which gives importance to this issue. We have already seen that, in the field of rent levels, the HLMs favour lower levels than seem appropriate to the government. The explanation of this difference of point of view is too obvious for it to be necessary to elaborate in great detail. It is the state which bears the responsibility and pays the political cost for the raising of revenue necessary to subsidize the HLMs and their tenants. With regard to selection, there is a conflict of opinion between local and central authority which may again be traced to the differing responsibilities of government and HLMs. The government has always taken the view that the HLMs are for those in need and it has defined 'need' almost always with regard to income and has suggested that the HLMs are inclined to reject the poorer tenant because of the inconvenience which he may cause if he does not pay the rent on the date due. The government will point to the social composition of HLM tenants and their income levels and will argue from time to time that these facts demonstrate that the HLMs are not fulfilling the social purposes for which the movement was originally created. The HLMs do not oppose this government point of view in principle but claim that they do in fact seek out those in need and that if they are unable to provide housing for the poorest sections of the community, it is only because the loans which are made available to them do not permit them to charge sufficiently low rents for their accommodation to attract the poorest-paid worker. But let us return to the question of why selection has become a question of political dispute in France whereas it has not done so in Britain and would not appear to be an issue inherently capable of political exploitation.

The explanation would appear to be that there has been no dispute in France about who is to be selected but there has been conflict about how selecting is to be done. As has already been indicated, the formula suggesting that the HLMs are intended primarily for the poor has always been adhered to by political parties and both government and HLMs. The dispute has been more a reflection of the distrust which exists between the government and those upon whom it must rely for the execution of its policies and also of the distrust between the public at large and those in authority within the HLM movement. Everyone is agreed on the formula, vague though it may be, but no-one is really confident that the principles agreed are being applied in practice. One finds references in the press from as early as 1952 to the fact that HLMs are being distributed to those who do not really deserve them, and it is also occasionally alleged that political considerations enter into the selection of tenants, although the latter accusation is now rarely heard [14]. The view that the conflict does not concern selection as such but turns rather on the question of the relations between the public and authority and between the government and its executive agents is borne out by the nature of the conflict which has always concerned procedures for selection rather than the principles to be applied. Central authority, reflecting popular distrust, has alway sought to impose procedures which reduce the area of discretion open to the local HLM office. This has been done either by the attempt to introduce mathematical formulae or by transferring the authority for selection to officials in whom the government has greater trust, such as the prefect.

In a report prepared by the Economic Council in August 1953, M. Houist complained that although power to regulate conditions of entry into HLMs had been granted in the Law of 24th May 1951, no decrees of application had yet appeared [15]. Agitation over the question was particularly acute during the winter of 1953–4 when the Abbé Pierre began his campaign in favour of the homeless which included attacks on the HLM movement for failing to provide accommodation for those most in need [16]. The Government was broadly in sympathy with the content if not the tone of the Abbé's remarks and published a *Décret-Loi* of the 27th March 1954, which imposed a compulsory points system on all HLM allocations. The points system was one which defined various types of need and awarded points to candidates in relation to their existing housing difficulties. Its rigid application would have meant that the applicant with the greatest number of points would be selected when a tenant was sought for each available new dwelling. As with the rent proposals of the previous year, the implication of the new procedures was a substantial diminution in the discretion which the local HLM organizations might exercise, and the reaction of the movement was equally hostile on this occasion. Within only two months of the appearance of the Government's legislation a report had been submitted to the National Assembly which was entirely sympathetic to the HLM point of view and the Government soon felt itself under an obligation to withdraw the points scheme, all the more so because the HLMs had done nothing in practice to apply the scheme which was legally obligatory.

The Government's retreat was formalized in the Decree of the 26th July 1955 and even the briefest consideration of its terms makes it clear that the solution adopted was not so much a compromise between the Government and the movement as total capitulation on the Government's part. Whereas the scheme of the previous year had made the points scheme obligatory, it was now to be used only at the discretion of the HLM organization in question. This meant in practice that it was not applied anywhere. The original scheme had also contained provision for appeal where a prospective tenant felt that he had not received correct treatment. There was no provision for such appeals in the Decree of 26th July 1955. The original government scheme had also attempted to enlist the support of public opinion against the HLMs and in favour of more just selection policies by making information about recently allocated HLMs publicly available. The *Décret-Loi* of 27th March 1954 had said that such information should be available to members of the public at the HLM local office. This in itself had been a concession to the HLM for the Government had wished to make the information available at the *mairie* but had modified the clause at the request of the movement [17]. In the Decree of 26th July 1955 no provision was made for the availability of information to the public at large.

The only safeguard which remained to the minister was a duty imposed in the Decree to provide him with full information on the process of tenant selection and he was empowered, if he was not satisfied with the information provided, to impose the points scheme as a penalty. If ministers had had the necessary authority to work this new system according to the letter, then there would have been no capitulation. But, as it was, this authority was lacking and no minister ever felt able to impose the points scheme as a penalty.

One is naturally inclined to ask what selection policies were being followed during this period of controversy by the HLMs. Were the HLMs doing the best possible in the framework of legislation laid down for them by the Government or was the minister correct in his assessment of their selection policies? There are some survey data available for the mid-Fifties and they tend to confirm the popularly held view that HLMs were often given to middle-income groups and even to the wealthiest sections of the community in defiance of the spirit of the HLM legislation [18]. So poor in fact was their performance in this matter that wealth appears as a positive advantage in the competition for an HLM tenancy. The evidence shows that as broadly defined a category as worker was under-represented in the HLM new housing as compared with the whole stock of housing, old and new. The group which appeared to stand the best chance of selection at this time and which was proportionally most heavily represented among new HLM tenants was that of middle management. Later evidence on the same question appears less decisive but still suggests that practice does not correspond with the spirit either of the HLM movement or of the legislation which is supposed to control selection practices [19]. M. Consigny, for example, writing in 1969, noted that the HLMs continued to exclude tenants whose income fell below a minimum fixed by themselves and that the household income of the HLM tenants was above the average for the nation as a whole [20]. It appears very doubtful, however, whether selection policies would be radically different if they were directly under the control of the minister. Some of the evidence for this assertion will be found in the succeeding pages of this chapter, but sufficient evidence is in fact available in the report on housing need and demand prepared as part of the work for the preparation of the Sixth Plan, which contains calculations designed to estimate the proportion of the population who may legally be selected for HLM tenancies, bearing in mind the maximum income ceiling which has been imposed in this sector since 1958. These calculations suggest that the ceiling, which is fixed by the minister, allows between 70 and 80 per cent of the population to be selected for HLM tenancies, the figure varying somewhat with the category of housing under discussion [21]. The excessive liberality of this ceiling the determination of which is a ministerial responsibility, strongly reinforces the argument, which has been developed here, that central local conflict is not concerned so much with the substance of selection policy but rather with who selects.

Since 1955 there have been occasional skirmishes between the government and the HLMs over the qestion of tenant selection, but no essential changes have been made. Continuing disquiet did prompt the government to publish an *Arrêté* in 1968 but an examination of its terms confirms the view that the central authorities are either unwilling or unable to do more than tinker with this problem.

In the first place, the *Arrêté* only applied initially to the Paris region and has been cautiously extended to some other large cities since. Secondly, although the *Arrêté* provides that the prefect shall prepare a list of priority cases and then communicate it to the HLM organization in question, the HLMs are only obliged to allocate a minimum of 30 per cent of new dwellings and 50 per cent of relets to applicants on this list. These are the Paris percentages and elsewhere one invariably finds lower figures. Again, the list which the prefect supplies must always name many more families than there are dwellings available so that the HLM organization is always left with considerable discretion [22].

The government and its advisers are fully aware of their failure in this area of policy. A special report on the housing of foreign workers prepared for the Sixth Plan deplored the fact those provisions of the 1968 *Arrêté* relating to foreign workers were ignored by HLMs in the Paris region despite a threat to withhold loans [23]. Not content with criticism alone the planners suggested the *contrat de programme* as a way out of the difficulty. This would be, according to the planners' suggestion, a contract to be agreed between the minister and the HLMs. It would define on the one hand the general level of tenant income, choosing a level well below that which is at present to be observed among occupants of HLMs, and in return for this concession from the housing authorities the minister would grant a certain fixed level of aid for the future and greater autonomy in other less essential areas. As may be seen, the experts have concluded that a system of command is not politically possible and that therefore greater success may be achieved by openly admitting the contractual nature of the relationship between the central authority and those upon whom it must rely. The *contrat de programme* is a bold attempt to break away from the unsuccessful coercion which we have described but its boldness seems so far to have prevented its being adopted. Although 1971 brought some HLM reforms, a number of which had been requested by the Housing Committee of the Sixth Plan, no *contrat de programme* were signed. Ministerial policy at present is concentrating on strengthening the hand of the prefect by slow administrative action in those areas where this is felt necessary rather than seeking to make any fundamental changes in the relations between minister and HLM.

When the President of the Republic, M. Giscard d'Estaing set up the Barre Committee to examine housing policy in 1975, one of the matters which concerned them most was the way in which state subsidies were not reaching the poorest sections of the community because these people were not sufficiently represented among HLM tenants. The committee observed that 14.7 per cent of the French population earned less than 10,000 francs p.a. but that this section of the community only constituted 5.9% of HLM tenants [24]. Although they repeated the criticisms made in earlier investigations of the failure to apply penalty rents, and of the continued selection of tenants who ought to have been able to pay their way elsewhere, they saw no remedy either in the *contrat de programme* or in more widespread use of the prefectoral system of housing allocation. They felt that the blame for the wastage involved in existing arrangements lay not so much with the unwillingness of the HLMs to house the poor, but in the financial barriers in the way of such a policy, and that increased aid could only be provided for this section of the population through a new, more selective form of housing allowance, which would remove any danger of inability to pay and which could be paid directly to the HLMs by the Administration on behalf of the poorest tenants.

The Barre Report therefore recommends that the subsidies which public housing receives through low interest loans should be gradually withdrawn, and that in their place a housing allowance should be provided which will make possible increased aid to the poorest tenants.

These are radical recommendations and have yet to be officially adopted as Government policy. All that we can say on this subject to date is that there has continually been dissatisfaction about the unwillingness of the HLM authorities to select the poorest tenants but that nothing substantial has been done about this since the abortive attempt to impose a points system in 1954.

Before leaving altogether the question of selection of new tenants, some mention should be made of an important aspect of the HLM system of finance which is at least partly responsible for the failure of the HLM movement to live up to the ideals to which it aspires. New construction is financed in large part but not entirely by funds at privileged rates of interest. Since 1966 these come from the *Caisse des Prêts aux HLMs* which in turn draws them from the *Caisse des Dépots et Consignations*. The movement is, however, obliged to seek funds elsewhere in varying proportions according to current government financial policy, and is in fact normally anxious to do so since, if it is able to borrow additional funds from private sources, these will serve to increase the size of the building programme. Much of this outside investment comes from companies which, since 1953, have been obliged to devote 1 per cent of the firm's total wage bill to some form of housing each year. To make these compulsory investments available to the HLM movement is convenient to many companies. In return for these investments, however, the companies demand and are entitled to a share in the dwellings to be provided. The nomination of tenants by companies which have provided investment in the above manner is naturally inclined to divert the HLMs from their truly social function. Neither the HLM movement nor the Government seem particularly anxious to put an end to this practice as may be judged by the modesty of the proposals made in January 1968 by the Under-Secretary of State responsible then for housing, M. Nungesser. He suggested that the share of dwellings which might receive tenants nominated by private investors ought to be limited to a maximum of 40 per cent of new HLM buildings. The number of tenants whom they would be entitled to nominate would be related to the percentage of initial finance which they had provided. The 40 per cent share was to correspond to investment amounting to 15 per cent of the cost of the project. One is entitled to conclude that the Government was not showing an over-zealous concern for reducing the size of this problem [25]. It should also be noted that this reform was only made necessary by the change in financial arrangements which had been recently adopted and which had increased the share of state finance in the HLM programmes, thus reducing the share which would come in future from the private sector and hence making necessary an adjustment of the privately nominated quota. The reform was therefore more an adjustment to changed technical circumstances than a deliberate attempt to limit the distortion of the principle of selection according to need brought about by the existence of private investment in what is normally regarded as a public and social service.

Both central government and the HLMs have their own reasons for wishing to retain these arrangements. The government will get more dwellings than it otherwise would for a given level of investment. As far as the HLMs are concerned, the advantage of allowing companies and local authorities to help them is that it relieves them of some of the constraints which would arise from being obliged to cover all costs with a loan of fixed size coming from national funds. The central government is naturally concerned to control inflation in building costs and therefore fixes exactly the amount of living space that must be provided for a given size of loan. Supplementary finance enables the HLMs to provide a little more or spend more in order to raise the standard of accommodation.

IV  *The Sur-Loyer*

In our examination of both rent level controversies and conflict over the processes of tenant selection, we have noted the continuity of certain problems which appear to be insoluble. The weakness of the State when faced with determined opposition has also been clearly apparent. The same features of the pattern of policy development may be clearly distinguished when we turn to a new area of political conflict closely related to the question of tenant selection just examined. Most of the controversy concerning tenant selection concentrates on the process of allocating newly available dwellings. There is, however, another aspect to this problem which is the possibility of reallocating dwellings which are already occupied but whose occupants are considered to be capable of providing themselves with either an unsubsidized form of housing or, at any rate, a form of accommodation which is less subsidized than the HLMs. The principal instrument of government policy in this area is what is termed in France the *sur-loyer*. The French term must be used and explained as no equivalent institution exists in Great Britain, nor has it ever been discussed in either political or housing circles. The *sur-loyer* is an additional rent which the tenant must pay on top of the standard rent charged for his accommodation. It is in the nature of a penalty which is imposed on the tenant because his income is judged to be too high for the class of accommodation which he is occupying. In theory, the imposition of the *sur-loyer* is supposed to provide the tenant with an economic incentive to leave his HLM accommodation and move elsewhere. The institution of the *sur-loyer* was first introduced into the French housing system in 1958 [26]. The date is, of course, politically significant and one might be inclined to presume at first sight that the political changes of that year had in fact had some impact in the more mundane area of housing policy. As we shall soon discover, any appearance of a decisive change in policy designed to bring about a transformation in the class of HLM occupants is shown by an examination of later developments to be illusory.

Little was heard of the *sur-loyer* during the early years of its existence. It appears to have been unwelcome to the HLM organizations, and ministers between 1958 and 1965 made little attempt to oblige them to introduce in practice the innovations which had been adopted by the government in principle. In those sections of the Fifth Plan which deal with housing, one finds reference to the problem of rent levels, and particularly the *sur-loyer*, in both the general report and recommendation, and the special report on financial problems. The Commission observed the necessity for higher rents and particularly for the application of the *sur-loyer* [27]. They were unhappy to observe that the *sur-loyer* was not being applied in any but an insignificant minority of areas. These comments were made in 1965 and reflect a situation which had existed for some time. Ministers in the 1960s frequently complained of the refusal of the HLMs to apply *sur-loyer*, but could apparently do nothing about this [28].

In the autumn of 1968, another newly arrived minister, M. Albin Chalandon, was apparently shocked to discover the situation with regard to the *sur-loyer*. He declared his intention to encourage a much more thorough-going application of the existing legislation, and even suggested, as earlier ministers had not done, that those who paid the *sur-loyer*, but did not move out as required, would, after the elapse of a certain period of time, be evicted [29]. This rather more heavy-handed approach immediately stirred up opposition from the Left, the HLMs, and from some deputies from within the minister's own Gaullist Party [30]. These objections seem to have had the desired result for in the spring of 1969 the reforms were modified in such a way as to cease to have any significance whatsoever [31]. In particular any reference to eventual eviction was dropped entirely.

As with the case of tenant selection problems, the Barre Report effectively abandons the hope that progress can be made through better enforcement of existing legislation. Their remedy, much higher rents coupled with an allowance which can be adjusted with changes in the recipient's income, has the merit, from the Government's point of view, of dealing directly with the tenant rather than passing through the HLM organizations as intermediaries. This will make it easier to withdraw aid when it is regarded as no longer necessary. Past experience with the HLM movement is undoubtedly one of the principal reasons why the thinking of government ministers and senior civil servants is moving in the direction of providing aid more directly and in a more flexible form.

### v  *Financing the HLMs*

We have already cited innumerable examples of the persistence of the same problems in the sector of publicly rented housing in France, but a particularly striking example of continuity is available if we examine the terms on which government loans are made available to the HLMs. Before 1961 finance was normally granted at 1 per cent, repayable over sixty-five years. This does not give an altogether accurate description of the real charges which the HLMs faced since they have always had to use some supplementary sources of finance for which they must normally pay a market rate of at least 5 per cent. This supplementary finance was, however, kept within what were considered reasonable limits before 1961, and normally did not represent more than 10 or 20 per cent of the loans which the HLMs raised. Between 1961 and 1966, the nominal rate charged by the Government remained 1 per cent, but the quantity of supplementary finance which was required to meet the building programme which the Government assigned to the movement increased rapidly and hence the effective charge to be met out of rents increased also. This increase was made more important by the government decision in 1961 to shorten the period of repayment from sixty-five to forty-five years [32]. In 1966, the administrative arrangements for HLM loans were changed, and the *Caisse des Prêts aux HLMs* was set up. This was a natural time at which to reconsider the terms of financial aid and a new interest rate of 2.6 per cent was fixed. This increase of interest rate was coupled with a further slight shortening of the repayment period from forty-five to forty years [33].

One may well ask how the figure of 2.6 per cent came to be selected. It appears that in discussions between the minister and the HLMs, it was agreed, by way of compromise, that the new interest rate would represent overall the rate which the HLMs had earlier been effectively obliged to pay as a consequence of the mixture of government and supplementary finance, the former being at 1 per cent and the latter at 5 to 6 per cent. The 1966 system has proved no more permanent than those which preceded it. In 1970 the interest rate was raised from 2.6 to 2.95 per cent. This change was brought about by the increase in the interest rate paid by the *Caisse d'Epargne* which has always been one of the sources of finance used by the HLM movement [34]. It hardly needs to be stressed that the changes in these financial arrangements have been extremely slight, but that they have always tended in the same direction: a steady erosion of the privileged position of the HLMs. So frightened has the Government apparently been of decisive change in this area that much of the development has been given a mechanical character. By this I mean to refer, for example, to the steady increase in the effective interest rate which resulted from the increasing reliance on supplementary finance. When the Government attacks what it regards as HLM privileges by these means, it demonstrates clearly its inability to adopt more decisive changes in policy. Such decisive changes would need to be justified politically. The compromise reached in 1966 which was based quite arbitrarily on the practice of preceding years also provides evidence of the Government's weakness. Nor is it possible to argue that the Government accepts the financial terms on which aid is granted as satisfactory. The constant development of policy in the direction of less favourable terms for the HLMs suggests strongly that the Government does not believe in this form of financial assistance, at least not on the extremely favourable terms which have traditionally been available. It would rather concentrate on forms of personal income support, linked to housing needs such as the housing allowance, and direct less aid through the HLMs. Continuity arises therefore because the government is unwilling to incur the unpopularity which it feels would result from a confrontation with the HLMs. The startling continuity of the pattern of government aid to the HLMs will stand out even more clearly when we have described the sharply varying forms of aid which have been a notable feature of policy in Great Britain.

VI *Selling to tenants*

Additional light may be thrown on the French pattern of policy
development in the area of public housing if we examine the problem
of the sale of HLMs originally built for renting. Of all the issues in
this sector of housing policy, the question of the sale of publicly
rented dwellings to their tenants is the one which is generally approached in the most obviously political spirit. This is true of both
Britain and France. The comparison between the two countries on
this issue is particularly instructive but will be left until chapter X.
Here we shall examine the course which policy has followed and the
difficulties which the Government has encountered in France.

The bill providing for the possibility of selling HLMs to sitting
tenants originated with the UNR group in the National Assembly
in 1964 [35]. It was strongly opposed by the Left and by some deputies within the majority, particularly in the Senate and was
amended substantially as a result [36]. The most important of these
amendments made it necessary that a two-thirds majority in the
*conseil d'administration* of the HLM organization in question be obtained before any dwellings could be sold. The opposition to the bill
served notice on the government that the application of this measure
was to be no easy matter. The opposition of the UNFO–HLM, on
behalf of the movement, could not stop the bill becoming law, but
it was no less effective for that. At the annual conference of the HLM
movement in 1969 M. Albin Chalandon, the responsible minister,
before an openly hostile audience, expressed frankly his frustration
as the total failure to achieve any significant number of sales [37]. An
official estimate suggested that after four years only one HLM in
a thousand had been sold [38]. In 1970 and 1971 the government
promoted new legislation in this area, the essence of which was the
awarding of a power to the minister to appoint an ad hoc administra-
tor who would be able to execute HLM sales without the authority
of the HLM organization in question [39]. This legislation failed to
reach the statute book.

The question of the effective opposition to the selling of HLM
dwellings is in some ways exceptional in that parliamentary opposition is important. But the decisive factor here as elsewhere, seems to
be the inability of the government to achieve administrative execution after a law has been passed.

VII  *Differential rents*

In the previous chapter, one of the issues which were considered inherent in the public sector was that of the possible operation of differential rent schemes. The first appearance of this issue in political debate in France was in 1958 when the newly appointed minister, M. Pierre Sudreau, referred sympathetically to the principle and suggested, in an important press conference, that steps should be taken to bring about its application to the HLM sector [40]. M. Sudreau was to remain in office for four years and he had therefore the political security necessary to initiate new policies. His advocacy of a policy of differential rents was natural in the circumstances. Whereas, under the Fourth Republic, Ministers with responsibility for housing had accepted without demur that aid for housing, which was destined for many different social categories, was necessary, their successors since 1958 have inclined to the view that, in principle, it should be directed preponderantly to those in the greatest need. But, as we have already noted, there are innumerable examples to show that the change is usually one of rhetoric rather than one of policy. The case of differential rents conforms precisely to this pattern. M. Sudreau was certainly genuinely convinced of the desirability of the new policy as an equitable means of redistributing the rent burden in the public sector as between the poorer and wealthier tenants. The policy was also advocated at this time in a report prepared by M. Houist for the Economic Council. But it was not to be. After the press conference little more was heard of differential rents and it is important to ask why the policy was not adopted at this time and has never since been anything more than a perennial talking-point.

Part of the answer lies certainly in the existence in France of a housing allowance, the operation of which has some effect on the rents effectively paid by tenants of different incomes. The size of the allowance varies with the tenant's income and the rent which he must pay. The existence of such an allowance satisfies to some extent the demands of a policy of aid to the needy, but only partially, since the housing allowance is only one of the forms of government assistance from which an individual may benefit and most of the others are much less directly related to either the housing or financial circumstances of the recipient. But the housing allowance itself is not a pure aid to those in need for either overcrowding or poor housing can disqualify potential beneficiaries. The allowance therefore has more the character of a stimulus to better housing than an aid to those who suffer from poor housing or overcrowding. Most critics of the present housing allowance are also of the opinion that it extends far too high on the income scale and is therefore proportionately less valuable to the poor who might otherwise receive a greater share of the money available. Nevertheless, the existence of a housing allowance in France has taken some of the urgency out of the campaign for a differential rent.

The most likely source of opposition to the new policy seemed to be the HLM organizations themselves for they would have had to bear the brunt of inevitable tenant hostility. A differential rent scheme requires some investigation of individual incomes and this is always regarded as an extremely difficult process in France, especially when dealing with the self-employed. It may be that the HLM organizations were not enthusiastic about the new policy but the evidence on this point is indecisive. The movement appears to have been divided on the question. As we shall see, in 1960 M. Langlet, the General Secretary of UNFO, advocated the development of an alternative system to that of differential rents. But in recent years he has changed his view on this question and now appears to prefer the differential rent approach to the problem of the poor tenant [41]. Decisive opposition seems to have come finally not from the HLM movement but from the Ministry of Finance. In order to understand this opposition we must examine its attitude to publicly financed housing. To those responsible for government finance, the public programme of house construction represents an enormous call on resources available for investment. They are concerned, particularly when inflationary dangers seem most acute, as was the case in 1958, to limit the size of this programme. But they are also concerned to make sure that the government retains control of the total cost of projects which it approves. The cost to the State is not only represented by the construction costs and the loans which they make necessary but is also affected by the level of return which is demanded for these loans, that is to say, the rate of interest which the government demands from the HLMs. In Britain the government commitment from revenue has normally been fixed in absolute terms so that the financial authorities can estimate fairly exactly, and well in advance, the charge which the housing subsidies will represent in future budgets. The case is not quite so clear in France for HLM organizations are allowed both to accumulate surpluses and also to run deficits from time to time. The size of these dificits and surpluses is however strictly controlled by the fixing of minimum and maximum rents, a responsibility which is shared between the Minister of Finance and the minister responsible for housing. The financial authorities are therefore directly concerned with the level of income from rent in France in a way in which they are not in Great Britain. In Britain the central government fixes its contribution for the future in pounds, shillings and pence per house per year. This then leaves the local authority with the responsibility of making up the necessary income for debt servicing and repayment either from rents alone or from some combination of rent and rate income. In France central government does not fix its future liabilities in such a clear-cut fashion. In the French case, cost to the central authorities will depend on the minimum and maximum rents, which are naturally revised frequently, and also upon the share of HLM investment which is financed by central government lending. (It will be recalled that the HLM will invariably find a certain part of the necessary capital from non-governmental sources.)

M. Sudreau argued in favour of the differential rent approach on the grounds that it would be cheaper for the central government. His argument was based on the premise that income lost through setting lower rents for the poorer tenants would be more than balanced by the increased rent demanded of average or wealthy tenants. The question is in part technical and depends simply on the details of any individual differential rent scheme but it is also political since one must form a judgment as to whether it will be possible to impose the higher levels of rent on the majority of tenants in the way implied in the differential rent policy. The Ministry of Finance apparently had doubts concerning both aspects of the problem and therefore rejected the proposal to adopt differential rents on the grounds that it would increase the effective charge of new and existing housing to the State. It was felt, no doubt, that although M. Sudreau might easily succeed in lowering the rents paid by poorer tenants, he would have great difficulty in raising the rents paid by other tenants.

Faced with this obstacle, those responsible for the formation of housing policy were obliged to seek alternative solutions and these came from the HLM movement and were elaborated in the annual report which M. Langlet presented to the UNFO–HLM congress in 1960. He recommended that three categories of HLM should be created. The principal category of dwelling would receive loans at a rate of one per cent, as had been the case for HLMs in the recent past, but two new categories were proposed, one of a superior quality which would be financed by loans at three per cent, and one of an inferior quality which would receive loans on which the Government would demand no interest. In all cases it was suggested that the loans would continue to be repaid over a period of 45 years [42]. The system proposed by M. Langlet on behalf of the HLM movement was not new. In the past the HLM organizations had built different categories of dwelling, each destined for a distinct income bracket and with its appropriately adjusted loan terms. The implications of these proposals were not simply financial. It was implied that in future there would be three types of HLM dwelling, each with its own form of finance, its own physical specifications, and its own requirements with respect to the category of tenant which might be normally selected. The scheme had the advantage of providing at least some flexibility in rent levels, which was the aim of the differential rent policy, but it clearly involved social segregation of an extremely blatant character. Nevertheless the new system of three categories outlined by M. Langlet was adopted by the Government and the Decrees of the 3rd of June 1961 in fact reproduced exactly, with respect to interest rates, the demands of the HLM movement expressed one year earlier [43]. Although the social segregation involved in a system of this sort excites some criticism in France, the general opinion is that some such differentiation of types of HLM is inevitable. For example, the inhabitants of the *bidonvilles* (shanty towns) who must be rehoused when these areas are cleared and slum-dwellers subject to redevelopment, are considered to require special types of housing which, although they may be provided by the HLM organizations, are described as sturdy and have lower rents than the standard HLM dwelling [44]. These flats will be in blocks of their own, apart from the other HLMs.

Since the institution of these three categories of HLM in 1961, the system has continued very much as it was first established, although the precise definitions of each category change from time to time. Despite continued criticism of the social segregation involved in these arrangements, both in the Consigny and Barre Reports, nothing has yet been done to bring it to an end [45].

VIII  *Abbé Pierre*

It will be clear from all that has been said in this chapter that the public debate about housing in France usually involves only specialists and those directly involved in policy-making or administration. This does not mean that political ideas do not play a part in this debate but it does mean that the government is rarely under pressure from public opinion to innovate in one direction or another. It is all the more important, therefore, to examine the events of 1954 and 1955 when, for a short time, the Abbé Pierre succeeded in making housing an issue of national concern.

His campaign began with a letter to the minister, published in *Le Figaro* early in January 1954, inviting him to attend the funeral of a baby who had died partly because his parents were living at the time in a disused bus in Paris [46]. Intense emotions were stirred up at this time. The result was that a succession of ministers was hurried into building extremely cheap accomodation. The first dwelling type included in such a programme was to cost only one sixth of the standard HLM [47]. In a matter of months these dwellings were condemned as totally inadequate and a new programme, still of very cheap housing, was launched. This process continued until three programmes had been launched and abandoned [48].

IX *Conclusions*

What conclusions are we entitled to draw from the events of these years in relation to our study of the pattern of policy development in the public sector? It so happened that at the very moment when public attention was, for the first time, drawn to the housing problem, the Government had just completed the process of setting up the mechanisms and institutions which were to provide the basis of post-war French housing policy. If public opinion or the political debate were to have any influence on housing policy, it would have been necessary to develop this public interest at a much earlier date. As we have seen, the key decisions were taken in 1948, 1950 and 1953, and unless the whole framework was to be called into question, there was very little which a government in 1954 could do by way of response to public demand. Faced with this problem, a succession of ministers allowed themselves to be rushed into ill-prepared programmes which proved to be a waste of public money and also a disappointment to those who saw in them some miracle solution to the problem. A series of programmes, each announced with a fanfare and heralded as a great new step forward towards the solution of the problem, were followed by disillusion. House-building was booming during these years and there was very little which the Government could have done to increase the phenomenal rate of expansion witnessed at this time. This expansion was, however, based on the foundations laid earlier by Messrs Claudius-Petit and Courant. The

## Table VIII.1

*France*

*Housing completions by sector*

Source: Ministry of Development, Regional Policy and Tourism

| | Recons-truction | HLM | | semi-public subsidized | | Private unsubsidized | Total |
|---|---|---|---|---|---|---|---|
| | | To rent | For sale | Logécos | other subsidized | | |
| From the Liberation until 31 Dec. 1953 | 166,876 | 47,015 | 21,069 | 840 | 84,396 | 168,906 | 489,102 |
| 1954 | 37,214 | 20,154 | 10,399 | 11,940 | 61,084 | 21,202 | 161,993 |
| 1955 | 34,658 | 36,037 | 14,187 | 34,631 | 70,379 | 25,157 | 215,049 |
| 1956 | 32,561 | 30,407 | 15,255 | 51,669 | 78,527 | 22,918 | 231,337 |
| 1957 | 32,946 | 54,537 | 18,657 | 67,416 | 78,417 | 21,760 | 273,733 |
| 1958 | 24,230 | 68,690 | 18,916 | 73,929 | 80,429 | 25,496 | 291,690 |
| 1959 | 17,095 | 82,776 | 18,120 | 86,618 | 87,600 | 28,232 | 320,441 |
| 1960 | 12,716 | 77,026 | 18,811 | 89,043 | 87,642 | 31,326 | 316,564 |
| 1961 | 11,850 | 70,795 | 20,680 | 98,965 | 81,677 | 32,080 | 316,047 |
| 1962 | 8,266 | 68,322 | 20,876 | 103,355 | 74,205 | 33,897 | 308,921 |
| 1963 | 3,853 | 78,937 | 22,498 | 112,754 | 79,196 | 38,946 | 366,184 |

**Table VIII.1 (Contd.)**

| | HLM | | | with Crédit Foncier loan | | other subsi-dized | Private unsubsidized | Total |
|---|---|---|---|---|---|---|---|---|
| | Recons-truction | To rent | For sale | immed-iate | defe-rred | | | |
| From the Liberation until 31 Dec. 1953 | | | | | | | | |
| 1964 | 2,391 | 92,295 | 24,929 | 137,655 | — | 69,647 | 41,882 | 368,799 |
| 1965 | 1,344 | 95,803 | 28,645 | 148,101 | — | 78,915 | 58,791 | 411,599 |
| 1966 | 728 | 96,900 | 30,122 | 125,874 | — | 75,875 | 84,672 | 414,171 |
| 1967 | 310 | 105,330 | 31,452 | 114,862 | 9,006 | 69,238 | 92,680 | 422,878 |
| 1968 | 100 | 116,553 | 31,773 | 99,555 | 16,552 | 60,661 | 85,789 | 410,983 |
| 1969 | — | 116,784 | 31,286 | 103,396 | 23,341 | 55,160 | 96,994 | 426,961 |
| 1970 | — | 121,290 | 34,077 | 112,651 | 34,843 | 52,073 | 101,340 | 456,274 |
| 1971 | — | 127,848 | 38,368 | 110,012 | 39,326 | 56,185 | 103,970 | 475,709 |
| 1972 (*) | — | 126,900 | 49,400 | 124,700 | 39,300 | 69,600 | 136,100 | 546,000 |
| 1973 | | 109,000 | 55,000 | 129,100 | | 207,400 | | 500,500 |
| 1974 | | 121,700 | 60,000 | 122,700 | | 196,000 | | 500,400 |
| 1975 | | 111,500 | 58,000 | 124,300 | | 220,500 | | 514,300 |

(*) an overstimate of about 30,000 caused by changes in tax law

whole episode no doubt contributed to the already widespread disillusion with political authority and particularly with its capacity for planned intervention to deal with serious social problems. With respect to the theme of continuity and rigidity the episode was to some extent the exception which proves the rule. The low-priced public housing programmes were a policy innovation but proved a failure and short-lived. The basic instruments, however unsatisfactory, remained the HLMs, and the public outcry at this time against the inequity of the HLM tenant selection policies had, as we have seen, no impact on these organizations.

The conclusions which one is entitled to draw from the foregoing account are too obvious to need heavy underlining. The continuity, which is so marked a feature of French housing policy in general, and also of this sector, is exhibited in numerous areas. Table VIII.I shows that, despite great quantitative changes in the scale of the HLM programme during the fifties and sixties, the distribution between those HLMs which are rented and those which are sold remains very much what it has always been. Some changes have been made in tenant selection procedure but these have been of a partial character and have fallen far short of the wishes of central government. The financial arrangements made available to the HLMs have undergone some, very gradual, change as a result of constant government pressure. There has been certainly considerable effort to reduce the importance of politics in the day-to-day running of the HLMs and the Gaullist majority has sought representation within the movement. But the progress towards depoliticization has been limited. One may well ask what types of new policy might have been adopted if the existing rigidities had not made this impossible. Some of the desirable changes which might have reoriented the HLM system are only too clear because they have been at one time or another, government objectives. But there are other changes, which seem desirable to informed critics of the French housing system, which have not only failed to be implemented but have failed also to attract the attention of ministers. For example, the problem of social segregation is disquieting. M. Consigny expressed this problem in the following terms: 'L'objectif de la politique du logement ne peut être un objectif purement quantitatif de multiplication des logements d'un certain type correspondant à la solvabilité d'une certaine catégorie de la population .... Le développement de la construction dite sociale ne doit pas se faire au prix de l'éclatement de la communauté nationale en catégories et en zones géographiques. Il doit être au contraire l'instrument d'une plus grande homogénéité sociologique au sein des agglomérations' [49]. He goes on to argue that this can only be achieved by means of abolition of the sub-types of HLM dwelling and the establishment of a differential rent scheme. Despite ministerial sympathy for this point of view, M. Consigny's recommendation still awaits implementation [50].

Another change which many critics of the HLM movement demand is the abolition of HLM building for sale, since here the movement is duplicating the work of the *Crédit Foncier*, an organization which, after all, specializes in this sort of activity. If the object of the public system is to aid those who are most in need, it would appear a strange anomaly that about 20 per cent of new building in the sector is sold only to those who can provide a substantial deposit from their personal savings. Other changes in HLM practice, which have not been canvassed but which one may anticipate will be issues in the future, are not lacking. The HLMs are so far only marginally involved in the problems of slum clearance, redevelopment, and rehousing. They will have to take on this work at some point. They might usefully be asked, at some future date, to interest themselves in the renovation of existing housing of poor quality. I mention these points only in order to demonstrate that the rigidity and consequent continuity which we have observed in the public housing sector are not in the least the consequence of universal satisfaction with existing arrangements. As to the explanation of this rigidity, it would seem best to follow the practice adopted earlier and leave the discussion of this until we are able to use, as a basis for our conclusions, both British and French experience.

*References*

1. *Bulletin Statistique du Ministère de la Reconstruction et de l'Urbanisme*, No. 12, 30 June 1952 (La Documentation Française); *See* table VIII. 1, p. 148.
2. *Le Monde*, 11 April 1958.
3. *La Politique du Logement en France* (Documents et Etudes du Centre de Recherches Economiques et Sociales, May-June 1964), p. 8.
4. ibid., p. 9.
5. Pierre Dumont, *Rapport Présenté au nom du Conseil Economique* (Avis et Rapports du Conseil Economique), 14 December 1963, p. 802.
6. *La Vie Française*, 26 June 1953.
7. *Les Nouvelles Economiques*, 16 August 1947.
8. Debates of the 13th and 14th of August 1947, *J.O., Débats*, pp. 4289-90 and 4283-4.
9. *Syndicalisme*, 4 January 1951.

10. G. Houist, *Étude Générale sur le Problème du Logement*, *Journal Officiel*, *Avis et Rapports du Conseil Economique*, 21 August 1953, p. 719; *Le Monde*, 4 June 1953.

11. See Table VIII. 1.

12. G. Houist, *Logement des Travailleurs de Faible Revenu* (*Journal Officiel*, *Avis et Rapports du Conseil Economique*, 25 February 1956), p. 65.

13. ibid., Annexe V; *Le Figaro*, 5 November 1953.

14. *Combat*, 11 April 1952.

15. G. Houist, *Étude Générale sur le Problème du Logement*, *Journal Officiel*, *Avis et Rapports du Conseil Economique*, 21 August 1953.

16. *Le Figaro*, 7 January 1954.

17. G. Malignac, 'Le Logement des Faibles: Evincement Progressif et Formation d'un Sous-Prolétariat', *Population*, April-June 1957, pp. 237–60. This article summarizes invaluably the early post-war conflicts in this area.

18. A. Sauvy, 'Les mal-Logés', *Population*, Oct.-Dec. 1957, pp. 589–90.

19. P. Consigny, *Rapport sur l'Aide Publique au Logement* (*Groupe de Travail sur l'Aide Publique au Logement*, 1969), pp. 17–23.

20. ibid., p. 24.

21. *Rapports des Commissions du Vle Plan, 1971–75: Rapport de la Commission de l'Habitation*, Vol. I.

22. E. Crivelli and J. Bouret, *Les HLM* (Editions de l'actualité Juridique, 1975), pp. 325–36.

23. *Rapports des Commissions du Vlème Plan, 1971–75: Rapport de la Commission de l'Habitation*, Vol. II: *Les Travailleurs Etrangers*.

24. *Revue de l'Habitat Sociale*, No. 5, p. 20. This issue is useful since it contains the full text of the *Rapport Barré*, accompanied by a critical commentary which represents the point of view of the HLM movement.

25. *Le Monde*, 31 January 1968.

26. 'Logement', *Information Sociale*, 1970, No. 3; *Combat*, 1 and 2 August 1959.

27. *Rapport Général et Rapports Spéciaux Annexes de la Commission de l'Habitation du Vème Plan*, pp. 153–7.

28. *L'Aurore*, 12 and 13 May 1962; *Le Monde*, 26 September 1962 and 19 September 1966.

29. *Le Monde*, 21 September 1968. *Le Figaro*, 21 December 1968.

30. *Le Monde*, 19 March 1969.

31. *Le Monde*, 3 and 8 March 1969; *Le Figaro*, 10 March 1969; *Combat*, 23 December 1969.

32. *Le Monde*, 4 June 1961.

33. *Combat*, 11 February 1966; *Le Monde*, 23 March 1966.

34. *Le Monde*, 17 November 1970.

35. *Combat*, 17 December 1964.

36. *Libération*, 6 November 1964; *L'Humanité*, 29 November 1964. For full text of UNFO—HLM objections, see *Démocratie*, 13 May 1965; *Le Monde*, 11 June 1955.

37. *Le Figaro*, 30 September 1969.

38. *Le Monde*, 19 April 1969.

39. *Projet de Loi*, No. 1449, *Annexe au Procès-Verbal de l'Assemblée Nationale*, *J.O.*, 24 November 1970; *Le Monde*, 5 June 1971.

40. *Le Figaro*, 13 June 1958; *Le Monde*, 12 June 1959.

41. *Le Monde*, 10 June 1970; *Le Figaro*, 4 January 1972.

42. *Le Monde*, 19 May 1960.

43. *Le Monde*, 4 June 1961.

44. J. Baschwitz, 'La lutte contre L'insalubrité, *Notes et Études Documentaires*, 4051, January 1974.

45. P. Consigny, *Rapport sur l'Aide Publique au Logement* (Groupe de Travail sur l'Aide Publique au Logement), pp. 32–40; *Rapport Barré, Revue de l'habitat sociale*, No. 5, p. 17.

46. *Le Figaro*, 7 January 1954.

47. *Le Monde*, 24 January 1954.

48. The whole episode is described in G. Houist, *Logement des Travailleurs de Faible Revenu, Rapport présenté au nom du Conseil Economique* (Avis et Rapports du Conseil Economique), 25 February 1956.

49. Cited in *Le Monde*, 19 December 1970.

50. O. Guichard, *Le Monde*, 12 May 1973.

# IX

# The Public Sector: Britain

## 1 *1945–51*

Whereas large-scale public housing was a post-Second World War phenomenon in France, the council house has been a familiar sight and topic for discussion in British politics since immediately after the First World War. The housing problem received the attention of politicians immediately after the war and the Act known as the Addison Act was passed, thus giving birth to the council sector.

Whereas the HLMs in France have always been presumed to be in need of subsidy in the form of loans at reduced rates of interest, the public sector in Britain has never had the advantage of such stable financial arrangements. The terms on which finance has been made available have always been a subject of open political conflict and, perhaps more important than this, governments have always been able to bring about decisive changes in these arrangements when they have wished to. Such has been the case during the post-Second World War period which we shall examine in this chapter and such was also the case in the inter-war era. The changes in these arrangements may be viewed as reflecting a changing balance of advantage and disadvantage as between the three parties principally involved: the local authorities, their tenants and the central government. In the first scheme under the Addison Act rents were fixed with regard to the level of rents pertaining in the private sector in the neighbouring district. The local authority was in addition called upon to make a fixed contribution independent of the cost of the housing. The deficit still remaining after these two sources of income had been taken into account was to be paid by the central government. This was a scheme which was clearly advantageous to the local authority and the tenant. Their liability, in the form of rate contribution and rent respectively, was fixed in absolute terms. Any deficit was met by central government. This arrangement was very soon replaced by one which limited the financial liabilities of the central government in exact terms and left the deficit to be paid for either from the rent or the rate income. Such was the approach of the Wheatley and Chamberlain Acts. In the 1930s a third scheme came into operation under which the fixed subsidies of the Wheatley and Chamberlain Acts were withdrawn and local authorities only received subsidies for specially defined housing purposes. A detailed discussion of these developments is not within the scope of this study but they have been briefly recalled here in order to demonstrate that the purposes and the financing of local authority housing have always in Britain been subjects of political debate and areas of policy in which political change regularly expresses itself [1].

We may now consider the housing policy of the Attlee Labour Government of the immediate post-war period. Its policy with regard to the public sector may be considered as a piece since there were only slight alterations in the basic orientation of their policy during the six years in which they were in power. The keynote of Labour policy was the allocation of all available houses, whether built to rent or for sale, according to need. This concept was translated into practical policy by giving an absolute priority to the council sector and only allowing the building of houses for owner-occupation on the granting of a licence to be obtained from the local authority. Such a licence was only granted when the ultimate owner of the house was known and the authority satisfied that the case was one of need. This Labour policy meant in effect that the speculative building in anticipation of future demand which had been so much a feature of the building boom of the late 1930s was forbidden. Although individual local authorities were entrusted with the decisions as to who was to receive the licences to build in the private sector, the Minister fixed a ratio of council to private building at the national level. In this period, Mr Bevan established a ratio of four council houses to every house built privately for owner-occupation. This of course contrasts sharply with later Labour and Conservative policies which have aimed at a building programme equally divided between the council and private sectors [2].

It may appear that this policy was an extremely doctrinaire approach but in fact in this period of severe housing shortage, following on the almost total absence of housing construction during the war, there was no great difference of view between the two major political parties. At this time the policy being pursued by Labour was not generally regarded as a Socialist policy and therefore open to criticism from the Conservative point of view. A Conservative Party report on the post-war housing problem produced in 1944 (*Foundation of Housing*) recommended that the first one million dwellings to be constructed after the war be predominantly built within the public sector. The rationing approach was much more widely accepted than one would ever imagine, reading the pronouncements of Conservatives only ten years later. The generally accepted sentiment on the question was well expressed by an official, questioned by the Estimates Committee in 1946, who, speaking of his own council's building programme said: 'They [the councillors], entirely of their own volition, took the view that, in view of the number of people who required houses and also the number of people who required houses but could only afford to rent them and not to buy them, who were very greatly in the majority, their programme should come first [3]. Nor was the Labour Party convinced at this time, as it was to be later, that all forms of housing must be subsidized. Subsidies were greatly increased in the Housing (Financial and Miscellaneous Provisions) Act in 1946 but, at the outset at least, this increase was considered to be the unfortunate result of temporarily inflated costs. Official policy did not recognize subsidy as normally involved in public housing. The *New Statesman* expressed the Labour view early in 1946 in the following terms: 'Subsidies at the proposed rate would be simply intolerable if they were to continue long; for they would eat up so high a proportion of our national and local resources as to make it quite impossible to tackle other tasks hardly less urgent than housing – for example, the building of schools and community centres and the effective formation of town planning schemes [4].

Whereas since 1955 the political arguments about subsidy for council housing have been conducted largely on matters of principle, the earlier discussion followed much more in the tradition of the inter-war period when subsidy had been regarded as a useful instrument of policy by both Labour and Conservative governments, an instrument the use of which must be determined largely in the light of economic circumstances, notably housing costs and the interest rate due on money borrowed for housing purposes. Both the 1946 Act for which Mr A. Bevan was responsible and the Housing Act of 1952 prepared under the direction of Mr Harold Macmillan, the Conservative Minister, fixed the level of subsidy according to a mathematical calculation based on the principle that it was reasonable on average to demand that the wage earner contribute 10 per cent of his income in the form of rent for his council house. The remaining charge necessary for the house was then shared in both Acts between central and local government. The consensus which was established between Conservative and Labour front bench spokesmen is also evident in the agreement of the Coalition Government to provide a subsidy for new housing construction, although Coalition policy, unlike the Labour policy, involved a subsidy to both private and public forms of house building [5].

As well as accepting the element of subsidy in council house building most Conservative critics also agreed that the need principle was the correct one in circumstances of grave shortage and this meant that they largely accepted the predominant position given by Labour to council house building and the use of the licence system for the private sector. 'Technically private enterprise is a much superior instrument for actually building houses. Whether it is better for disposing of them is a matter for argument' [6]. This is the view of a future Conservative front bench housing spokesman and illustrates well that, at this time, Conservatives accepted the allocation of all new housing, private as well as public, according to need, although they continued to criticize the uneconomic and inefficient methods of local authority 'direct labour establishments'. Some local authorities have always used 'direct labour establishments', that is, have built their own estates rather than contract with private firms.

Most Conservative criticism of the Labour housing programme was directed not so much at the fundamental principles of subsidy and allocation which it represented but at the capacity of the Government to plan effectively and at the relative weight given in the investment programme to housing as against other priority areas. Conservatives tended to argue that more houses could and ought to be built both because housing had received an insufficient priority in the government investment programme and also because with the same expenditure, it should be possible to build more. The discussion of housing during this period treated policy as an exercise in national economic planning, and the Conservatives claimed that the Government was vulnerable to criticism on this score. Given the existence of a consensus on principles, debate centred around the size of the programme. In this field there was a constant conflict between the popular demand for more housing and the Government's wish above all to safeguard the balance of payments which was threatened by the import of raw materials needed in housing construction. In 1947 the annual housing target was fixed at 240,000, only to be reduced shortly afterwards to 140,000. This was increased to a figure of 170,000–180,000 dwellings in 1948 and in July 1949, the Minister of Health announced the adoption of 200,000 houses per annum as the target for the future. Only three months after this, Sir Stafford Cripps reduced the building rate to 175,000, although this more austere target was again pushed up to 200,000 by the spring of 1950 [7]. The Labour Government was conscious of its vulnerability on this aspect of housing policy and therefore undertook in the spring of 1950 not to alter the housing target again within the next three years [8].

## II  1951–55

With the Conservative victory in the general election of 1951, an important turning point is reached in the development of housing policy. There were no outstanding initial changes but within a short period of time it was clear that the change of government was going to have considerable impact on the housing programme. We shall see in examining the development of Conservative policy that this is in fact the case, although the first major piece of Conservative legislation, the Housing (Subsidies) Act of 1952, continued directly in the line of Labour subsidy policy and increased subsidies to a level substantially above that pertaining in the latter years of Labour rule and one that surprised many contemporary observers. In part the explanation for this Act, and for the unusual Conservative policy of the first four years of Tory rule, lies in the events of the Blackpool Annual Conference which took place between the elections of 1950 and 1951 [9]. On this occasion, amendment to the official party statement on housing which was proposed from the floor was carried against the clear wishes of the front bench spokesmen on housing. The amendment stated the desirability of a target of 300,000 houses per annum. It should be remembered that at the time this amendment was adopted, the rate of house building was about 200,000 per annum and that therefore the new policy represented an increase of 50% on what many experts had considered to be an ambitious programme. This policy was adopted by the leadership of the party before the subsequent election and therefore became an electoral engagement which Mr Macmillan was charged to fulfil. The adoption of this target was a clear victory for the more intransigent Conservative critics of Labour's housing policy. If, for example, one examines the

Conservative position in March 1950, before the new target had become official party policy, one finds that official party spokesmen were extremely loath to be drawn into a precise engagement on future housing policy and gave the impression that such increases as the Conservatives would achieve would result mainly, not from increased housing investment but from a better use of resources already committed in this sector [10]. The increase of the housing target by 50 per cent implied much more than a more efficient use of existing investment in housing.

The events at Blackpool were decisive for early Tory policy because they rendered impossible any rapid return to the traditional Tory housing policy of reduced subsidies and reliance on the speculative builder [11]. There was, it will be remembered, only a very modest privately financed building programme in progress at the time of the Conservative victory and it was clear that, if the 300,000 target was to be reached within reasonable time, the Government could not rely on this sector. Mr Macmillan therefore accepted that it was necessary to increase council house building and also to provide a larger government subsidy for such building. This policy was clearly unpopular with doctrinaire Tories but it was certainly necessary if the promise given at the 1951 election was to be fulfilled and the policy undoubtedly proved enormously successful politically [12]. The target was reached and easily surpassed well before the 1955 election and in doing so the Conservative Government proved that they were as capable and willing to carry out extensive construction of council houses as their Labour opponents [13]. To have relied so heavily on the public sector ran counter to many basic Conservative principles. It meant first and foremost that owner-occupation did not prosper during these years. It also meant an increasing budgetary contribution year by year to the housing bill and commitments of future expenditure on subsidies which could not be avoided in the future, even if later council house construction was not subsidized as generously.

Although Mr Macmillan's term as Minister for Housing and Local Government (1951–55) was characterized by a continuation of the previous stress on public housing, this period also saw some policy changes that were more consistent with pre-war Conservative practice. Immediately after the election victory of 1951 the ratio of four council houses to one owner-occupied was changed to three to one, and, before long, the licensing of private building was abandoned altogether so as to permit expansion. These measures were taken in a spirit of economic liberalism which did not, however, extend to the more fundamental lines of housing policy such as the size of housing subsidies, the importance of the public building programme, or the continuation of rent control in the private sector. These years saw the application of policies that were distinguished both from Labour and from later Conservative policy. What Mr Macmillan did in essence was to modify Labour policy in a Conservative direction. The really decisive break with the past did not come until Mr Sandys' announcement in September 1955 that subsidies for council housing would be cut.

## III  *1955–61*

No important change in housing policy could have been foreseen by any observer of the 1955 election campaign. Mr Macmillan had already shown that the Government was unwilling to accept unlimited expansion of the financial commitment to the council sector by announcing a small reduction in subsidy during 1954 which was to come into effect early in 1955 [14]. This slight modification reflected the Macmillan conception of housing policy and gave no inkling of the major changes to come under the new minister and in the new political situation created by the increased Conservative majority and the economic difficulties of the summer of 1955. Mr Sandys announced in the autumn that the Government was introducing legislation in the forthcoming session of parliament which would do away with the general housing subsidy as it had existed during the past nine years. He took the view that the housing shortage was now much less acute and that subsidy should be used for particular purposes such as the housing of slum-dwellers. A slum clearance programme was to be started and was to become the main aim of public intervention in housing in the future. An element of subsidy was also to be maintained for the housing of old people. In line with these changes in the financial involvement of the central government in housing, changes were also made in the local government involvement. Whereas previously local authorities had been legally obliged to make a contribution from the rate income to housing costs, they were to be free in future to determine the size of their contribution and, if they wished, to contribute nothing whatsoever. The implication of this change in policy, which was embodied without modification in the Housing (Subsidy) Act of 1956, can hardly be overestimated. The most immediate consequence was that council rents were bound to rise. Existing subsidies would continue for houses already finished, but when central and local subsidy to housing is cut, council rents for existing and future tenants must rise. This is because most authorities pool their rents and therefore the burden of new unsubsidized housing falls on all their tenants. The impact on rent levels was all the more important because of the rising interest rate of the fifties and the Conservative view that housing authorities could not expect any special treatment for their borrowing.

Perhaps even more important were the long-term implications of these decisions for the purpose of the council sector. Mr Sandys' new conception of the purpose of council housing was radically different from that of both his Conservative and Labour predecessors. In his view the private sector was capable of providing housing for almost all future need and the council sector was to be purely residual, catering for those who could not find alternative forms of housing. His approach implied that the bulk of future council tenants would belong to special categories, such as slum-dwellers, the elderly, or perhaps in a minority of cases those in general housing need who lived in areas where shortage still persisted. This new conception of council housing justified and even suggested a smaller programme, and demands for this, which had already been made in 1955, were to prove even more intensive in the struggle in 1957 and 1958 to maintain the parity of the pound and combat inflation. The Sandys' view of the function of council housing did not remain a statement of pure Conservative doctrine never to be implemented in fact. There was no general subsidy for five years and, even more important perhaps, the size of the council housing programme was reduced in successive years. Particularly important were the cuts made in November of 1957 by the then minister Mr Henry Brooke. So rapid was the decline in the public sector that it could not even be fully compensated by the expansion of the private sector which was taking place during the 1950s. The council house sector was certainly vulnerable at such a time for the double reason that it involved heavy capital investment and also that it did not square easily with Conservative values. The argument was now heard, when capital expenditure programmes were drawn up, that for political reasons housing had been given an exceptional priority in the early fifties and that now other programmes, notably roads, must be allowed a larger claim on available resources.

There was an additional handicap under which the council house laboured in the political and economic atmosphere of the late fifties.

In many areas expenditure depends closely on the policies adopted and this means that short-term incremental adjustments are difficult to achieve. But in housing one is dealing with a programme which is made up of a large number of units which are not interdependent, and hence cuts can be made more easily. It is important to note that this change in the Conservative Government's policies for public housing occurred at the same time as the moves to decontrol rents in the private sector. In our earlier discussion of the Rent Act it was pointed out that a view of this legislation which took into account the historical perspective led to the conclusion that the Act was particularly radical and went well beyond what might normally have been expected from a Conservative government. The same conclusions are justified with respect to changes in the public sector taking place at the same time. The Baldwin Government of 1924–9 for instance, had not repealed the housing legislation of the preceding Labour Government, and, when housing subsidies were finally discontinued for general purposes in 1932, it was in economic circumstances that were far more serious than those confronting the Conservative Government in 1955. The importance of the change in policy in the public sector is further underlined if one considers simply the quantitative change to which it contributed. By the late 1950s the council programme had declined to a level of output of less than half that of the Macmillan era and, moreover, it was composed in large part of housing for the elderly and for slum-dwellers, categories which had not benefited greatly from council housing in earlier years [15]. We have indicated that British housing policy is periodically marked by decisive changes of direction of a political character. Such was clearly the case in 1955 and 1956. This was no ordinary change of policy comparable to that which took place after the Conservative victory in the general election of 1951. The scope of change in the public and private sectors, the period of time during which new policies were maintained, and the plainly ideological nature of the new orientation, show this to be the most important turning point in the post-war development of British housing policy.

IV *1961–64*

The Sandys policies were never abandoned in one conscious change of direction as the Macmillan policies had been but were slowly eroded in a gradual fashion. Some change of approach was noticeable in the Housing Act of 1961 [16]. This legislation abandoned the

Sandys principle that there was no longer a need for a general housing subsidy in the public sector. New council building was in future to qualify for subsidy of some kind regardless of its purpose. Other aspects of policy demonstrated on the other hand the continuity of Mr Brooke's 1961 policy with that of his predecessor. The White Paper which accompanied the new legislation stated that there could be no overall increase in the quantity of investment in housing, thus restricting the reorientation of policy to the purely qualitative area [17]. Mr Brooke also made it clear in introducing the Bill that authorities would be called upon to demonstrate that there was a definite need within their area before loan sanction would be given for new housing projects [18]. In this statement he repeated the Government's commitment to a construction programme giving a clear priority to the private sector.

Mr Brooke left the Ministry of Housing and Local Government during 1961 and, after a short period in which Dr Hill was responsible for housing policy, Sir Keith Joseph replaced him and remained in charge of Conservative housing policy until the general election of 1964. During the period of Sir Keith Joseph's occupation of his post the pressure for increased housing output was evident and the Government began to find that its recent performance in the field of housing was becoming a political liability. As we have already pointed out, the agitation of this period centred around particular problems of harassment and extortion in the privately rented sector, but this criticism spilled over into other fields of housing policy. The problem of the homeless came to the fore for the first time. This was a problem which had previously been regarded as one of individual inadequacy. But now homelessness was a political issue and research showed that the cause of the difficulties of many families lay in recent housing policies and not in their own inadequacy [19]. It appeared from the work carried out by Mr J. Greve and also as a result of the research undertaken for the Milner-Holland Report that the Sandys policies were beginning by the early sixties to produce severe problems in London and, to a lesser extent, in other central city areas. Council house building in such areas was difficult and was running at either the same level as that of the early fifties or lower. It was now also accompanied by slum clearance and therefore few if any of the newly built dwellings were available for those on the general waiting list. The problem was further aggravated by decontrol which had served to encourage landlords to sell their property and thus to increase owner-occupation at the expense of the privately rented sector, in this way diminishing occupation rates per dwelling and rendering more acute the shortage of housing for the poor who could neither buy nor find council accommodation. New problems also appeared to which the Government seemed to have no answer. The Labour Party, for instance, concentrated a good deal of attention on the rapid increase in the price of land for housing development. This problem, like that of homelessness, was made more acute by the demand for centrally situated development land for purposes other than housing.

The appearance of these new types of housing problems posed serious difficulties for the Conservative Government. As we have seen, as far as the Rent Act was concerned, there was little that the Government felt able to do. It was publicly committed to a policy and little modification was possible, short of total renunciation of principles which had been affirmed in the teeth of the most virulent opposition. The situation was not the same with regard to the public sector. The implications of the criticisms levelled at the Government were clear. The public building programme had been allowed to fall too rapidly, especially in areas of continuing shortage, and it need-ed to be increased substantially, particularly if the Government intended to continue with its slum clearance programme. In other words, the reply to criticism was in part quantitative and did not involve renouncing previously avowed principles and therefore the Government felt itself able to respond to pressure. The way in which the adjustment of the housing programme took place during the early sixties demonstrates not only the slow erosion of the Sandys principles but also the clearly political character of policy-making in this area of housing.

In February 1962 the Government affirmed the long-standing housing target of 300,000 houses per annum, adding that this was considered a sufficient rate of new construction to cope with all needs for the next twenty years [20]. By December of the same year this attitude had been only slightly modified. Sir Keith Joseph now stated that the rate would be slightly increased for 1963 to 305,000 and that increases above this figure could be expected for later years [21]. In 1963 a government White Paper dealing with future housing policy established a target for the near future of 350,000, 150,000 of which were to be houses in the council sector [22]. In October of the same year Sir Keith Joseph raised the target once again to 400,000, thus implying that building in the council sector would have to rise well above the previously established target of

150,000 [23]. This affirmation brought the process of increase to an end for the time being. The steady upward revision of the housing target in these years completed the abandonment of the Sandys principles which had begun with the reintroduction of a general needs subsidy in 1961.

The modifications in housing policy effected in the early sixties entitle us to distinguish the period 1961 to 1964. It is important to bear in mind that the changes of these years were linked with other developments in social and economic policy. The Sandys principles as applied both to public housing and to the Rent Act were an expression of radical Tory economic and social policy in the mid-fifties. As we have seen, these policies created new problems some years later in the field of housing just as they did in other spheres and the response in the two spheres was to some extent parallel. In economic policy the Government felt obliged to concern itself directly with the levels of wages and prices and to seek out new instruments for influencing them. In these innovations there was no sign of a return to the strict physical controls of the war and immediate post-war period. In housing also, the emergence of new problems made the area once more one of political controversy, thus obliging the Government to accept increased responsibility.

## v 1964–70

When the Labour Party took office in 1964, it had no clear commitment with regard to council housing equivalent to that which existed in the field of privately rented accommodation. Nevertheless, any observer basing himself on the policies of the earlier Labour Government and on Labour criticisms of Tory policy could easily have concluded that it would be a high priority for Labour to increase the subsidy made available for council housing and to push forward public construction. Labour has always been committed to the subsidy although the party has been less in agreement as to its exact purpose. One Labour view was expressed by the party's spokesman in 1956 in opposing the Sandys subsidy reduction policy: 'We think there ought to be subsidised housing, not only for those who stand in sore need of it, but for the citizens of this country as a whole' [24]. This view has been the dominant Labour view and was accepted by the party unanimously when it was defined in opposition to the Conservative policy of aid only to those in need, that is to say to those who belong to particular categories. But the principle of a general subsidy, available for all forms of housing, is not accepted without qualification by all Labour members of Parliament. In particular, front bench party spokesmen have for long favoured rent rebates in the council sector. Such a policy implies concessions to the principle of aid to those in need. Labour's White Paper setting out the housing programme reaffirmed the party's commitment to the principle of the rent rebate [25]. The general and selective justifications of the housing subsidy are not of course incompatible, for policies may often combine a subsidy to most or all householders with an additional element of aid to those in greater need. This compromise approach was in fact followed by the Labour Government although, if one contrasts its use of the subsidy with that of the Conservative governments which came before and after it, one may observe a much greater emphasis on general subsidy and a much less marked priority for directing subsidy towards those in the greatest need.

Mr Crossman, the first Labour minister responsible for housing, decided on a subsidy increase and, although the necessary legislation did not become law until 1967, subsidies were back-dated to the date of the 1964 election. It is quite possible that, even if the Conservative Government had been returned to power in 1964, there would have been an increase in the housing subsidy, since Sir Keith Joseph had been engaged in a review jointly with the Association of Municipal Corporations (AMC) for some time prior to the election. The form of subsidy which was adopted by the Labour Government showed clear signs of being a Labour measure. There had been considerable criticism prior to 1964 of the blanket way in which the subsidy was distributed without, it was alleged, sufficient regard for varying local circumstances. The view that the old form of subsidy expressed in pounds per house per year was clumsy and wasteful is now generally admitted and will probably be reflected in any future Labour legislation. But the party had not adopted this point of view in 1964 and therefore the subsidy only took note of particular local conditions to the extent that this had been traditionally the case, as for example in the expensive site subsidy  or the subsidy for high building. A second characteristic of the form of subsidy adopted was that it was calculated so as to reproduce the conditions of local authority borrowing at $4\frac{1}{2}$ per cent, that is to say, the subsidy was to be sufficient to close the gap, between $4\frac{1}{2}$ per cent and whatever rate local authorities as a whole were obliged to pay on their outstanding housing debt. The reason for the attractions of this form of subsidy to Labour is not hard to find. A constant theme of Labour criticism during the thirteen years of Conservative government had been the burden under which authorities laboured as a consequence of continually rising interest rates. In adopting a form of subsidy which automatically protected local authorities against changes in the interest rate, Labour was only following through the logic of its own complaints. The hostility to high interest rates is deep-seated in the Labour Party and in fact the constant maintenance of a low interest rate had been a feature of its own earlier economic policy [26]. It is important to stress this continuity in policy, for it demonstrates that the ideological differences, which may so easily be observed between the two parties, have a real and not a merely verbal significance. This is an important point, particularly when one is concerned with the British-French differences, and will be discussed at greater length in the next chapter.

But if tradition played its part in the formation of certain policies, there were also quite naturally signs of evolution in Labour thinking about housing problems. As already indicated, there was no possibility of a return to the strict supremacy for council housing which had been maintained in the immediate post-war period. The Government's view, set out in its White Paper on the Housing Programme, was that construction should be equally shared in the short run between the public and private sectors [27]. This in fact meant only a slight modification of the practice of the Conservative Government in the early 1960s [28]. In the long run the Government declared itself in favour of a diminished role for the council sector. This revisionist point of view had no practical significance during the period of Labour's rule however, because government policy admitted that during the period of continuing national shortage it was necessary to maintain the 50 per cent share for the public sector.

The most publicized aspect of Labour's housing policy was certainly the commitment adopted in the short-lived national economic plan to reach a target of half a million houses a year by 1970. This target was accepted as entirely reasonable by the Conservative Party who in fact went one better in their 1966 Election Manifesto, in promising to reach this target by 1968. The target was adopted in 1965 and the policy seemed already to be running into difficulties as early as 1966, although it was not formally abandoned until after the devaluation of the following year. The explanation of how this failure came about is not so much a question of housing policy as of economic policy and therefore it is not of great interest to us in this study. Nevertheless the adoption of this extremely ambitious target and its acceptance by the Conservative Opposition is ample evidence of the political demand at this time for more housing, a demand the equivalent of which it would be difficult to find at any time in recent French history.

A number of factors helped to make council rents a national political issue in the late 1960s as they had never been previously. There was first and foremost the attempt to reach some form of agreement with the TUC in which council rents had to play a part. In addition, after the poor Labour showing in the local elections of 1967, many authorities were Tory-controlled and began to raise rents. The combination of these two factors was enough to bring about a break with the long-standing tradition of local autonomy in rent matters. Policies and incomes legislation in 1968 imposed maximum limits on council rent increases, despite the protests of local authorities [29]. The controls were dropped by the end of 1969 but this incident illustrates the way in which economic policy can affect housing policy. It is also worth noting that the clash between Labour central government and Tory local authorities over rents, and the recommendations of the Prices and Incomes Board that in the long run council rents ought to rise considerably sparked off an important debate about rent and subsidy [30]. This was to lead to the Conservative Housing Finance Act. These events and the discussion surrounding them showed how fundamental questions were open in Britain whereas in France the national debate on such matters has only begun with the publication of the Barre Report in 1975.

The combination of inter-party with central–local conflict also served to bring back into the political arena the issue of the sale of council houses, which had lain dormant for more than a decade. For a time Mr Greenwood, Mr Crossman's successor as Minister for Housing and Local Government, did not intervene·to stop sales despite the demand from the left-wing of his party that he should do so, particularly at the 1967 Party Conference [31]. But in July 1968 he did place a limit on the number of sales that would be permitted in stress areas [32]. After 1970 the Conservative Government removed these centrally imposed limits thus re-enacting an incident of just nineteen years earlier when another Conservative minister had done exactly the same. Such is the party political and ideological intensity of this and many other housing issues.

Enough has been said already about Labour policy on the vitally important question of subsidies and on the less important but politically explosive question of council house sales to show the link between

Labour Party housing policy and the housing policy of the Labour Government. Nevertheless the picture must be completed by indicating some of the areas of continuity with earlier Conservative policy and also areas in which policies advocated by members of the party, particularly the left-wing, were not adopted by the Labour Government. The Party's strong attachment to the council house system had borne fruit in the new legislation on subsidies, but when compared with the policy of fifteen years earlier, the decisions in this area of the Wilson Government appear in some respects to be moderate. Throughout the six years of Labour rule the aim was to split the annual construction programme approximately equally between public and private sectors. Some Labour critics of Conservative policy make play with the conflict between these two forms of housing, suggesting that it is necessary at times to limit the activity of the private sector in order to allow the public sector to expand without hindrance. This view of conflict between the two sectors was never adopted by the Labour Government. One may also note a moderated attitude towards the relation of public to private construction in the official Labour policy on building in Scotland. Traditionally Scottish new housing has relied much more heavily on the public sector than is the case in England and Wales. The Labour Government recognized this, not as an advantage but a handicap to the future economic growth of Scotland and stated as its aim the encouragement of private construction for sale in Scotland, so as to reduce the relative weight of council building [33].

In order to balance the picture of Labour policy one must also refer to a number of suggested innovations which were rejected. Labour was committed before 1964 to the establishment of regional authorities which were to carry out some housing functions [34]. Nothing was heard of this commitment between 1964 and 1970. If it had been implemented it would have challenged local authority pre-eminence in the public sector. Some radical suggestions coming from the left-wing of the party also found expression in the report of the Estimates Committee which appeared in 1969 [35].

These included the establishment of a centrally financed and controlled building agency for England and Wales, comparable to the Scottish Special Housing Authority, new centrally designed procedures for the definition of housing need, and new powers to be used by the minister in the case of authorities who failed to embark on a sufficiently ambitious building programme. None of these suggestions appeared to meet with the approval of Mr Greenwood.

VI *Policy since 1970*

We may now consider the most recent phase in the development of housing policy in the public sector which covers the period since the Conservative general election victory of 1970. As one might have expected, the number of council houses completed annually fell somewhat following the election and the ratio of public to private building for housing purposes was modified considerably in favour of the latter. But by far the most important policy innovation was the Housing (Finance) Act which was without doubt the most important piece of post-war legislation since it broke entirely with some traditions of housing policy of as much as fifty years' standing. Although this Act was repealed by Labour following their return to office in 1974 it deserves considerable attention because of the political controversy which it caused and because, despite its repeal, it has left a permanent imprint on national policy.

The fundamental position adopted in this new legislation was that there was no longer any general justification for a subsidy for council housing. It was no longer accepted that the tenants of council houses were in some way a special category who needed financial assistance. Such assistance, as was made available under the Act to the tenants of council houses, was based not on their status as council tenants but on their incomes in relation to the rent which they paid. The Act applied this principle to public and private tenants alike, extending a national rent rebate scheme to both. The Act therefore treated council and private tenants in the same way and both had rents fixed according to the fair rent formula contained in Mr Crossman's legislation of 1965. This meant that local authorities lost ultimate responsibility for overall rent levels which became the concern of the Fair Rent Committees. The parallel between the fair rent mechanism as established by Labour for the private tenant and as intended by the Conservatives for the public sector is not exact. Under the 1965 Rent Act a fair rent was only fixed after application by either the landlord or the tenant. Under the legislation of 1971 fair rents were fixed for all council tenants according to the terms of the legislation rather than at the request of either the tenant or the landlord.

In addition to the withdrawal of earlier housing subsidies and the imposition of the fair rent system, the legislation provided for a rent rebate scheme of national scope which applied in the same form in all local authority areas in England and Wales. This scheme was widely regarded as considerably more generous than those previously operated by a number of local authorities and the Government un-officially estimated that, by the year 1975–6, 40 per cent of all council tenants would be receiving rent rebates [36]. Although the general subsidy for new housing was to cease, the legislation did accept the principle that slum clearance was a national problem and therefore special help in the form of a subsidy was made available for future clearance operations, which were to remain a high government priority.

A brief description of the principles involved in the new legislation hardly gives an adequate impression of the far-reaching nature of the new system. In earlier years a fundamental point which had remained constant under a variety of different subsidy regimes had been that the local authority was under an obligation to balance the housing revenue account. This meant that legislation did not permit authorities to raise council rents so as to accumulate a surplus on housing which might be used for other purposes. Since the fair rent system was now to apply throughout, it was certain that surpluses would be created in some areas, and that these would not remain with the local authorities but would be centralized and used for the financing of the national rent rebate scheme. From the point of view of the local authorities this meant that they would not only be deprived of the subsidies which they previously received and be subjected to a national rebate scheme, but they would also see local rents raised to a level sufficient to create surpluses on their housing account which would be taken and used for national purposes. This gives some idea of the considerable break with the traditions of local autonomy which existed in the field of local authority housing and also explains why there was so much hostility to the new Act, not only in the parliamentary Labour Party but also from Labour-controlled councils.

The exceptional character of this legislation is particularly brought out if we compare it with the legislation passed by the minister ten years earlier, which represented at that time official Conservative thinking on such questions as local autonomy, rent rebate, and the housing subsidy. Mr Brooke and his predecessors as Conservative ministers responsible for housing were without exception and without qualification favourable to some form of rent rebate scheme for the public sector. But it was always argued, mainly in defence against criticism coming from the right-wing of the party, that however desirable such schemes might be, their introduction must be left to the local authorities concerned since the fixing of rents was a matter for local discretion. This remained the official view, despite the fact that the number of authorities who offered a rent rebate scheme to their tenants only increased slowly with the years and these schemes varied very greatly in their details and in the extent of their generosity. As already explained, the 1971 legislation completely abandoned this point of view and imposed the principle of a rent rebate scheme in all areas. With regard to possible reductions in the levels of subsidy, Mr Brooke had argued that some subsidy would be needed and that in any case one could not modify the implied contract which already existed between the central and local authorities in the form of the earlier legislation which had generally promised fixed subsidies for a period of sixty years. He gave evidence of his belief in this principle in his own legislation by guaranteeing the new subsidy which was then established for a period of ten years whilst reserving the power to alter or abolish it after this period. In taking this action he was acknowledging in legislation what was generally understood to be the case during the 1950s and early 1960s, that is, that a government had the political right to choose its own form of subsidy for current building but that local authorities were entitled to rely on the continuation of existing subsidies for their full period of sixty years as promised. As explained, the 1971 legislation did not accept this point of view as the Government not only refused any future general subsidy but also did away with existing subsidies on houses constructed under earlier and more favourable financial arrangements.

The radical departure from established practices embodied in the new legislation is also brought out if we make the comparison with the legislation of 1961 with respect to the principle of selectivity. Aid only to those in need is an oft repeated and long-established Conservative slogan. It found some but varied expression in both Acts. In the Act of 1961 two levels of subsidy were provided, with the more generous provision being intended for poorer local authorities. Need therefore in this case had referred to the need of the particular local authority but need in the legislation promoted by Mr Walker ten years later referred to the financial need of individual council tenants. The radical implications of this second approach produced changes in the system of housing finance which go far beyond anything envisaged in 1961. Previously, subsidy had been given to all authorities who were left free to dispose of it among their tenants as they saw fit. In the new legislation a more radical adherence to the selective principle brought to an end this division of work between central and local authorities and established a direct relation between the central government, which is responsible for the national rent rebate scheme, and the citizen. In the area of rents at least, the local authority ceased to play the role of intermediary.

Before leaving the Housing (Finance) Act, something should be said of the political controversy surrounding its enactment and the difficulties which arose in the early stages of its implementation. With respect to the response of the Labour Party, the events of 1957 were to some extent repeated fourteen years later. The party opposed the measure from the outset and undertook to repeal it [37]. Numerous objections were made to the Act but, during parliamentary consideration, Labour spokesmen stressed its inflationary consequences and the contradiction between the Government's attitude on prices in general and its attitude to the level of council house rents [38]. The Government recognized that the Housing (Finance) Act was one of its most important pieces of legislation and, despite pressure from the Opposition, made no important concessions and refused to accept arguments based on the general economic interest and the need to fight inflation. It in effect insisted that housing was an area of policy-making in its own right rather than simply an aspect of economic policy. It was prepared to take this stand despite grave inflationary problems and demands in negotiations with the TUC for the suspension of the Act. This is important as it would seem that, if housing is treated as accessory to economic policy, one is likely to have a more continuous and unbroken development of policy, avoiding sharp increases in government spending and rents. This attitude towards housing policy helps to maintain the distinctively British pattern of policy development. If housing policy were more closely tied to economic policy, contrasts in party policies would be less clear-cut.

But the Act was not only attacked for the rent increases which it produced. All the perennial questions of the equity of the financial arrangements made in each housing sector were re-opened. The Government protected itself against criticism demanding equality for private and public tenants by providing rent rebates for both. But more difficult problems of equity as between the sectors are posed when we consider that the majority of council tenants were not to benefit from the rebate scheme. Under the Act they were to pay a fair rent which was thought to be about the level made necessary by historic costs. This was difficult to justify since the owner-occupier who buys his own house pays only the historic cost and receives in addition an income tax allowance on the interest due on his mortgage. The council tenant was to receive in future no subsidy the function of which could be considered parallel with the tax advantages afforded the house buyer. Whereas therefore the Labour Government of 1964–70 was open to criticism, mainly on the ground of comparison between the two rented sectors, the Conservatives proved more vulnerable with respect to the lack of equity existing between the two rented sectors on the one hand and house buyers on the other. The problem of equity between the different sectors once again is seen to stimulate changes in housing policy as the Labour Party is now edging its way towards the imposition of income ceilings which would limit the tax advantages of house buyers [39].

Nor were the principles embodied in the new legislation criticized only on the ground of equity between the different sectors of housing provision. Labour critics of the Act pointed out that, in effect, the council tenant was being asked under the new system to contribute part of his rent to the financing of the national rent rebate scheme. To some extent this has always been the case for, even when there was a general housing subsidy, any authority which decided to operate a rent rebate scheme was entitled to do so without financing it from the rates and, in this case, to operate the scheme meant charging a higher rent to council tenants than would otherwise have been necessary. Nevertheless the old system was fairer to the council tenant since, even if his rent was higher as a consequence of the introduction of a rent rebate scheme, it remained a subsidized rent. All that happened when the scheme was introduced locally was that a tenant lost some of the benefit of his subsidy. Under the Housing (Finance) Act he was to pay above cost, and some of the profit which was thereby produced was to help to pay for the rebate scheme. It should be noted with respect to the Labour criticism of new rent levels that, although they condemned the profit element which now played a part in council rents, they did not take up a firm position on the question of the true principles which should determine such rents. Since the Labour victory in the general elections of 1974 there has been some talk of 'resonable' rents and of giving the council sector aid comparable to that received by owner-occupiers [40]. But these formulae do little to answer questions about Labour's ultimate intentions.

During 1972, when the Act first began to have a direct impact on council rent levels, there was considerable opposition from Labour-controlled local authorities. The Lambeth borough council tried the method of using legal loopholes in the legislation but was unsuccessful when challenged in the courts [41]. A large number of authorities protested individually to the Department of the Environment and many of these succeeded in negotiating smaller initial increases. The more militant authorities carried their opposition to the extent of refusing altogether to operate the Act and in so doing defied the law. Provision was made in the Act for this eventuality and housing commissioners were appointed in some areas to take over the duties of those authorities who proved uncooperative. The question of illegal conduct in the resistance to the Act was discussed at annual Labour Party conferences and also at a special housing conference of local government authorities concerned at Cheltenham in February of 1972. Mr Crossland, the party's housing spokesman, consistently refused to encourage authorities in unlawful resistance to the principles of the Act. Firmness was shown in the appointment of housing commissioners under the Act and the high priority which was given the measure, despite its political unpopularity, was made clear when council rents were placed outside the scope of the price freeze of the autumn of 1972.

Although a number of local authorities initially refused to apply the Housing (Finance) Act, Clay Cross achieved the greatest notorriety because its defiance was particularly outspoken and was not confined to the area of housing. Mr Mitchell argues that events in Clay Cross show how weak central government is when faced by determined local opposition [42]. I cannot agree.

It seems important to me not to see Clay Cross in isolation but to ask instead the more vital and more general question: 'Did local hostility to the Act prevent its being applied as originally intended?' On this question the facts seem to speak for themselves. No major urban authority in the United Kingdom refused to apply the Act and the thirty-five smaller authorities which initially expressed their intention to resist all eventually agreed to implementation or had higher rents imposed on them by a Housing Commissioner [43]. The total sum involved was only one and a half million pounds and this was not a loss to the Exchequer because much of it was later repaid, either by council tenants or ratepayers in the areas concerned.

The notion of fixing fair rents for the public sector no longer represents government policy but this is not because of the defiance of Clay Cross but because the Labour Party, as promised, has repealed the Housing (Finance) Act and replaced it by legislation which subsidizes council rents more heavily. There is nothing here which can compare with the successful defiance of government policy embodied in legislation on numerous occasions, accounts of which can be found in the earlier chapters dealing with France.


## VII  *Tenant selection*

Considerable attention was paid in chapter VII to the political character of disputes about the selection of tenants for publicly constructed housing. Despite the great concern of both Labour and Conservative Governments for the financial arrangements which govern public housing, no post-war Government has been much concerned with the selection policies followed by the local authorities. A number of official reports have criticized tenant selection policy and particularly the operation of local residence requirements. There is an astonishing lack of information about the policies which are in fact pursued and the consequences to which they give rise. An official survey of policy with regard to the public sector has devoted considerable attention to the problem of tenant selection but no important recommendations involved intervention by central government and therefore there was no break with the long-standing practice of regarding tenant selection as a purely local matter [44]. Disapproval of the practice of excessive local residence requirements was once again expressed but neither professional opinion nor any of the three political parties has suggested that there is a need for any change in this area. Not that such information as is available gives an entirely satisfactory picture of the selection process. The Milner-Holland Report emphasized once again what had been known for many years prior to 1965, that the poorest families rarely found their way into the council sector despite the existence in some areas of rebate schemes designed in principle to encourage them [45].

In my view, the reason for the lack of political conflict on this very important subject is the changing composition of the groups concerned and their lack of any clear political identity. If selection policy is ever to become a subject of public concern and political debate it seems that it will be as part of the general question of race relations for there is clear evidence that immigrants, and particularly coloured immigrants, suffer from negative discrimination in the allocation of council housing and demands have been made on behalf of this group which would allow them some guarantee of fairer treatment [46]. In the French atmosphere of distrust between central and local authorities, as we have seen, something approaching a quota system

## Table IX.1

*Britain*

*Housing completions by sector*

(England and Wales)

SOURCES: J.B. Cullingworth, *Housing and Local Government*
(Allen and Unwin, 1966), p. 52.

*Handbook of Statistics of the Department of the Environment*
(H.M.S.O., 1970), p. 8

| | Public | Private | Total |
|---|---|---|---|
| 1945–46 | 21,878 | 30,657 | 52,535 |
| 1947 | 87,915 | 39,626 | 127,541 |
| 1948 | 175,213 | 31,346 | 206,559 |
| 1949 | 147,092 | 24,688 | 171,780 |
| 1950 | 145,784 | 26,576 | 172,360 |
| 1951 | 150,497 | 21,406 | 171,903 |
| 1952 | 176,897 | 32,078 | 208,975 |
| 1953 | 218,703 | 60,528 | 279,231 |
| 1954 | 220,924 | 88,028 | 308,952 |
| 1955 | 173,392 | 109,934 | 283,326 |
| 1956 | 149,139 | 119,585 | 268,724 |
| 1957 | 145,711 | 122,942 | 268,653 |
| 1958 | 117,438 | 124,087 | 241,525 |
| 1959 | 102,905 | 146,476 | 249,381 |
| 1960 | 107,126 | 162,100 | 269,226 |
| 1961 | 98,466 | 170,366 | 268,832 |
| 1962 | 111,651 | 167,016 | 278,667 |
| 1963 | 102,413 | 168,242 | 270,655 |
| 1964 | 126,073 | 210,432 | 336,505 |
| 1965 | 140,935 | 206,246 | 347,181 |
| 1966 | 151,978 | 197,502 | 349,480 |
| 1967 | 169,958 | 192,940 | 362,898 |
| 1968 | 158,453 | 213,273 | 371,726 |
| 1969 | 150,788 | 173,377 | 324,165 |
| 1970 | 145,182 | 162,084 | 307,266 |
| 1971 | 130,000 | 180,000 | 310,000 |
| 1972 | 103,000 | 184,000 | 287,000 |
| 1973 | 89,634 | 174,413 | 264,047 |
| 1974 | 111,547 | 129,626 | 241,173 |
| 1975 | 138,313 | 140,381 | 278,694 |

for immigrants has already been attempted, although with little
success. The low political priority given by all parties to questions
relating to tenant selection tends to suggest that British housing
politics turn essentially around questions of income and wealth
distribution and the political ideologies associated with different
views on this question and that, when such issues are not raised, much

of the steam is taken out of the political controversy on housing questions.

At a number of points in this account I have had occasion to refer to the most obvious contrasts between the British and French pattern of policy development. These will be the subject of the next chapter.

## References

1. M. Bowley, *Housing and the state 1919–44* (Allen & Unwin Ltd., 1945), pp. 2–181.
2. *See* table IX. 1.
3. *Fifth Report from the Select Committee on Estimates, Housing Expenditure*, Session 1945–46 (London, H.M.S.O., 1946), p. 208.
4. *The New Statesman and Nation*, 23 February 1946.
5. *Housing*, Cmd. 6609 (H.M.S.O., March 1945), p. 5.
6. E. Marples, *The Financial Times*, 23 November 1950.
7. *The Times*, 5 May 1950.
8. *The Financial Times*, 23 June 1950.
9. R.T. McKenzie, *British Political Parties* (London, Heinemann, 1955), pp. 197–8.
10. *The Times*, 11 October 1950.
11. This was Conservative policy between 1931 and 1939.
12. The policy was condemned as 'unwarranted' by *The Times*, 3 March 1952.
13. *See* table IX. 1.
14. *The Financial Times*, 30 June 1954.
15. *See* table IX. 1.
16. *Housing in England and Wales*, Cmnd. 1290 (H.M.S.O., February 1961). This White Paper explains the provisions and purpose of the Act.
17. ibid., para. 37.
18. ibid., para. 33.
19. J. Greve, *London's Homeless*, Occasional Papers on Social Administration No. 10 (G. Bell and Sons, 1964).
20. *The Times*, 8 February 1962.
21. *The Times*, 14 December 1962.
22. *Housing*, Cmnd. 2050 (H.M.S.O., May 1963).
23. *The Times*, 10 October 1963.
24. *The Times*, 1 October 1959.
25. *The Housing Programme: 1965–70*, Cmnd. 2838 (H.M.S.O., November 1965).
26. J.C.R. Dow, *The Management of the British Economy 1945–60* (Cambridge University Press, 1964), pp. 7–12.
27. *The Housing Programme*, Cmnd. 2838 (H.M.S.O., November 1965), p. 8.
28. *See* table IX. 1.
29. *The Times*, 22 May 1968.
30. *Increases in Rents of Local Authority Housing*, Prices and Incomes Board Report, No. 62, Cmnd. 3604 (H.M.S.O., April 1968).

31. *The Times*, 22 March 1967.

32. *New Society*, No. 306, 8 August 1968.

33. *Housing-Action*, Labour Party, 1967.

34. *The Times*, 23 February 1963.

35. *Fourth Report from the Estimates Committee, Housing Subsidies*, Session 1968–69 (H.M.S.O., 1969).

36. *New Society*, No. 493, 9 March 1972.

37. *The Guardian*, 3 October 1972 and 4 October 1973.

38. *The Times*, 4 November 1970. The NFC criticized the Act on a much broader basis: *The Times*, 9 August 1971.

39. Anthony Crosland in the debate on the Queen's Speech, *The Guardian*, 3 November, 1972.

40. *The Times*, 4 June 1974.

41. *The Times*, 8 and 12 August 1972.

42. A. Mitchell, 'Clay Cross', *Political Quarterly*, XLV, 2.

43. *The Times*, 25 March 1975. Figures supplied by Mr Crosland in the House.

44. *Council Housing—Purposes, Procedures, Priorities: Ninth Report of the Housing Management Sub-Committee of the Central Housing Advisory Committee*, (London, H.M.S.O., 1969).

45. *Report of the Committee on Housing in Greater London*, Cmnd. 2605 (H.M.S.O., March 1965) pp. 49–55 and 124–36.

46. J. Rex and R. Moore, *Race, Community and Conflict* (Oxford University Press, 1967), pp. 19–43; E. Burney, *Housing on Trial* (Oxford University Press, 1967); *The Housing of Commonwealth Immigrants* (London, The National Committee for Commonwealth Immigrants, 1967).

# X
# The Public Sector: Conclusion

Before embarking on the explanation which is the essential task of this chapter, it is as well to remind ourselves of the differences which we have observed, both the constant differences and the contrasted patterns of development. The French pattern has been marked by deadlock on certain problems which have remained a constant preoccupation and by slow and even development of policy in established directions with respect to others. The British pattern, on the other hand, has been one of sharp twists and turns in policy on a variety of issues and frequent and important reorientations. With respect to one of the issues of the greatest importance in the public sector, namely that of the terms on which government finance is made available, these contrasted patterns are particularly evident. In the French case there has never been any question of a total withdrawal or even substantial reduction in the amount of subsidy granted the HLM system by means of reduced interest charges. This is so despite the fact that, unlike the comparable British form of provision, the HLMs receive a form of hidden subsidy which comes to them via the housing allowance made available to the poorer of their tenants. A certain amount of government hostility to the privileged form of finance made available to the HLMs is observable but this has only been translated into occasional and slight adjustments in the terms of loans always tending to raise slightly the interest charged and diminish the number of years allowed for repayment. In the British case one may observe statutes every four or five years which make substantial alterations in the terms on which finance is made available, and the most recent of these has even attempted to withdraw altogether any form of subsidy for housing as such, confining aid to those cases where income support is considered necessary [1].

The contrast in approach is equally evident in the area of rent levels. In France, after some initial conflict and uncertainty in the late forties and early fifties, the situation has remained without substantial modification since 1955, with the rent burden being distributed among tenants by means of the weighted surface area system and the general level of rents being fixed by ministerial decree determining minimum and maximum rents per square metre applicable throughout France. The British system has produced considerable changes from time to time. Until 1968 rents were directly influenced by central decisions on the size of the housing subsidy so that their level was affected by the fluctuations referred to above, and since 1968 there has been intervention for economic reasons, and more recently a total abandonment of the system of local autonomy and its replacement by a system which fixed council rents throughout the nation according to a formula defined by statute.

In the area of tenant selection the contrast does not altogether parallel that already described. In both countries a large degree of discretion has been granted to the local authorities. In the British case this has been a publicly adopted and justified policy which has been little criticized. In the French case there has been constant government and public disquiet at the policies adopted by HLM organizations and there has been spasmodic government effort to reduce abuses. This has succeeded in reducing the area of discretion available to those locally responsible but has not gone so far as to decisively transfer responsibility from the locality to the centre. Whereas therefore the continuity in Britain has rested on political agreement, its basis in France has been political deadlock.

As to the general purpose of the public sector, particularly in relation to other sectors of housing provision, there has been no change in the post-war period in France and only a little more in Britain. The official French position has always been that the sector should provide for the poorer section of the community who will find alternative forms of provision more difficult to obtain. In practice, as we have seen, this has not been the case and paradoxically many HLM organizations apply to all applicants the test of a minimum rather than a maximum income [2]. Under Conservative rule in Britain the official view has always been the same as that of the French Government but the Attlee Labour Government took a much wider view of the role of the council sector and there is also a substantial body of expert opinion in Britain today which favours a wider role for the sector, particularly now that being a council tenant is not necessarily associated with the receipt of indirect income support [3]. On this question, therefore, our observations tend to confirm that the housing policy is more open to change and development in Britain, and more rigid in France.

This view of the basic contrast between the two systems is further reinforced by an examination of the changing allocation of functions as between central and local authorities. In broad outline, the British history has shown a period of concentrated central direction, followed by a rapid relaxation and development of local autonomy, followed again by a tightening of controls from the centre at the expense of local rights. This fluctuation has not been a feature of the French case where centralism has remained firmly entrenched and only recently has there been the slight possibility of decentralization as part of a policy of regionalization. Although the possibility of regionalizing some aspects of housing policy has been under discussion since the late 1960s, and was given some prominence in the Sixth Plan, it remains as yet no more than a potential threat to well-established central direction.

In both countries attempts have been made to meet the problem posed by tenants of publicly owned housing with widely varying incomes. In a society in which inequalities of income are quite readily accepted but in which, nevertheless, it is felt necessary to modify them by a variety of means, the differential rent or rent rebate scheme would seem to be an inevitable solution. By a process of development, slow at first in the forties and fifties but more rapid since then, this solution has been adopted in Britain. In France many of those responsible for housing policy regard this solution as appropriate, with modifications necessary in order to take account of the existence of the French housing allowance. But for a number of reasons to be examined more fully presently, there has been little progress to date on this issue. The interim solution of a variety of categories of HLM developed since 1958, is not generally regarded as satisfactory because of the lower construction and space standards which are permitted for the cheapest of the categories, and because of the social segregation involved.

Sufficient has now been said to remind the reader of the principal contrasts existing between the British and French pattern of policy development and we may now proceed to attempt some explanation of this difference. One may begin with the most obvious explanatory point to which I have already referred in describing the course of events in France. This first point is the apparent power of the HLM movement, as represented by the UNFO–HLM, to resist successfully government innovations in policy. There is no difficulty in understanding the reasons for the successful use of this power prior to 1958. This was a period of weak coalition government, and the HLMs had considerable public sympathy and support from among the deputies, as we observed in describing the rejection by the HLMs of the points system which the government wished to impose on them.

Since 1958 the situation has been more complicated. It is certainly true that the Law relating to the sale of HLMs, to which the movement is whole-heartedly opposed, has been effectively sabotaged. But it may be that this has only been possible because of the support which the HLM movement has received from some prefects and senior ministry officials. Nor should one forget the incident during M. Maziol's period of responsibility, which reduced the representation of the tenants and other outsiders within the HLM movement, again against the wishes of the movement. However, there are clear indications that the Government has been unable to achieve all its policy objectives, particularly with respect to tenant selection, terms of finance and the sale of HLMs. One may conclude that, although the veto power of the HLMs is not as absolute as it once was, nevertheless it remains an important obstacle to the undiluted application of government policy. In my view, however, one should not overestimate the defensive power of the movement in explaining the continuity and rigidity of French housing policy development. If there existed the necessary political will to bring about the desired changes it seems to me that the HLM movement would not be a serious obstacle. In existing conditions the ability of the movement to obstruct is of some importance but only because it is reinforced by other tendencies which work in the same direction.

In order to bring out fully the importance of the HLMs as a restraining force on government policy it is useful to make a direct comparison with the parallel British body, the Association of Municipal Authorities (AMA, previously AMC). The AMA is parallel to the UNFO–HLM in the sense that both are concerned to represent the views of those entrusted with carrying out public housing policy at the local level. The parallel is not of course complete because whilst the UNFO–HLM deals only with public housing the AMA must represent views of its member authorities on a variety of subjects. In the representative institutions of British local government there is an Association of Education Committees but no such specialized representative body exists in the housing field. All the evidence suggests that the AMA is much less important than the UNFO–

HLM. It would seem almost absurd to even ask whether the AMA has an important voice in decisions concerning basic matters such as the way in which local authority housing is to be financed. These are matters which are so important to government and are generally recognized as having such serious political implications that the organization which represents the local authorities would not expect to have an important say. After a careful examination of the representations made by the AMA on housing matters over a number of years, Targett cautiously concludes: 'It must be conceded that rarely is policy altered following representations from, or amendments submitted by, the association' [4]. In fact one might substitute the word 'never' for 'rarely' in this citation. The evidence provided by Targett's thorough study suggests that the Government frequently ignores representations by the AMA even on purely technical or administrative matters. When the association was discussing the terms of the Housing (Improvement) Act of 1964 with Sir Keith Joseph, it suggested that the compulsory powers which it was proposed to give the local authorities in the new legislation should extend to allowing the authority to insist on the installation of certain electric points [5]. The substance of these representations was not included in the legislation and the Bill in fact passed in a form which the local authorities regarded as much too complicated to be of any use. The AMA was certainly pleased with the new subsidies introduced by Labour but cannot be credited with any influence on this legislation. Since 1965 the whole trend of housing legislation has been unwelcome to those whose overriding preoccupation is the maintenance of local responsibility. More specifically the AMA protested at the Labour Government's decision to refer council house rents to the Prices and Incomes Board and the association is entirely opposed to the provisions in the 1971 Housing (Finance) Act which deprive the local authorities of their powers with respect to the fixing of rents in order that the fair rent formula may be applied nationally [6]. There is therefore a great difference in the political significance of the bodies which represent those directly responsible for the execution of housing policy in Britain and France but, as I have stated above, it seems to me that this factor should not be considered as decisive and should certainly not be treated in isolation.

When dealing with the privately rented sector, it was pointed out that there was a fundamental economic difference between the French and British situations which had political consequences. In the French case, policy had to be adjusted to the existence of both an existing stock of privately rented accommodation and a current construction programme which relied on the rental mechanism for some of its financing. In the British case, only the former sector was of any importance, there being no significant building to rent for profit. With respect to the public sector no such obvious cause of difference can be observed since the State in both countries is permanently committed to substantial public programmes. Both are therefore involved in the management of an important economic activity. But on closer examination this similarity proves superficial since its consequences are not the same in the two cases.

There is first of all a clear difference in the post-war history of the British and French economies. Both have experienced periods of inflationary crisis but the problems created by stop-go policies have been less acute in France. At times of difficulty there has not been the same imperative need to cut public investment. Certainly in 1952, as part of the Pinay plan for the control of inflation, investment in public housing was severely cut back. But this limitation was recognized as purely economic and was never defended as desirable in principle. In this respect there is a sharp contrast between the cutback in France in 1952 and the cuts made by the Conservative Government in the period 1955–8. In the former case, since the justification for the reduction was purely economic, once the situation had been mastered, the level of investment was restored and in fact continued to rise rapidly [7]. In the slightly later British case the cut was not regarded as a simple matter of economic management but was additionally justified by reference to more general political principles, that is the desirability of encouraging ownership rather than reliance on a publicly provided service. Hence, even when the economy showed signs of recovery, the level of investment was not restored as rapidly as in France [8].

The same has been observable in the case of more recent economic difficulties. In 1963 the French economy was once again faced with severe inflationary problems and M. Giscard d'Estaing prepared his stabilization plan. Despite the urgency of the problem no cut in the public housing programme was envisaged and, in fact, reference to the available statistics for this period show that, between 1962 and 1965, HLM building expanded rapidly [9]. Whether one considers the problem of 1952, 1958 or 1963, it is true that in France there has never been even the slightest tendency to suggest that publicly provided housing will no longer be necessary on the same scale as previously. Admittedly in 1958 there were substantial cuts in the HLM programme, but, once the crisis had passed, investment returned to its former level and expansion was allowed to continue. This is a fundamental difference between the British and French cases. In the former, cuts imposed by a Conservative Government, will be justified politically as part of an overall strategy for housing. In the French case no such overall strategy is in question. Part of the permanent French settlement is the existence and steady expansion of the public sector. There is a general consensus on this point which has survived all manner of political changes in the post-war period. No such consensus exists with regard to the council house sector in Britain.

But the very different reaction by Government to economic crises is not the only aspect of the relation between State and economy which it is important to examine for our purposes. There is, in addition, a substantial and permanent difference in the nature of government involvement in economic activity in the two countries. It is true that there is no great difference between France and Britain with respect to the size of the public industrial sector, but nevertheless the French Government intervenes more persistently and in a more systematic fashion in the private sector. On the dimension of the degree of State involvement and acceptance of responsibility, France is consistently more *dirigiste* than Britain. We have yet to examine the relation between the State and private building for owner-occupation, but it is necessary here to make clear that, whereas in Britain the State's involvement in current construction is polarized into two sectors, one of complete control and the other of very little control, in the French situation there is a gradation which implies the existence of a large sector of construction, the financing of which involves a combination of public and private funds, and which therefore depends heavily on government policy. This intermediate sector, largely associated with the *Crédit Foncier*, has no parallel in Britain. The character of French State involvement in the house-building industry is therefore typical of the French economy as a whole. The official French view of this situation is that perhaps in principle the large extent of involvement is undesirable, but that it is only possible to reduce it gradually and this process of withdrawal should take place from the intermediate sector first and that therefore it should not affect the HLM sector at all. As we shall see in later chapters, Governments of the Fifth Republic have taken certain cautious steps in the direction of financial disengagement from the intermediate sector, but the stage has not been reached yet where this withdrawal is at all complete, and therefore the HLMs are not threatened or affected by what has so far been done to re-orient and concentrate State aid to housing. In Britain the situation is quite different. When demands are heard for a shift in housing policy from an emphasis on the public sector to a situation in which private demand plays a larger part, the council house sector is directly threatened and affected. The contrasting character of state involvement in economic activity, taken together with the more acute economic problems which have been encountered by post-war British Governments, certainly go some way towards explaining the comparative stability of policy towards the public housing sector in France and particularly the steady expansion of public investment.

The differing degrees of state intervention in Britain and France are naturally associated with different official attitudes. Extensive state intervention in economic activity in general, and even more so in house-building, has been maintained without serious challenge in France during a period of more than thirty years and under Governments of a variety of political persuasions. Most frequently these have been Governments of the Right or centre Right and therefore the association between parties of the Right and liberal economic doctrine, which we take to be natural in this country, is weak or non-existent in France. For example, although one might plausibly describe Gaullist attitudes on constitutional questions as right-wing, the party has never championed *laissez-faire* or even moderate state withdrawal from economic intervention. French economic liberals are more often to be found in the weak Centre parties, currently in opposition, than in the parties of the Right. The absence of liberal economic ideas supported by a powerful political party is an important stabilizing element, particularly with respect to French policy towards the public housing sector. Such ideas require that one constantly review the size of the publicly owned and financed sector in order to discover whether it would not be possible for it to be reduced so as to allow a wider area of private provision. Such an approach also implies strict policies for the selection of public tenants and a definition of general aims for the public sector which regards it as residual, and catering only for those who cannot provide for themselves by other means. The liberal approach also implies that there be a clear distinction between public finance and public purposes, on the one hand, and private finance and the private sector, on the other. The liberal accepts unwillingly that public money should be spent on groups that are not strictly defined according to need and he opposes generally intervention which is not justified as designed to maintain a strict minimum standard [10]. Official French thinking on social and economic matters does not accept these liberal views of the function of the State and accepts the need to make public money available, not only for social purposes strictly defined, but also to maintain economic expansion by aiding industry, not simply to avoid unemployment but also to assure future expansion. As we have indicated this does not mean that the authorities in France are content with the waste of public resources which they observe both in the intermediate and the entirely public sectors at present, but their hostility to existing arrangements is not one of principle and nor could it be described as primarily political. They are simply anxious that the State obtain a better return for its investment in terms of social gain. The letter addressed in 1975 by the French president to M. Barre, then simply a noted economist and public servant, stresses particularly this point [11]. Both the letters and the deliberations of the commission make it clear that official French thinking, even in the most recent period, since the raising of oil prices, and even now that housing shortages are less general than they were, is not concerned to cut public spending on housing but simply to redirect it. It is clear that this attitude is much less potentially radical and less inclined to bring about sharp changes in policy within the public sector. An acceptance of even moderately liberal policies would have extremely radical consequences for the existing system of housing finance and administration in France.

The situation is altogether different in Britain. Some students of the Conservative Party stress that its views on economic questions are a mixture of *laissez-faire* liberal economic views and Tory paternalism [12]. This is a doubtful generalization and certainly does not apply in the field of housing where, with certain politically motivated exceptions such as its support for the tax deductibility of mortgage interest payments, the party applies economically liberal policies with respect to housing as far as this is politically feasible. This approach naturally implies a certain suspicion of the public sector and this tendency is further reinforced by the great respect within the party for house ownership. Some idea of the expectations which Conservative supporters hold with respect to their party may be gained from the following quotation from *The Times* during the period of the Attlee Government: 'The main features of the Conservative alternative are the raising of private rents; a larger annual output of houses; the removal of restraints on private building, with its corollary an imposing of restraints on the council building' [13]. The then current Conservative speakers' manual proclaimed: 'The private enterprise builder works best when he works at his own risk; but at present he has no incentive to finish his house quickly in order to find a customer for it, since he may only build when he has a customer; and his selling price is tied to the inflated level of local authority costs' [14]. As we have seen, these expectations were initially disappointed but finally realized when the party had assured itself of a stronger majority. The hostility towards the council sector is quite evident and also the link between this hostility and the acceptance of liberal economic principles.

There are other liberal arguments the consequence of which is also general hostility to the local authority sector. A recent Bow Group pamphlet states with reference to housing policy: 'The subsidies discourage the provision of private rent accommodation and thus reduce freedom of choice in housing and create an undesirable social division' [15]. In addition to the purely liberal economic arguments, the party's spokesmen stress the social division involved in two quite different forms of housing provision for different sections of the community. Reference is also sometimes made to a more balanced community or a balance of tenures and on these occasions it is normally argued that the council house sector has become too large and must be reduced, both by sale of existing council houses and by the reduction of the relative importance of the council building programme in favour of private provision [16]. These attitudes, and the Labour opposition to them, are clearly the basis of many of the changes in policy which we have observed in post-war Britain.

One has great difficulty in finding anything comparable in France. If, for example, one examines the speeches of the Gaullists and Independent Republican deputies in the great debate on housing which took place in June 1971, a debate which spread over several days, one does not find, with one or two rare exceptions, the sort of hostility to the HLM movement which can be seen in the parallel situation in Britain [17]. The Independent Republican deputies, for example, were more interested in direct defence of the tax advantages obtained by the building industry, and also supported a Bill sponsored by their own parliamentary group which sought to alleviate the difficulties building firms working on public contracts by making some alterations in the system of advanced guarantee payments [18]. Many deputies within the majority in fact eulogized the HLM system in an apparent attempt to win the approval of those who saw their future as HLM tenants [19]. I believe that we have identified here an important cause of policy changes in Britain and the absence of such change in France. Sharply contradictory attitudes towards the public provision of housing as between the two major parties are clearly a necessary condition in Britain of the pattern of policy development which we have observed. The Labour attitude is in some ways less important since it simply defends the council house system and rejects the Conservative arguments.

But it is not sufficient to point to the attitude of the Conservative Party and the absence of any parallel phenomenon in France. To some extent the polarized conflict between the two British parties in their attitudes towards the council house sector is only a reflection of class conflict although certainly the parties and their attitudes and actions serve to accentuate the division into two opposed camps. We have already noted that financial arrangements in Britain consist of two distinct and opposed systems, whilst in France there is enormous variety in the forms of finance and modes of management employed. One may give numerous examples of the variety of forms to be found in France and the absence there of the pure form of polarization to which we in Britain are accustomed. We may take as an example the division between building for rent and for sale.

In the British case this distinction corresponds exactly with the division between public and private ownership. With very few exceptions all council houses are publicly financed, owned and rented and all privately constructed housing is sold. In France there is a sector of HLMs which are built and financed in the way which is normal for the HLM sector but are then sold to selected buyers on advantageous terms and with special loans. If there were to be a parallel to this practice in Britain it would be the building of council houses for sale. But neither party seems much interested in developing this type of policy in Britain and it remains insignificant, despite the occasional local experiment which has attempted to escape from the dichotomy of either building publicly for rent or leaving all to the private sector [20].

There is also a long-established tradition in France of *Sociétés Co-operatives d'HLMs* which are given the use of low-interest public loans but who build accommodation which then becomes the property of the co-owners. Some effort has been made in legislation promoted by the Conservative Government in 1964 to establish a sector of co-ownership housing in Britain. The experiment has so far been a success, though on a modest scale, but the small scale on which this new venture has inevitably operated in its early days, by comparison with the established programmes in the council and private sectors, means that it has not as yet made the slightest impression on the increasingly polarized British scene, divided as it is between council and private estates. Despite the declared hostility of the Conservative Party to this polarization and the misgivings of many who are not politicians, the process seems to be continuing ineluctably with the declining size of the privately rented sector and the consequent increase in proportional importance of the other two sectors.

Other examples of the more varied pattern to be found in France are the *Sociétés d'Economie Mixte* which use private and public funds to build for renting but at higher rents than are charged in the HLM sector, and the SCIC which uses publicly controlled funds and builds for rent, but whose housing constitutes in some ways a sector inter-mediate between the HLM and the owner-occupied sector since rents are again higher than those charged by the HLMs. Mention should also be made in this connection of the *Crédit Foncier* which, as previously explained, is a semi-public institution which uses publicly controlled funds to aid owner-occupation. All these French institutions and the attitudes which are naturally associated with them, are a powerful reinforcement for existing French arrangements. Although the activities of the HLMs in building for sale are a cum-bersome duplication of work carried out by the *Crédit Foncier* it has never been suggested that the *Crédit Foncier* take over these respon-sibilities. Such a suggestion would certainly be strongly opposed by the HLM movement as a whole. On the other hand, the *Crédit Foncier* does not seem to put up active resistance to changes in govern-ment policy which affect it. With respect to the intermediate rented sector there have been signs that any attempt at change here would be strongly resisted by some Gaullists [21]. In the French case we there-fore see a variety of factors at work, all of which tend to stability: the vested interest of institutions in retaining functions previously assigned to them, the support of certain social groups for practices which benefit them in particular, and government fear that any changes in financial arrangements are likely to affect construction adversely, at least in the short term.

In order to illustrate some of the points which I have made in this chapter, it is useful to examine the memorandum submitted by Manchester City Corporation to the House of Commons Estimates Committee in 1969 [22]. The public at large and politicians in both parties treat the housing subsidy as a controversial question and regard it as a form of welfare. To many Conservative politicians it has been an unjustified form of income support. To most Labour politicians the subsidy represents a means by which people of modest income may be permitted to enjoy housing standards which they would not otherwise be able to afford. In both cases, let it be noted, the emphasis is on the transfer of income involved. The approach adopted by the Manchester City Council was quite different. The case for having a housing subsidy of some sort was made out much more in terms of what society needs and much less with regard to the needs of particular individuals or classes of individuals. It is argued that redevelopment of central city areas is absolutely necessary and that this redevelopment will not be carried out by private means to any significant extent. It is therefore necessary to allow public bodies to do this work and to erect houses on the land which is made available by this redevelopment. Certainly individuals will live in the houses so provided but society as a whole will have benefited from the reconstruction of the city thus accomplished and it is natural therefore that society, that is to say here the general body of taxpayers, should contribute significantly towards the cost of this redevelopment. Not only housing costs will be involved since a variety of facilities will be made available in the redeveloped areas and non-housing costs will include the holding of land out of effective use for long periods and its clearing and replanning. The argument of the memorandum is that rents should not be fixed at too low a level for the houses provided as a result of redevelopment but that it is illogical to relate the rents of individuals to the cost of a project which is beneficial to the community as a whole. The argument here is that the transfer of income from taxpayers to council tenants which is necessarily involved in the existence of a housing subsidy is, to some extent, merely accessory and accidental and that the merits of particular forms of subsidy ought not to be decided by arguments which refer to the categories of individuals who pay or receive the subsidy.

If this approach were more widely accepted in Britain, much of the political steam would be taken out of many issues surrounding public housing provision. The Manchester approach, if we may so call it, is not in the least typical and in fact one would expect to find arguments of this sort much more frequently in French discussions of the same problem. The French point of view with respect to the element of subsidy involved in public or semi-public housing programmes has always been that, whilst it was desirable to concentrate the subsidy on those in the greatest need, it should also be recognized that the country as a whole was in need of a large and increasing building programme and that no changes in the arrangements for the use of public funds could be adopted if these were likely to limit the development of the construction programme, whatever the arguments in terms of equity might be. After all, it is argued in France, it should be admitted openly that almost any form of housing subsidy is unjust since it is unlikely to go to the poorest members of the community. This is because subsidized housing is, despite the element of subsidy, nearly always still more expensive than older and poorer existing property, and therefore, whilst the poor take existing property, those with slightly higher incomes take the newly built and subsidized accommodation. There is in theory a filtering-down process at work by which aid given directly to one section of the community benefits also its poorer members. The poor gain because they can move into housing vacated by those who have been rehoused. On this view it does not matter quite so much who receives the subsidy initially since society as a whole benefits [23]. The adoption of this sort of approach by French policy-makers, and its rejection in favour of a more politicized approach by their British counterparts, goes a considerable way to explain the different policy development patterns which we have observed.

The policy recommendations contained in the Barre Report of 1975 do show a slow change in official French thinking because the commission tends to concentrate more exclusively on the income transfer involved in subsidized housing. But there is still a considerable distance between the Barre Report and Conservative thinking of either the mid-fifties or earlier seventies. Barre envisages no overall reduction in subsidies to the public housing sector, nor does it see public housing being confined to special groups like the elderly or those whose housing has been demolished in a slum clearance programme. Since writing this Report, M. Raymond Barre has been appointed Prime Minister and so the Report is clearly an excellent guide to likely future developments in housing policy. There is no sign in the Report that public housing provision in France is likely to be reduced or redirected in the fundamental way to which we are accustomed from time to time in this country.

In the preceding paragraphs attention has been directed towards a number of apparently unassociated factors: the polarized character of provision in Britain as compared with the French situation, the strength of economic liberalism in Britain and its weakness in France, and the varied and complicated pattern of French institutional arrangements as compared with the simple and symmetrical system operated in Britain. It may be however that these differences, all of which tend to aid in the explanation of the very different patterns of policy development, are part of a more general pattern. When an examination of a number of different facets of the politics of housing tends to reveal a variety of factors, all of which point towards polarization in Britain and variety in France, one is inclined to believe that this is not a coincidence and that what one is observing is only proof of some underlying difference which has produced so many parallel differences. The politics of housing in Britain seems preoccupied with class. Arguments are concerned constantly with the impact which suggested arrangements will have on either the working-class council tenant, or the middle-class owner-occupier and taxpayer. The French do not seem so preoccupied with this perspective on housing policy. But, it may be objected, it is one thing to say arguments about housing policy are polarized and quite another to associate this polarization with class conflict.

Evidence that class plays a part in British housing policy, which it does not play in France, may be found in the treatment of the problem of the wealthy tenant of public housing. In both countries it is recognized that where such cases exist, and there may be arguments about their frequency, they are to be regretted. But, despite this common disapproval, the reaction in Britain and France is from this point onwards very different. The British Conservative, especially the back-bencher, is constantly preoccupied with this question and returns to it again and again [24]. His conclusion is generally that this is a vice of the system, that public money is being unwisely used, and that individual cases are symptomatic of a general difficulty, i.e. that of council tenants who are being unjustly subsidized by others who often have lower incomes than those council tenants themselves. The solution can only be to take away that unjust and unnecessary subsidy and put everyone on the same footing, that is to make everyone pay the cost of the housing which they occupy. In this argument the Conservative critic of council housing builds his attack on the system and its injustices on observation of individual cases but he arrives finally at a more general and sweeping conclusion.

His Labour opponent naturally takes a very different view of the matter. He argues that the flagrantly unjust cases to which the Conservative refers are exceptional and untypical. He insists that the council tenant is paying as much rent as his modest wage will permit and that the subsidy must therefore be maintained at its present level, or perhaps even increased. In both cases the argument concludes with the necessity for abolishing, or maintaining, the housing subsidy. But what of the French reaction to the very same problem of the rich HLM tenant? The Vth and VIth Plans both devote considerable attention to this problem. The remedy must lie in the devising of more effective forms of *sur-loyer* and more effective control over the selection policies of the HLMs. Note the contrast between this approach and that just described above. The problem remains one of individual circumstances. Someone is unjustly enjoying a privileged situation and means must be found of taking this privilege from him. There is no suggestion that the system of subsidy as a whole is at fault because policy-makers distinguish between the general level of HLM rents, which, they believe, must be kept as low as possible, and the individual wealthier tenants who must be forced out of the sector. Whereas in Britain one begins to talk immediately of privileged groups, in France one talks of unjustly privileged individuals. The French approach clearly limits the scope of disagreement and shelters the HLM system from attack. In Britain the climate of opinion seems to make it possible for critics of the council house sector to use individual cases as a stick with which to attack the whole system of subsidy. As we have seen in chapter VIII, throughout the history of conflict over the question of the *sur-loyer*, ministers have attacked the HLMs not as institutions or as part of an unjust and inefficient system, but rather for not applying particular rules. The ministerial diagnosis has always been one of individual privilege which could be corrected by stronger regulation. It is significant that the institution of the *sur-loyer* is unknown in Britain and that there is not even a convenient English translation of the term. The Barre Report departs to some extent from the accepted view on this question because it despairs of ever getting the *sur-loyer* properly applied but as explained earlier, it still rejects the British Conservative answer to this problem.

I have already referred to the importance in this discussion of the absence of any strong liberal tradition of thought in France on social and economic matters. This is true not only in relation to national economic policy but also to the field of social policy. One of the basic concerns of the British system of social security has been, by way of the Supplementary Benefits Commission, to make sure that no one falls below a nationally established minimum. Although this safety net approach is also necessarily a part of the French social security system, a much greater emphasis is placed on achieving a greater degree of justice as between different groups within the community, even when the question of absolute poverty does not arise. Family allowances are, of course, much larger in France, and play a more important role in the system of social security. The justification of family allowances is that the family with five children will be unfairly disadvantaged as compared with a family with only one child if both are in receipt of the same income. Whether the family of five children is in absolute poverty or not, it is felt desirable to increase their real income, by means of the system of family allowances, in order to achieve greater justice. The acceptance of this approach, which justifies payment to those who are not in absolute poverty or need more readily than a more strictly liberal approach to welfare problems, helps to support existing French arrangements in the housing field, and protects them from possible criticism on more liberal lines [25]. In this connection one thinks particularly of the housing allowance, which is specifically designed so that it cannot be of much use to the poorest families and is received by many families of well above the average level of income. Liberal doctrine is also flouted by the continued availability of the benefits of rent control to occupants of near-luxury apartments and the high income ceilings set for aid through both the HLM and *Crédit Foncier* systems.

In this chapter I have concentrated on those explanations of stability, or rigidity, in French policy and repeated changes in policy orientation in the British case which appear to be the most significant when dealing with public housing. In so doing we should be careful not to forget entirely the factors which were discussed in chapter VI when dealing with the privately rented sector since explanations may, to some extent, apply to more than one sector. Much of what has been said in this chapter concerning traditions of French thought and practice in the social and economic fields naturally bears on both the privately rented and publicly owned sectors. Nor should we forget the most important conclusion to come out of our earlier discussion concerning the role of the political party and its comparative weakness in France as a link between state and society.

The importance of housing for the British political parties and the consequent support which ministers of housing will often receive from the Prime Minister in Cabinet is an outstanding feature of British policy-making. Crossman repeatedly refers to the strong support he received from Wilson which enabled him to expand the public sector despite the opposition of the Chancellor and other spending ministers [26]. In sharp contrast to this, the weak link between French political parties and society deprives housing ministers of the crucial support which they need to bring about change, and the lack of cohesion of the Gaullists, for example, and the rigidity in policy to which it gives rise are not difficult to illustrate.

In recent years in France there has been a good deal of discussion between advocates of what is called *aide à la pierre* (aid designed to encourage construction and going to those involved in building) and *aide à la personne* (aid which goes to the individual buyer or tenant and not to the organization which is providing the housing). The first of these types of aid is typified by the low rates of interest made available to the HLMs, and the latter form of aid is particularly well represented by the housing allowance in France which is received by tenants and mortgage buyers and is related to their individual incomes. On behalf of *aide à la pierre* it is argued that one can oversee its use easily and make sure that it goes where it is intended and produces the desired results. Against this approach it is argued that *aide à la pierre* does not always sufficiently take into account variation in individual circumstances, and that therefore there can be a good deal of aid wasted on those who do not need it. On behalf of *aide à la personne* it is argued that it respects more closely the freedom of the consumer because he is left still to choose his housing and then will receive financial help if his circumstances suggest that this is necessary. Against *aide à la personne* it is argued that it is inflationary, because it involves the allocation of money without giving the public authorities the same control over costs as they might have in a public project.

In Britain the position is that both parties tend to accept the approach suggested in the formula of *aide à la personne*, although the Conservative Party is very much more convinced of the value of this approach than Labour. The unanimity of view on this ideological question within the Conservative Party has made possible the bringing forward of the Housing (Finance) Act which embodies, in a radical form, the philosophy of *aide à la personne*. In France, although the governing majority has for long had a Conservative complexion, particularly on matters of social and economic policy, no such definite choice has ever been made or even seemed likely. Nor is this simply a question of differences of view between the different parties which have made up the government coalition. If, for example, one takes the great debate of June 1971 one will find quite contrasted points of view expressed on the controversy by M. Nungesser and M. de Préaumont. The former disapproved of the Government's decision to transfer some of the funds previously allocated for the

HLMs to the financing of the housing allowance. He argued that, liberal in principle as the housing allowance might be, he felt it simply lined the pockets of landlords and developers and did not get more houses built, whereas more money budgeted for the HLMs would be sure to produce the dwellings required [27]. M. de Préaumont, on behalf of the Commission on Cultural and Family Affairs, stressed on the contrary, the advantages of a system which left the tenant free to find the housing which suited his needs best and then gave him a housing allowance if need be. He therefore approved whole-heartedly the budgetary transfer which his fellow Gaullist, M. Nungesser, had criticized [28]. Little wonder that, where there is a lack of a strong corporate view on questions of principle, ministers find it harder to make difficult choices and carry their parliamentary supporters with them. It should also be stressed here that these two Gaullists were both prominant deputies and that M. Nungesser's opinions were particularly entitled to respect since he had previously held the post of Under-Secretary of State responsible for housing.

The point has now been reached when we may draw together some of the most important conclusions which have emerged from this discussion. At the outset, stress was laid on the different roles as-signed in the British and French political systems to local and central authorities. It was concluded then that no significant political opposition on any matter related to housing could be found in the British case to come from local government. In France, on the other hand, the opposing attitude of the HLM movement is always a factor of importance constraining the development of housing policy and sometimes a critical factor. Emphasis has also been placed on the quite different economic environment within which housing policy has developed in Britain and France, and more especially on the different role adopted by the State in these two countries with respect to intervention. In this connection we have drawn attention not only to the way which the state has behaved but also to traditions of thought and the radical opposition between liberal and socialist approaches to be found in Britain, an opposition which is of no practical importance in French political life. Finally I have pointed to the importance of a polarized and symmetrical system of finance in Britain which facilitates policy oscillations. This structure is to some extent a reflection of class values, and the political expression of class conflict is the motor of much change in British policy. In the French situation many practices and institutions overlap the boundary bet-ween renting and owning, and between the public and private sectors, and would be threatened by policies designed to draw these boundaries more clearly.

## References

1. *Fair Deal for Housing*, Cmnd. 4728 (H.M.S.O., July 1971).

2. P. Consigny, *Rapport sur l'Aide Publique au Logement* (Groupe de Travail sur l'Aide Publique au Logement, 1969), p. 24.

3. D.V. Donnison, 'A Housing Service', *New Society*, No. 476, 11 November 1971.

4. A.J. Targett, *The Association of Municipal Corporations in the Field of Housing Legislation, 1963–1970*, M.A. Thesis submitted to the University of Kent, 1970, p. 116.

5. ibid., chapter II.

6. *The Times*, 22 May 1968 and 14 July 1971.

7. *See* table VIII. 1.

8. *See* table IX. 1.

9. *See* table VIII. 1.

10. J.E. Powell, 'Conservatives and Social Services', *Political Quarterly*, Vol. XXIV (1953), pp. 156–66.

11. *Revue de l'habitat social*, 5, p. 3.

12. W.J. Biffen, 'Party conference and party policy', *Political Quarterly*, Vol. XXXII (1961), pp. 257–66.

13. *The Times*, 17 February 1950.

14. ibid.

15. J. Nelson-Jones, *Home Truths on Housing, Costs, Rents and Subsidies* (The Conservative Political Centre, 1966), p. 39.

16. J. Morton, 'Selling-off council houses', *New Society*, No. 220, 15 December 1966.

17. Debate of 10, 11, 12 and 14 June 1971, *Journal Officiel, Débats*, pp. 2642–2905.

18. ibid., pp. 2653, 2660–62, 2681.

19. ibid., pp. 2656–8, 2671–2, 2675–6.

20. *Council Housing-Purposes, Procedures and Priorities: ninth Report of the Housing Management Sub-Committee of the Central Housing Advisory Committee* (H.M.S.O., 1969), chapter XI. The report recommends that such practices be more widely adopted.

21. *Proposition de Loi No. 98, Annexe au Procès-Verbal de l'Assemblée Nationale, J.O.*, 19 January 1968. This Gaullist proposal suggested the creation of a new rental sector just above the HLM sector.

22. *Fourth Report from the Estimates Committee, Housing Subsidies*, Session 1968–69, Vol. II, Memorandum submitted by the Corporation of the City of Manchester.

23. Interview with M. Eugène Claudius-Petit, *La Croix*, 27 April 1958.

24. *The Times*, 29 March 1958 and 21 May 1958. Thirteen Conservative backbenchers asked the Government to set up an official inquiry to establish how much council accommodation could be freed by the removal of wealthy council tenants.

25. P. Laroque, *Succès et Faiblesse de l'Effort Social Français* (Armand Colin, 1961).
26. R.H.S. Crossman, *The Diaries of a Cabinet Minister* (Hamish Hamilton & Jonathan Cape, 1975), pp. 108, 153–5, 169.
27. Debate of 10th June 1971, *Journal Officiel, Débats*, pp. 2656–8.
28. ibid., pp. 2649–50.

# XI

# Repairs and Improvement

It is necessary to examine this aspect of housing policy separately since it does not belong exclusively to any of the three major housing sectors. In France the policies designed to promote repair and improvement of existing property have been aimed almost entirely at the privately rented sector whereas in Britain they normally relate to all three sectors of housing provision.

This aspect of housing policy is also particularly interesting because it provides some of the most striking examples, in Britain, of the changes of attitude of the major parties, at times violently opposed to one another on the principles to be applied in this area of policy, and at other times more or less in agreement. The examination of the French case provides further evidence of the low political priority of housing policy in France, and also throws light on the consequences of the neglect of this issue by political parties. The French case may conveniently be examined first.

## France

Whatever the defects of later French policy with respect to the problem of repairs and improvements, an early start was at least made. The *Fonds National pour l'Amélioration de l'Habitat* (FNAH) was established soon after the cessation of hostilities and was put into operation in the late forties, at first on an extremely modest scale. The resources of the fund came principally from a five per cent tax raised on all private rents [1]. The basic philosophy which underlay this institution was that, because of extreme shortage, landlords were being obliged to accept controlled rents and that justice demanded that some recompense be rendered to them. The limited resources of FNAH meant that it could only provide cheap loans for the repair or improvement of 10,000–20,000 dwellings a year in the 1940s and 1950s, and this at a time when houses without basic facilities were numbered in millions. One may conclude from the scale of its operations, and from the fact that FNAH was only established as a quid pro quo offered to landlords in exchange for rent control, that governments of this period felt unable to make any serious contribution towards dealing with the maintenance or improvement aspect of the housing problem.

During the fifties and early sixties very little was said about repair policies. The FNAH existed and continued to operate but was not a subject of political discussion, let alone controversy. Government ministers appear to have felt that the real solution lay in higher rents and that the FNAH represented a mere palliative, whose scale of operations could not hope to match the size of the problem. This was certainly the aim of the policy initiated by M. Sudreau in 1958 [2]. He relied on repair coefficients to give landlords an incentive to improve.

In March 1966 the Secretary of State for Housing, M.R. Nungesser, took the initiative in the field of repairs and improvements and set up a round-table discussion involving those government departments interested in the problem, and private non-profit making groups [3]. Two recommendations coming from these discussions were adopted by the government. Interest on loans used by landlords for improvement were made deductible from income for income tax purposes, and landlord and tenant law was amended so as to make it easier for either to proceed with repairs without the consent of the other. A third recommendation, to increase the scale of the activities of the Fund, was not accepted [4]. Achievement was then, to say the least, modest, and several fundamental inadequacies in policy were not even touched on. In the first place, aid through FNAH, the government's most important instrument for house improvement policy, was still confined to dwellings with controlled rents. There were fewer and fewer of these. Secondly, nothing was done to develop policies applicable to the owner-occupied sector.

It was not long before the Government explicitly recognized the inadequacy of its own recent reforms in this area and once again called together the interested parties in a round-table discussion, on this occasion enlarging the participation to include tenants' and landlords' representatives. In a number of ways the discussion which took place underlined the lack of importance attached to repairs and improvements policy. M. Morane, for example, speaking on behalf of the CNAHE (*Confédération Nationale pour l'Amélioration de l'Habitat Existant*) expressed the following cautious point of view: 'Il ne serait pas réaliste d'imaginer que des crédits budgétaires puissent jouer dans ce mécanisme un rôle important' [5]. These doubts were amply justified by the expressions of opinion of both M. Vivien and M. Chalandon, the last of whom insisted firmly that on no account could one expect to obtain more budgetary aid for the type of housing activity which was under discussion [6]. But it was not only in the realm of possible governmental financial assistance that caution was evident. From 1966 onwards the Government had involved itself with CPACT (*Centre pour la Propagande et l'Action contre les Taudis*), a private non-profit-making organization in operations designed to bring about the renovation of small districts. These operations were limited in number and regarded as experimental. During the discussions of the round-table in 1969, despite the established character of the co-operation between Government and CPACT, it was not suggested by any of those present that the Government should assist agencies like CPACT actively to promote improvements in many more districts, building on the knowledge provided by earlier experimental projects. In fact there is plenty of evidence in the Liure Blanc describing these discussions and their outcome, that neither the Government nor the organizations with which it was working envisaged departing from established practice in any radical way. The initiative in future operations was to remain with either the tenant or the landlord. The role of any supervisory organization, apart from the experimental operations of CPACT, was to be simply that of providing publicity and of dispensing the necessary financial aid when application was received. No one involved in French housing policy, either as an active participant or as critical observer, appears to have envisaged giving a much greater degree of initiative to a public authority which would intervene, not simply in order to provide finance, but actively to promote repair and improvement in selected areas.

But the discussions of 1969 did have some repercussions in that the decision was taken by the Government to bring the restricted field of application of FNAH to an end and to enlarge its activities to the whole of the rented sector. The organization was now renamed *Agence Nationale pour l'Amélioration de l'Habitat (ANAH)*, and its resources drawn from a tax of three and a half per cent on the rents of all privately rented accommodation built before 1948. Once again the Government did not feel able to contribute financially to the resources of the agency but the new tax produced much more revenue than its predecessor, for it was no longer confined to those houses the rents of which were still controlled. The limitation of the agency's action to the privately rented sector was maintained [7].

The low political saliency of improvement policy was underlined once again when it took more than two years to set up ANAH. Apparently the problem was an interdepartmental disagreement between the development ministry and the ministry of finance. The latter was most concerned that ANAH's activities might increase inflationary pressure by raising rents [8].

In 1975 the Nora Report on housing improvements appeared. If its recommendations are accepted it will mean much increased spending on this area of policy and a much more active rôle for the public authorities. M. Nora wants the local authorities to play a larger role, as they already do in Britain, and he asks that aid be less dispersed between a variety of agencies, many of whom spend very little on housing, and that improvement be actively promoted as an alternative to new building [9]. But we shall return to the significance of the analysis contained in this report in a moment.

## Britain

In contrast to the French situation, in Britain there is some new legislation relating specifically to repairs and improvements every four or five years. Local authorities have been expected actively to promote improvement policy since at least 1964 and many were doing so before this date. Another way of stating the contrast is to say that in Britain, unlike France, improvement is constantly on the agenda, and every four to five years sees an effort to improve the effectiveness of policy. Authorities may be given more legal powers, grants may be raised or made available for new purposes, or activity may be more geographically concentrated. Whatever the changes made, there is a constant interaction between politicians and officials on the one hand, and the problem of ill-equipped, dilapidated houses on the other. To talk of continuous interest and activity is no exaggeration. Legislation dealing with improvements and/or repairs was promoted in 1949, 1954, 1957, 1959, 1961, 1964, 1969 and 1974. In the early 1960s between 110,000–120,000 grants were made annually and this number has now risen to a figure of over 250,000 [10].

Between 1953 and 1961 the Labour opposition was committed to a policy of taking all privately rented property into municipal ownership in order to improve it [11]. Although no attempt was made by the Labour Government of 1964–70 or by that in power since 1974 to execute this policy it is of considerable political interest. The policy of municipalization may be regarded as a doctrinaire socialist policy which owed more to economic considerations of a general character than to any appreciation of the housing problem. In my view, the extension of public ownership envisaged as part of this policy is by no means comparable with the Labour commitment to a limited degree of nationalization. It should first be remembered that according to Aneurin Bevan's own account the policy was adopted specifically in order to counter the Conservative initiative in the field of housing repairs and improvements in 1953 [12]. Secondly, it should be borne in mind that some Conservatives at least sympathized with a good deal of the reasoning which lay behind the policy of municipalization. Mr Macmillan, for example, in his 1953 White Paper, insisted on the need for authorities to acquire for slum clearance not only unfit housing but also habitable privately rented accommodation [13]. His view was that local authorities should acquire such property in order to improve it so that it might better serve its occupants during the period which must inevitably elapse prior to its demolition. In such a period, the authority would be entitled to raise rents in order to assist with the cost of the repairs undertaken. This policy was not full municipalization but it accepted the essential logic of the Labour case: public ownership coupled with higher standards of repair and improvements and higher rents. It should also be borne in mind that the political justification provided by the Labour Party for their policy did not insist strongly on the contrast between private and public ownership in principle. The emphasis was much more on the practical benefits which might be expected from public ownership. Mr Callaghan, for example, speaking in the 1959 election campaign, said: 'The whole point about municipal ownership is to make sure that people get the bathrooms and indoor sanitation that they were promised under the Rent Act but which have never been forthcoming' [14].

The fact that a radical alternative to Conservative policy was adopted by the Labour Party is of the greatest interest to a student of the politics of housing. This is particularly so because the field of repairs and improvements is surely one of those which is most inclined to receive a purely technocratic treatment. Though at first sight it does not seem that such concrete problems must necessarily pose questions of political principle, in my view the adoption of this policy is significant in two particular ways. In the first place municipalization provides an example of a radical alternative policy adopted and canvassed in two general elections on a particular subject which might, on the surface, appear to be of little interest to politicians. The fact that the parties did fight over this issue testifies to the quite exceptional salience of housing in the British political system. The adoption of the policy also throws interesting light on the comparisons between the British and French Left. The Socialist parties in both countries have been committed since the early sixties to the public ownership of development land but whereas the Labour Party supported municipalization of privately rented property for a period, and now seems likely to readopt this policy, the French Socialists have never shown the slightest interest in the problem of house repair or improvements and would certainly never pronounce in favour of the acquisition of privately rented property by public authority of any sort.

But Labour was not destined to retain the commitment to municipalization. There was some apparent hesitation about what the policy actually was, and some outright modification of it in the 1959 election campaign [15], and in the parties' 1961 policy document *Signpost for the Sixties*, it was not mentioned. There was some protest at this, at the 1961 annual conference, but the front bench carried the day easily.

Once the policy of municipalization had been abandoned, there was no longer any difference of principle between the two parties with respect to their approach to the problem. The only markedly ideological feature of Labour's policy following the abandonment of municipalization was the suggestion in a policy statement which appeared in 1962 (*Labour's Plan for Older Houses*), that direct-labour organizations based on a regional area should play a large part in repair and improvement work. In fact repairs and improvements were not given a high priority by the new Labour Government which, as already indicated in earlier chapters, concentrated primarily on the land commission, the leasehold enfranchisement Bill, new financial arrangements for the public sector, and somewhat later on the Option Mortgage Scheme. Only in 1969 was the Housing Improvement Bill brought forward and voted into law. Nothing in the Act could be described as controversial except for a slight difference of opinion between the parties regarding the degree of compulsion which might appropriately be permitted. Conservative ministers, when preparing previous Acts dealing with the same subject, had always insisted that the best result would be obtained by good co-operation between the local authority and those involved. The Act of 1964, for which Sir Keith Joseph was responsible, provided for a limited degree of compulsion which might be exercised in order to obtain an improvement desired by a tenant but resisted by the landlord, and it had also provided for the use of compulsion to override the objection of one tenant in a tenement block whose refusal to accept improvement was obstructing the wishes of fellow tenants. The Labour Party had attempted to increase the permissible degree of compulsion in this Act without success, but when in office they accepted the recommendation of the Denington Report:

'Successive governments have tried to secure the voluntary modernisation of these houses but the response has been inadequate and disappointing. Present methods of compulsion, which apply in limited circumstances to tenanted property, have proved ineffective, perhaps because of the cumbersome and time consuming procedure. In our view there is a need both for effective compulsion to improve and maintain the better older houses and for more pressures for early clearance of the worst' [16].

An examination of the political context of repairs and improvement policies shows up extremely clearly the contrast between the French and British political treatment of this area of policy. In repairs and improvement policy in Britain, we do not find the same degree of difference between the policy followed in different periods as has been observed in other areas of housing policy but we do find, at least between 1953 and 1961, a strongly contrasted approach on the part of the two parties. The fact that by and large there have been only slight differences of emphasis in the policies pursued by the two parties in Britain does not mean that there is a lack of contrast between the French and British situations. The main difference, to which reference has already been made, is in the degree of salience of the problem. For long periods of time in France a well-recognized problem in the administration of repairs and improvements (for example the problem created by the continuously decreasing scope of FNAH during the 1960s), may not attract attention so that remedial action is not taken by the government. In the British situation, on the contrary, our account has shown that there is new legislation every four or five years and sometimes more frequently. This suggests that the problem is one which receives fairly constant attention from the politicians and officials involved, although it cannot expect to receive the priority reserved for new building. One might imagine that the explanation for this difference would lie in a lack of knowledge in France as to the extent of the repair problem. This is by no means the case, M. P. Sudreau, for example, soon after coming into office, admitted frankly in a press conference that there were at least two million slum dwellings in France which ought to be demolished as quickly as possible but he added at the same time that there was not the slightest possibility of making any impression on this problem within the foreseeable future [17]. Recent reports prepared for the Fifth and Sixth Plans by the commission responsible for housing have also insisted on the gravity of the problem and have underlined its extent with a wealth of statistics drawn both from the 1962 and 1968 censuses and also from surveys carried out by the National Institute for Statistical and Economic Studies [18].

Nor does the explanation lie in a differing attitude on the part of those who are obliged to suffer the inconvenience of poor housing conditions. If one examines public opinion as reflected in polls, one finds that the French population is markedly less satisfied with its housing provision than the British. A survey carried out during 1953 in France asked the population of towns of 10,000 and above whether they were, generally speaking, satisfied or not satisfied with their current housing situation. Almost one third of this population expressed itself as generally dissatisfied and the proportion was naturally higher than this in the larger towns and among the recently married [19]. By the spring of 1967 a survey asking substantially the same question found a diminished but still substantial level of dissatisfaction within the general population. Those expressing themselves as generally dissatisfied formed just under 20 per cent of the total population and this figure rose to 25 per cent in Paris [20]. Figures for Britain roughly comparable with the later French survey show only 13 per cent of the population as expressing themselves as either very dissatisfied or rather dissatisfied with their accommodation [21]. It would appear then that the greater dissatisfaction at the grass-roots level in France is just not translated into a political demand.

The evidence suggests clearly that there is a blockage which operates at some point between the level of individual dissatisfaction and social concern. This is of course by no means something particular either to the repairs and improvement policy area or even to French housing policy as distinct from other areas of policy. In my view, much of this difficulty, as has already been explained in discussing the public sector, is due to the peculiar role of the political party in France, a role sharply distinguished from that of the British political party. It may well be that a party operating within a multi-party system is so preoccupied with tactical questions, for example its relations with other parties, that it has that much less time to devote to bread-and-butter issues. In the previous chapter I tried to show how Gaullists were less likely to develop coherent social and economic policies because the party's identity had been defined from the outset in relation to constitutional and colonial problems. The pressures which are brought to bear on a party as a result of participation in a multi-party system will affect all parties. They will tend, I suggest, to increase interaction between parties but to reduce it between parties and the public. Whether this is the correct explanation for the neglect of repairs and maintenance in France or not, it is certainly an observable fact that, although the French public is more concerned about housing than the British, French political parties do not concern themselves as much with the problem as their British counterparts, and this lack of concern has particularly serious consequences in the most mundane, and therefore most easily neglected, areas of policy.

Before concluding, I should like to say something about the influence of executive institutions on policy formation. Between 1953 and 1961 the Labour Party was committed to the municipalization of all privately rented property as a solution to the repair problem. This radical policy gained greatly in credibility because it was envisaged that it could be carried out by local authorities who already had behind them much experience in the management and maintenance of large quantities of housing. Had the Labour Party had to use the HLMs for this purpose, I do not think that a policy of wholesale municipalization would ever have been adopted. The HLM movement does not have the geographical spread, managerial competence, or experience, to undertake such an operation.

Institutions of execution are important in explaining the French-British contrast in another way. Just as the existence of a local authority structure with experience in housing makes certain policies credible in Britain which would not be credible without them, so reliance on agencies with specialized functions inhibits certain policies in France. A senior French civil servant charged with studying the field of improvement and repair policy in 1975, came to the conclusion that one of the reasons for the neglect of this area of policy in France lies in administrative arrangements [22]. Improvement policy is concerned not with accomplishing a large number of standard acts, as is new building, but in dealing with very varied local situations. These two factors, the impossibility of standardization of procedures and the wide variation in the nature of the problem from place to place combine to render progress difficult to achieve in France. French administrative structures cannot easily cope with these characteristics of the problem, because of their centralization and because of the lack of any obvious co-ordinator at the level of the town. Repair and improvement policies demand by their very nature, a process of execution with careful local co-ordination of a number of different functions relating to housing, procedures adaptable to local circumstances, and it has clearly been easier for a ministry in Paris to design procedures for facilitating new building programmes than to tackle the problems of existing housing.

In discussing the owner-occupied sector, we shall find further examples of the influence of executive institutions on policy formation, but this examination of repair and improvement policy has provided a particularly striking, and politically important, example of the importance of this factor.

## References

1. *Notes et Études Documentaires*, No. 1971 (La Documentation Française, 1955).
2. *See* p. 53.
3. *Le Monde*, 20 October 1966.
4. *Le Monde*, 20 October 1966; *Combat*, 18 January 1967.
5. *Livre Blanc: Politique de l'Habitat Existant*, Table ronde du 25 September 1969, p. 23.
6. ibid., speech of M. Albin Chalandon.
7. *J.O.*, 31 December, 1960; *Le Figaro*, 12 January, 1971.
8. *Le Monde*, 28 January 1971.
9. S. Nora and B. Eveno, *L'Amélioration de l'habitat ancien* (La Documentation Française, 1975).
10. *Tenth Report from the Expenditure Committee*, Session 1972–73, (Environmental, Home Office Sub-Committee), Vol. II, 'House Improvement Grants', pp. 1–3.
11. The official Labour policy of these years is contained in *Homes for the Future—a Socialist Policy for Housing*, June 1956.
12. *The Times*, 1 October 1959.
13. *Houses – The Next Step*, Cmd. 8996 (H.M.S.O., November 1953), paras 52–64.
14. *The Times*, 7 September 1959.

15. *The Times*, 19 and 25 September 1959.
16. *Our Older Homes – A Call for Action*, Report of the Central Housing Advisory Committee (H.M.S.O., 1966), p. 5.
17. *Combat*, 15 July 1958.
18. *Rapport Général et Rapports Spéciaux Annexes de la Commission de l'Habitation du Ve Plan – Rapport relatif au Patrimoine Existant* (1966); *Rapports des Commissions du VIe Plan, 1971–75, Rapport de la Commision de l'Habitation*. See especially in Vol. II: *Les Personnes Agées*.
19. *La Vie Française*, 26 June 1953.
20. *Le Nouvel Observateur*, 1 March 1967.
21. A.A. Nevitt, 'The State of the Social Services: Housing', *New Society*, No. 262, 5 October 1967.
22. S. Nora and B. Eveno, *L'Amélioration de l'habitat ancien* (La Documentation Française, 1975), p. 63.

# PART IV

# The Owner-Occupied Sector

# XII

# Owner-Occupation: France

## 1 *The semi-public sector—Crédit Foncier*

It is outside the scope of a work of this kind to attempt to assess the shortage of housing which existed in France at the Liberation but it is necessary, if one is to appreciate political developments, to have at least some idea of the extent of the crisis. It was reliably calculated, for example, in 1950, that it would be necessary to build at a rate of 210,000 houses per annum to avoid the situation becoming worse, and it was suggested, then, that at a rate of 320,000 per annum one might hope to deal with the housing problem after thirty years [1]. This assessment was probably over-optimistic and a more accurate picture was drawn by M. Dumont in the report which he prepared for the Economic and Social Council in 1963 [2]. He calculated at that time that, although the targets of the plans had to that date been attained, the situation was then very much the same as it had been in 1945. This lamentable state of affairs was due to an official underestimate of the size of the problem, to a very slow start to house-building immediately after the war, and to gross official underestimation of internal migration which led to the abandoning of much rural housing. Since 1963 the targets set by successive plans have been more ambitious until the point has now been reached, at which over half a million houses are being constructed every year. The authors of the Sixth Plan were nevertheless able to state: 'Si l'on compare enfin cette situation à celle des pays qui ont atteint un niveau comparable de développement et de richesse, c'est à la France que revient le record de la vétusté, de l'étroitesse, de l'inconfort et du surpeuplement du logement' [3]. Given this situation of crisis, we must ask what was the reaction of politicians in the years immediately after the war. There was of course no very exact idea of the extent of the problem, but, nevertheless, there existed a widely held conviction that some initiatives were needed in order to encourage house-building.

The official view, and certainly that of M. Claudius-Petit, the first minister with responsibility for housing to be in office for any length of time, stressed the low level of rents as constituting the basic problem which needed to be tackled before all others in order that investment in housing should once again become profitable and building recommence. This line of argument implied that building for the owner-occupied sector was not considered, and certainly not as a matter of urgency. It was naturally assumed that, given the state of the economy, there would be no market for newly built houses for sale and the consequence was, as we have seen in earlier chapters, that the first post-war government initiatives were concerned with the HLMs, and soon after, with the privately rented sector. It was not until the summer of 1950 that the French Government took the first important steps towards re-establishing that part of the construction industry concerned with building for sale. Nevertheless in these early years it is interesting to examine the attitude of the principal political parties to the development of an owner-occupied sector.

The parties of the Centre and Right were keen that the Government should encourage building for owner-occupation although there was some difference of emphasis between them, the MRP (Christian Democrats) expressing a belief in the social and educational benefits of ownership as such, whilst parties of the traditional Right were more concerned to promote private economic activity of all sorts [4]. Support for owner-occupation from these parties is natural enough, but the Socialists were almost equally favourably inclined. They made it clear in February 1948, when putting forward their own proposals, that they had no dogmatic objections whatsoever to the development of this form of housing provision [5]. The attitude of all elements in French political life, with the exception of the Communists, was that the situation was so serious and the need for housing of any type so apparent, that any form of provision was to be preferred to none at all. We find here a situation which is parallel to that already described in dealing with the privately rented sector. The gravity of the problem is such that a consensus is created among parties which, on other questions, could never reach agreement. In the case of rents, they were so low that it was generally agreed that substantial rises were necessary. In the case of owner-occupation, the Socialists might normally have been expected to have some reservations about wholesale encouragement of the sector. But the situation was such that any form of housing was considered better than one. The French Socialists, unlike their British contemporaries, thought primarily in terms of quantity. They were willing to relegate to a lower plane questions about who was to benefit.

We see then, in the early post-war years, a consensus among the non-Communist parties in favour of the development of owner-occupation, but it was not until 1950 that this politically favourable situation was to bear fruit in the form of legislation. Why was this? In the first place, owner-occupation was not thought to be a likely source of substantial quantities of housing. It had never been in the past. Secondly, when reformers had tried, between the wars, to promote housing through state intervention, public housing had seemed the natural way in which this could be done. The legislative proposals already referred to all saw housing provision as either state-aided and therefore publicly owned, or privately financed by profit-seeking landlords. The first priorities were therefore to encourage private investment through higher rents, and to reorganize the HLM sector. Only when this had been done, in 1947 and 1948, did the minister begin to think seriously about whether the State might not do something by way of subsidy to encourage private building. Finally, there was the simple fact that, whatever might be the theoretical attractions of subsidizing private building, industrial investment, and not housing, received first claim on available resources.

I have already referred in chapter II to the Act of 21st of July 1950 which established the legal framework for the operations of the *Crédit Foncier* [6]. This legislation first provided a state guarantee for loans extended by the *Crédit Foncier* and arrangements were made in order to allow the *Crédit Foncier* to advance up to 60 per cent of the price of a new property. Previously, there had been a limit of 50 per cent of the selling price. The new scheme also redirected the operations of the *Crédit Foncier* so that it now dealt with the construction of new housing and not, as previously, primarily with the improvement of existing property [7]. The *Crédit Foncier* did not possess the long-term finance needed for house-buyers and so the Government agreed to the Bank of France's undertaking to re-finance these loans after five or seven years. This system of medium-term loans being used to finance long-term investment was borrowed from the industrial sector, where it had already proved successful. Although the original provision was for loans of a maximum of 60 per cent of the selling price, this was raised soon afterwards to 70 per cent. In addition to the provisions for loans, the new legislation also sought to aid buyers with the repayment of interest. This aid was in the form of a subsidy of six francs per square metre of floor area per year, and was payable for twenty years. The Act recognized that the slow raising of rents was not doing enough to encourage needed construction. It was novel in that it made state-guaranteed loans and subsidies available for the building of houses which were to remain in private ownership. From the first, the scheme was open to future owner-occupiers and those who wished to build in order to rent, but the former category soon came to predominate and, since 1950, the *Crédit Foncier* has been primarily a means by which public money is used to aid owner-occupation.

We are now in a position to examine the political reaction to this innovation. One might have expected some criticism from the Right regarding the quite new extension of state responsibility, particularly bearing in mind the clear preferences of this section of political opinion for private initiative, to which we have already referred in this chapter. Objections of this sort were entirely absent from the debates in the National Assembly, both in 1950 during the passage of the Bill setting up the new system, and in 1953 when there was important legislation modifying it. Clearly the situation was so serious that politicians of the Centre and Right were willing to forget the proposals which they had made in the immediate post-war period, and accept a more interventionist approach without reserve.

Nor was there any difficulty from the Left, except for the Communist Party. The Socialists might have objected and argued that public money, in the form of the newly established six francs per square metre subsidy, was being used to aid privileged sections of the community, and in fact to subsidize the construction industry. This attitude was not adopted, and in my view the explanation is very much that to which we have referred on other occasions when describing the wide consensus which existed at this period in France with respect to housing. The gravity of the problem meant that almost all shades of political opinion were willing to accept that any means, private, public or semi-public, which showed some possibility of producing housing, were acceptable. Communist opposition was to be expected. 'L'avenir démontrera que l'attribution de ces primes, qui aboutissent à faire payer des impôts par les locataires des taudis au profit des spéculateurs de la propriété bâtie, n'atténuera pas la crise du logement' [8]. But this quotation should be compared with the following: 'Notons que ces primes, *si elles ont permis á un certain nombre de petits gens de faire bâtir une maison familiale,* ont aussi et surtout servi à la construction d'appartements à deux ou trois millions la pièce, facilitant ainsi les fructueuses spéculations des sociétés immobilières' [9]. This change of tone, coming, as it does, five years after the establishment of the new system, demonstrates that even the Communist Party was not entirely immune from the consequence of the success of the new system.

Nor was the cautious official view of the Ministry of Finance a stumbling block on this occasion. It is important to understand why this department was willing to approve the 1950 legislation for, as we shall see later, when examining its opposition to savings incentive schemes, the department might well have proved a much more formidable obstacle than the Assembly. The reason for its consent lies in the difference between a savings incentive scheme and a scheme for loans and subsidies. In the former case, as we shall see, the Ministry was afraid that a successful scheme might attract savings that would otherwise have been placed with the *Caisse d'Epargne.* If this happened, the State would be deprived of an important source of finance for government borrowing. An additional argument against savings incentive schemes was that one could never foresee the quantity of savings that would be attracted, and therefore one could not know accurately in advance what the Government might lose. In the case of the 1950 scheme of loans and subsidies, however, there was a heading in the annual budget, and hence expenditure could always be held back if inflationary difficulties arose. Whereas, therefore, the economic impact of a savings scheme depends on how attractive it proves, the effect of the 1950 scheme could be monitored by the financial authorities and limited, if necessary. It was for these reasons that M. Claudius-Petit was able to establish an effective system of aid.

Early in 1953 substantial modifications were made to the *Crédit Foncier* system, and, as a consequence, what was known as the *Logéco* was created (*Logement économique et familial*). The idea of the Minister, M. Pierre Courant, was to create and foster a cheap type of house, which would nevertheless serve adequately the needs of the average family. He was entirely in sympathy with the principles of the system which had been established by his predecessor in 1950 but he felt that the quantity of housing which was being built was quite insufficient and that greater incentives and improved facilities were necessary if the rate of building was to be raised to a reasonable level. From as early as 1947 there had been an official target of 240,000 dwellings per annum but by 1953 the annual building total had not reached even half of this figure. In the minister's view the solution was two-fold. Firstly, the *Crédit Foncier* loan was to be increased from 70 to 80 per cent of the total purchasing price and the purchaser was to be entitled to a subsidy of 10 francs per square metre in order effectively to reduce the interest charged on the loan. In exchange for these increased advantages, the Government was to restrict the type of housing which could qualify for the new system and limit both its size and cost, hence the justification for the new term *Logéco*. This did not mean that the old surface area subsidy at six francs was abolished, but simply that in future the *Crédit Foncier* would be responsible for two separate systems. The *Logécos* were an immediate success and more than a million were built between 1953 and their abolition in late 1963. They encountered no substantial political opposition on the grounds of increased state intervention or on the grounds of the granting of unjustified privileges, but the radical character of what M. Courant did provoked some criticism.

The Socialists, on behalf of the HLM movement, protested that a subsidized form of owner-occupation already existed within the HLM structure, and that the minister was therefore duplicating this in his new scheme [10]. It is clear that M. Courant wished to avoid the difficulties associated with dealing with the HLM movement and that he thought the HLMs slow and cumbersome in this branch of their work [11]. He was able to ignore these Socialist criticisms of his new policy. The *Logécos* are important because they represent the philosophy of direct state intervention of a type which finds no parallel in the British owner-occupied sector. They are further evidence of the willingness of the State to intervene on a wide scale and in favour of a variety of social groups. As I have pointed out earlier, it is this approach, and the vested interest to which it gives rise, which help to strengthen the pattern of continuity in French housing policy and the absence of which reinforces the more cyclical pattern of British policy development. After the legislation of 1950 and 1953, we may observe a change in the pattern of political conflict in the newly created semi-public sector, identical to that which took place in the privately rented sector, after the passage of the 1948 Rent Act. Basic principles were accepted and further change can be described in terms of conflict between the State and the recently created vested interests, or between different Government departments.

The new pattern of politics is illustrated time and again in later years. Despite the financially unorthodox character of *Crédit Foncier* operations, governments of all shades of opinion allowed the system to expand. Typically, in the mid-1950s, it was providing at least one third of the housing programme [12]. But difficulties arose when restraint was needed to cope with the danger of inflation. Such restraint was certain to prove unpopular, and so control over the activities of the *Crédit Foncier* has often been exercised with great discretion. For example, in 1964 a ceiling was placed on the institution, limiting both the total amount out on loan and the quantity of money which could be made available in future in any single year. This potentially unpopular measure did not, however, come to the notice of the general public until much later, since no legislation or even decree was required. The ceiling was simply embodied in an agreement signed by the *Crédit Foncier*, the Minister of Finance, and the Bank of France. Reference to Table VIII. 1 will show the impact of the March 1964 agreement on construction in the semi-public sector. The agreement certainly contributed substantially to the stagnation of the house-building industry, which is noticeable between 1965 and 1968 [13].

The events described above would appear to show that the desired flexibility and control can be obtained in favourable circumstances. But the Government is not always able to act with such discretion and dispatch, as is amply demonstrated by the events surrounding other anti-inflationary measures adopted in 1957 and 1958. Twice in 1957 the Government found it necessary to raise the bank rate, first from 5.4 to 6.4 per cent and then again later to 7.4 per cent [14]. The result of these changes for house-buyers with outstanding loans was, as would appear quite natural to the British house purchaser, an increase in the rate of interest charged. The outcry was immediate. M. Couinaud wrote in a report prepared for the Assembly Committee on Housing, War, Damage and Construction in February 1958: 'Il est véritablement inconcevable qu'après avoir contracté avec un établissement public, le bénéficiaire d'un prêt à la construction puisse se voir opposer ultérieurement, par simple décision unilatérale, une aggravation de ses obligations' [15]. What was apparently unthinkable in France is something which is accepted as a matter of course in Britain. Even the left-wing of the Labour Party has never believed that the State could afford to protect buyers even partially against the consequences of a higher bank rate. The CNL does not seem to have been very active in this protest but the mortgagees' section of the CGL was very much to the fore and even received by the Minister of Finance in January of 1958. A national day of protest was threatened by this organization for later in the same month.

As I have already implied, it is quite evident that events similar to those in France in 1957 would not have produced the same results in Britain. A full explanation of this phenomenon will be provided in chapter XIV but it is necessary here to point to one mathematical aspect of the problem, which tends in itself to provide a partial explanation for the extent of public protest. Contracts for the repayment of mortgage loans signed by purchasers with the *Crédit Foncier* had always made it quite clear that, in the case of an increase in the bank rate, the full additional interest charge would be passed on to the buyer [16]. There was therefore no element of surprise in the 1957 increases, but there was an extremely sharp increase in the monthly payments which a buyer was called upon to pay, an increase much sharper than one would normally associate with an increase in interest of two per cent. The first reason for this steep rise was that during the first years of a typical loan, no repayment of capital was undertaken, so that the monthly charge consisted entirely of interest due and hence an increase in interest rate had that much more effect, at least if judged in terms of the percentage increase in monthly payments required. The second reason for the large proportional jump in payments was that Government assistance was a fixed sum rather than a proportion of the repayments.

These considerations, although important, certainly do not entirely explain the extent of the political reaction to the increased interest charges, but, as we have already seen, it is a feature of the French system that change is very frequently a stimulus to violent reaction. The protests of the mortgagees' section of the CGL have already been mentioned and, in addition, one should note the opinion of the Economic Council expressed in July 1957 prior to the second increase. It suggested in its recommendation that special steps be taken to reduce the impact of the increases for buyers of *Logécos*.

Protests, both official and unofficial, had their effect on the Government and, in the autumn of 1957, M. Pflimlin announced that the Government would take steps to avoid the passing on of the second of the two one per cent increases. The Government was not ready, however, to return to the rate applicable prior to April 1957. The political effect of the protests of 1957 and early 1958 was not limited to the particular events of those years. In order to avoid this direct confrontation between the Government and house buyers in future, a system was established in 1958, by which purchasers were guaranteed a fixed interest rate for the duration of the loan regardless of later trends in interest rate levels [17]. Such a system contrasts strongly with that operated by the Building Societies in Great Britain and means that the State, and not existing borrowers, must bear the full burden of increased interest rates. Such a system is almost universally regarded, by both politicians and housing experts, as entirely unsatisfactory, for it means that borrowers obtain special privileges in addition to the natural advantage which they derive from the process of inflation. Some minor steps have been taken in recent years to attempt to diminish the unjustified advantage thus obtained by allowing for sharp increases in the interest charged in the later years of repayment. But such attempts have been only on a modest scale [18].

The most interesting period for our purposes in the development of the activities of the *Crédit Foncier* is the period from 1963 to approximately 1967. Important changes of policy were announced in the summer of 1963 and enacted in Decrees which appeared in December of the same year [19]. These decisions were of real importance and appeared to presage a change of quite a fundamental nature in the principles governing the activity of the *Crédit Foncier*, but, as we shall see, the course of events was to bear testimony once again to the inflexibility of French policy, even when the Government clearly intends to make important changes.

The first measures to be announced were intended to take account of the criticism that much of the aid in the sector with which we are dealing, was going to purchasers whose incomes made it seem absurd for them to be benefiting from financial assistance. The argument was put in the following terms. In the early fifties it was reasonable to aid anyone willing to buy new housing since the money spent in this way could be regarded as necessary in order to develop the housing construction industry. In a sense, government intervention at this time could be justified on economic grounds, even if socially the aid seemed somewhat misdirected. Once the industry was properly on its feet and real individual income was rising rapidly, it was argued that aid of the sort embodied in the system of the *Logécos* and other *Crédit Foncier* loans could no longer be justified. In response to this criticism M. Maziol announced during the summer of 1963 that he was abolishing the system of *Logécos* and replacing them by a system in which purchasers of housing would only be entitled to *Crédit Foncier* loans if their income fell below a certain ceiling. This ceiling was naturally to take account of the size of the family to be housed. It is worth noting at this point, that the initial reaction of the National Building Federation (FNB) to these proposals, at its annual congress held in Deauville in June 1963 was favourable [20]. Later in the year, however, the attitude of the industry and of other observers of government policy changed radically as more details of the proposed reform were released. The Government, it seemed, proposed to deal with those whom they described as speculators. This meant that property to rent, built with the aid of *Crédit Foncier* loans, was to have maximum rent ceilings imposed on it. Previously, the conditions of these loans had referred only to the type and cost of construction. There were also to be measures designed to penalise those who bought *Crédit Foncier* housing and then resold it at a profit within a short period. In the weekly of the Building Federation during January 1964 a virulent attack was mounted on the Maziol reforms [21]. It was alleged, and there is some evidence to support this allegation in the timing of the additional reforms, that the rules against speculators were simply disguised deflation. The Government, instead of openly stating that the interests of the economy as a whole required a slowing down in the expansion of house-building, was enforcing such a slowdown by indirect means. The protest at the new measures was not confined, however, to the building industry. *Le Figaro* stated in April 1965: 'De plus en plus une crise grave s'installe dans la classe moyenne, secteur où l'aide de l'Etat est devenue pratiquement inexistante. Le cadre moyen, l'ouvrier qualifié, se trouvent, en effet, exclus des prêts spéciaux accordés par les pouvoirs publics, un système de plafonnement des ressources réduisant considérablement pour eux ce recours à l'aide officielle' [22]. Employer organizations also demanded that the 1963 measures be amended [23].

In 1965, an election year, the Government appeared to have second thoughts and to respond sympathetically to the protests which its earlier policy had provoked. The new modified policy was expressed in a series of measures which appeared during the summer of 1965 [24]. In October, M. Taittinger, in a report prepared for the Assembly on the budget proposals for 1966, with reference to the situation created by the December 1963 reforms, stated: 'C'est pour redresser cette situation qui suscitait un vif mécontentement, que le Gouvernement a pris en 1965 un certain nombre d'initiatives nouvelles qui, sans revenir sur l'esprit des textes de 1963, y apportent des compléments et des aménagements importants' [25]. This version of events is hardly consistent with the facts, as will become clear if we compare systematically the measures of 1963 with those announced during the summer of 1965.

It will be recalled that the 1963 measures imposed an income ceiling as a condition of receiving what were technically described as 'Special Loans' (*Prêts Speciaux*). This ceiling remained a feature of the 'Special Loans' even after the measures of 1965, but a new system was created of 'Differed Loans' (*Prêts Différés*) and entitlement to these loans was in no way made conditional upon the income of the beneficiary. One may describe the innovation as simply supplementing the former but in fact the 'Differed Loans' contradicted the principle of concentrating aid on the less wealthy, particularly when one bears in mind that the resources of the *Crédit Foncier* are limited and that therefore the 'Differed Loans' could only be financed out of money which would otherwise have been used for the 'Special Loans'.

Rules against speculation were another important feature of the 1963 reforms. As M. Taittinger explains in his report, the period during which resale was forbidden was shortened considerably in 1965, exceptions to the rules introduced, and penalties for those infringing them relaxed.

As to the third principal feature of the reforms, the imposition of rent ceilings on housing built with the aid of *Crédit Foncier* loans, these remained in force in 1965 but the reversal of policy was completed when they were lifted in January 1967 [26]. One is obliged to conclude with M. Mathieu that the concessions granted in 1965 constituted a total reversal of earlier government policy [27]. It is difficult to imagine any more telling testimony to the difficulties which face politicians whose aim it is to undertake reforms which are bound, in the nature of things, to prove unpopular in certain quarters. As for the present-day situation, if the recommendations of the Barre Report are accepted they will have the most profound consequences for the character of the semi-public sector of housing provision. It is suggested in the Report that the *Crédit Foncier* should no longer have a limited number of loans at priveleged rates of interest which it can dispense in principle to a clientele unable to afford less subsidized house purchase. Instead it will use the funds which it collects to lower interest rates for all house purchasers, thus encouraging competition between different lending institutions, instead of dividing the market for housing finance into a number of segregated markets. Essentially this will mean returning to the policy which was unsuccessfully tried in the mid-1960s, although this time with an intention to carry reform much further. It is too early yet to say whether the Barre Report will have the effect which its authors intend but the fact that M. Barre is now Prime Minister may facilitate its adoption.

## II  *Other forms of aid to owner-occupation*

The *Crédit Foncier* is the backbone of the system of state aid to owner-occupation, but it is not the only means by which the State intervenes in this area. A variety of incentive saving schemes are particularly worthy of attention.

The *Epargne Logement* (savings incentive scheme) has taken various forms since it was first introduced early in 1953 by M.P. Courant but, despite the variety of forms which these schemes have taken, the essential basis of the scheme has remained the same [28]. The aim has always been to produce supplementary resources to be spent on new housing provision in order not to rely only on state-controlled and financed lending. Normally an attempt has been made to encourage saving by offering some particular incentive to the saver. At the outset this incentive was a form of indexing applied to the sum saved. It was argued that, in a period of rapid inflation, when a saver could never be sure of the price of housing at some future date, it would be an important incentive to him if his savings could be indexed to the price of new residential construction. Incentives used in preference to indexing in the later development of this scheme have included a priority for the saver in the granting of *Crédit Foncier* loans, or more simply, a higher interest rate for contracted savings or savings which could be used only for housing purposes [29]. The slow and difficult development of the incentive scheme is of particular interest to a student of housing policy in that it gives an additional example of the slowness of change in French policy and the difficulties which innovators must confront. In the case of the incentive savings scheme, the difficulties encountered have not been those of sharp clashes of interest between different sections of the community, nor have they concerned the difficulties of relations between the State and its executive institutions. The blockage in this case has rather been interdepartmental, with the ministry responsible for housing policy pressing for the adoption of more attractive schemes, and the Ministry of Finance opposing this.

The character of the difficulties which were to beset the development of the *Epargne Logement* was clear from the outset. As early as 1950 a Bill to introduce the system was in course of being drafted under the supervision of M. Claudius-Petit [30]. Although drafting had begun in that year, the Government as a whole did not agree to the proposed legislation until late in 1952, and it appears that the minister was then only able to gain the acceptance of his cabinet colleagues by threats of resignation and public statements condemning unnecessary delays in introducing an important reform measure [31]. The party giving the minister constant support during this period of struggle against the financial authorities was the MRP who had tabled a Bill early in 1951 expressing support for the principle of the *Epargne Logement* [32]. It was characteristic of this group's approach to housing problems that their proposals stressed that the savings incentive scheme was not a capitalist scheme but one designed to encourage individual saving prior to owner-occupation. 'Il ne s'agit plus d'avoir recours à l'épargne des capitalistes. . . . C'est pourquoi nous proposons de faire appel à la masse des Français moyens qui se trouvent aux prises avec le difficile problème du logement pour eux et pour les leurs' [33]. Support also came for the minister from other sources outside the Government between 1950 and 1953. M. Dary presented in 1950 an important report to the Economic Council on the general problem of finding finance for a needed housing programme [34]. He stressed the importance of the incentive scheme and regretted that progress in drafting was so slow and that information, to which the Economic Council felt itself entitled, had not been available from the Ministry of Finance. Two years later in July 1952 another report prepared by M. Houist underlined that there was a wide political consensus in favour of the savings scheme and that the delays which had been experienced were all the more difficult to understand and regrettable [35].

As already mentioned success was finally obtained late in 1952 and legislation successfully promoted during 1953, but, before examining the details of the scheme that was established, it is important to ask why there had been so much difficulty and delay. The most important opponents of the scheme were certainly the senior officials in the Ministry of Finance. These officials were not opposed to savings incentive schemes in principle, in fact quite the contrary, for they were extremely anxious to encourage as much saving as possible in order to finance necessary industrial investment. But they were convinced that there was a fixed limit to the quantity of savings available within the country and that, therefore, a gain for housing would mean a loss for industry or for the Government. This argument was naturally strongly rejected by supporters of the savings incentive scheme within the Ministry of Housing and Reconstruction. Their view was that the total quantity of savings available within the country was not fixed, and that, on the contrary, new sources of supplementary saving could be discovered if the right incentive was provided. In the view of the supporters of the scheme, then, there was a certain proportion of the national income which might be be rechannelled from consumption into saving if the saver could be assured of improving his housing situation as a consequence of the effort undertaken. The Ministry of Finance was particularly concerned about the placing of government loans and the financing of industrial rather than housing investment. In an interdepartmental conflict of this sort it should be borne in mind that the Ministry of Finance is very much senior to the various ministries which have been responsible for housing and that Ministry of Finance officials are generally more competent and highly rated within the administration. The predictable outcome of this conflict was the delay to which I have referred but also a finally adopted scheme of a very modest character.

The basic concept embodied in the scheme as finally adopted was the indexing of savings placed in a special account to the cost of new construction. It was understood that the saver would eventually use these savings as part of the financing necessary for the purchase of his new house. This system continued in force for six years and during this period it proved a total failure since the amount of saving attracted was insignificant in relation either to the needs of the country as a whole or to the needs of the individual saver. The reader may feel that this account exaggerates the importance of specific objections raised by the Ministry of Finance. In support of my assertion I would only quote, in addition to the evidence already produced, the words of the Fifth Plan on this subject which were clearly designed, in the mid-sixties, to counter the same objections which persisted as a brake on the development of an attractive incentive scheme. 'On peut seulement regretter la timidité excessive des mesures qui ont été annoncées. Tout donne à penser en effet que des flots d'épargne très importants pourraient s'orienter vers la constitution d'un capital destiné à l'acquisition d'un logement pourvu que les garanties suffisantes soient données sur l'efficacité de l'effort entrepris' [36]. In addition to the complications of a scheme of indexing, which certainly must have discouraged many potential savers, the scheme enacted in 1953 also suffered from the defect that the savings used were only to benefit from the advantages of indexing if they were used for the purchase of new housing. A saver was, therefore, if he wished to profit from the scheme, obliged, several years in advance of his purchase, to undertake to buy a newly constructed dwelling rather than an existing one. This limitation was imposed at the wish of M. Claudius-Petit by way of amendment during the passage of the Bill, with the object of encouraging new building so badly needed at the time [37]. The consequence, however, of this well-intentioned amendment was certainly to render the scheme much less attractive to the general public.

The system for which M. Courant was responsible continued in force, despite its apparent failure, until it was replaced by the Decrees of the 11th of March 1959 [38]. These put an end to the system of indexation for reasons of general economic policy. By this time the major source of loans for those wishing to buy their own housing was the *Crédit Foncier* and it was thought consequently that the way to attract savings would be to offer the saver priority in the queue of those waiting for loans from this institution. This idea was put into practice in the new scheme and the possibility of obtaining a loan was used as bait. The interest rate offered was only two per cent, with some additional income tax relief, but the system soon proved to be, not surprisingly, as unattractive as its predecessor and only succeeded in producing a quantity of saving equivalent to three per cent of the total accumulated by the *Caisse d'Epargne* and the *Caisse Nationale d'Epargne*. Some attempt was made in April 1964 to improve the conditions by lenghtening the time over which the eventual loan would be repaid and increasing the size of the loan to which the saver was entitled from 10,000 to 15,000 francs. But these were only minor modifications and the size of the loan to which a saver was entitled was still such that it could only be regarded as supplementary finance useful to a saver who could obtain the bulk of the sum necessary elsewhere. In both the systems which existed between 1953 and 1965 there was a strict link between the size of the savings accumulated and the size of the loan to which the saver was thereby entitled. A reader familiar with British institutions may readily imagine how unattractive were the facilities offered in these years to savers if he considers how much saving the Building Societies in this country might collect if investors were not allowed to withdraw their savings without severe financial penalties, and if they were provided with no incentive to save unless they could be sure, several years in advance, that they were going to use their personal savings to buy their own home.

In 1965 the Government seems to have drawn the conclusions from its previous unsuccessful attempts to tap new sources of saving and decided to alter the terms of the *Epargne Logement* radically in order to render it much more attractive. The major improvement which the new scheme introduced as compared with its predecessors was that the saver was left much more free to use his savings as he wished. It will be remembered that in the scheme as it existed between 1953 and 1959 the saver was only permitted to use savings for the purchase of new housing and, in the 1959–65 system, maximum advantage was only obtainable if one agreed to use the scheme as a way of obtaining a loan from the *Crédit Foncier*. This meant in effect that the most expensive categories of new housing were inaccessible. The new scheme left the saver free to buy either existing or newly built housing and also to choose freely as between aided and unaided forms of construction. There was some response from the public to this more liberal regime but the scheme did not come into its own until much more liberalized, late in 1969, at the time of the devaluation of the franc [39]. It would appear that at this time the financial authorities were anxious at all costs to relieve inflationary pressure by attracting as much saving as possible. At this date the scheme was rechristened *Plan d'Epargne Logement* and the saver was left entirely free as to the use of his accumulated savings provided that he left them untouched with the savings institution during a specified minimum period. By this time the scheme had become more one of contractual saving and, as such, interested a far wider public. The authors of the report on housing contained in the Sixth Plan congratulate the Government on the success of the new scheme and note that the resources made available are now increasing rapidly in a way which contrasts sharply with the stagnation of the past. It should be borne in mind that, although the saver is free to use his accumulated savings as he pleases in the new system, the savings thus accumulated must be devoted by the institution in question to the finance of housing loans in some form or other. Much of the saving thus created has been channelled into the mortgage market created by the Government in 1966. It is worth noting that the financial authorities, rather than those primarily responsible for the formulation of housing policy, were as much responsible for the final successful establishment of an attractive scheme as they had been for the delay and timidity of earlier schemes.

III *Conclusion*

When attempting to come to general conclusions about the nature of the politics of the owner-occupied sector, it is necessary not to overemphasize policy rigidity. Some important innovations have taken place, to which it is only just to refer. The most important of these concerns the efforts of the Government to build up that section of the housing market which does not rely on any direct public aid, that is to say, benefits only from tax concessions. In the 1950s such a sector was almost non-existent but, in recent years, the share of housing production in this unaided sector has increased considerably and between 1966 and 1971 the share of finance coming from purely private sources rose from 40 to 56 per cent [40]. This progress has been made possible largely as a result of the success of the contractual savings scheme, already referred to, but also as a result of the successful establishment of a mortgage market [41]. It has for a long time been recognized that the basic weakness of the system of financing housing in France has been the absence of a mechanism capable of transforming liquid savings into long-term loans. In the United Kingdom, Germany and the USA, housing finance in the private sector is essentially of this type, although there is considerable variety in the institutions employed [42]. The provisions of the Act of the 1st of March 1967, designed to make the process of realization of mortgages more simple and rapid, and the establishment for private banks of a regulated market in mortgages which avoids liquidity problems, have begun to equip France with a mechanism comparable to that of her northern neighbours. These measures have been slow in coming. The first discussions of the necessary steps date from 1961 and changes in the regulations of the Bank of France, designed to encourage the intervention of private banks in this sphere were only made in 1966 [43]. Nevertheless, the size of the achievement should not be underestimated, and the privately financed sectors are certainly destined to further expansion. If this tendency continues uninterrupted for some time, it may eventually have important consequences allowing, perhaps, the Government to withdraw its support from the semi-public sector, without thereby causing a building slump. If this were to happen, a pattern of state intervention might establish itself, which would resemble much more closely that existing in Britain. But any such development must still be considered a future possibility rather than something which can be predicted with any certainty.

Nor should the purely quantitative aspect of the housing problem be neglected. In conformity with our thesis there has been no period in the expansion of house-building since the war which shows the booms and depressions which have been experienced in the United Kingdom, but nevertheless the total increase in production, with periods of stagnation from time to time, has now brought the annual figure of completions to the half million mark. There has also been a steady increase in the proportion of owner-occupiers although the Government has never expressed the same unconditional attachment to this form of tenure as have British Conservative governments. In the mid-fifties it was estimated that one third of all households were owner-occupied and by 1968 this figure had risen to 44 per cent [44]. The difference in political priorities is reflected in the more rapid transformation in the size of the owner-occupied sector as a share of total stock in Great Britain.

It is true to say that the conflicts to which we have referred in our discussion of the owner-occupied sector have not exhibited the same violence as elsewhere. It is also true that in France, as in Great Britain, the owner-occupied sector probably arouses less controversy than either of the other two sectors. We have been able to observe great stability, and sometimes inflexibility in policy. Among the forces resisting change, we have particularly noted interdepartmental friction, and the power of vested interests created by state intervention. It has been amply demonstrated in this chapter that some of the political characteristics to which we have already referred in discussing other sectors are not absent from the owner-occupied sector. It may be less controversial but the characteristics of French political life which make for inflexibility seem as evident here as elsewhere.

*References*

1. G. Mathieu, 'Logement, notre honte', *Le Monde*, 11 March 1958.
2. P. Dumont, *Rapport présenté au nom du Conseil Economique et Social, Avis et Rapports du Conseil Economique et Social*, 14 December 1963.
3. *Rapports des Commissions du VIe Plan (1971–75), Rapport de la Commission de l'Habitation*, Vol. I, p. 18.
4. *Proposition de loi déposée par le PRL, Annexe au Procès-Verbal de l'Assemblée Nationale, J.O.*, 26 June 1946; *Proposition de loi déposée par le MRP, J.O.*, 29 August 1946; *Proposition de loi déposée par le RGR, Annexe au Procès-Verbal du Conseil de la République, J.O.*, 19 July 1947.
5. *Proposition de loi déposée par la SFIO, Annexe au Procès-Verbal de l'Assemblée Nationale, J.O.*, 13 February 1948.
6. *See* above, p. 17.

7. P. Champion, *Crédit Foncier de France* (Editions de l'Epargne, 1966).
8. *L'Humanité*, 28 July 1950.
9. *Proposition de loi No. 11089 déposée par le PCF, Annexe au Procès-Verbal de l'Assemblée Nationale, J.O.*, 30 June 1955, p. 3 (my italics).
10. Debate of 20 March 1953, *J.O., Débats*, pp. 2118–21, and debate of 21 March 1953, *J.O., Débats*, pp. 2168–70.
11. *Projet de loi Annexe an Procès-Verbal de l'Assemblée Nationale, J.O.*, 6 February 1963 (*see* especially the *Exposé des Motifs*). M. Courant discusses this problem in the Debate of 17 March 1953, *J.O., Débats*, p. 1994.
12. *See* table VIII. 1.
13. For details of this agreement, see *Notes et Études Documentaires*, No. 3301 (La Documentation Française, 1966).
14. Jean Meynaud and Alain Lancelot, 'Groupes de Pression et Politique du Logement', *Revue Française de Science Politique*, Vol. VIII (1958), No. 4, pp. 849–50.
15. M, Couinaud, *Rapport fait an nom de la Commission de la Justice, des Dommages de Guerre et du Logement, Annexe au Procès-Verbal de l'Assemblée Nationale, J.O.*, 7 February 1958, p. 2.
16. M. Aroud, *Rapport présenté au nom du Conseil Economique, Avis et Rapports du Conseil Economique*, Septermber 1957.
17. The outcome of this struggle is described by the effects evaluated by G. Houist in the *Rapport présenté au nom du Conseil Economique et Social, Avis et Rapports du Conseil Economique et Social*, 9 July 1965.
18. *Le Figaro*, 16 November 1971, all this and other important matters relating to the *Crédit Foncier* are very clearly explained in M. Dresch, *Le Financement du Logement* (Berger-le-Vrault, 1973), ch. 2.
19. *Le Monde*, 31 December 1963.
20. *Le Monde*, 12 June 1963.
21. *Combat*, 7 January 1964.
22. *Le Figaro*, 7 January 1964.
23. *Le Monde*, 13 March 1965; *La Vie Française*, 18 December 1964.
24. *J.O.*, 16 July 1965; *Le Monde*, 17 July 1965.
25. J. Taittinger, *Rapport sur le Projet de loi de Finances de 1966, Annexe au Procès-Verbal de l'Assemblée Nationale, J.O.*, 2 October 1965, p. 10.
26. *Le Monde*, 19 January 1967.
27. ibid.
28. Debate of 18 March 1953, *J.O., Débats*, pp. 2031–37.
29. E. Halbout, *Rapport au nom de la Commission de la Production et des Echanges, Annexe au Procès-Verbal de l'Assemblée Nationale, J.O.*, 10 June 1965.
30. *Le Monde*, 21 April 1950.
31. *Combat*, 25 October 1952; *Le Monde*, 10 December 1952.
32. *Proposition de loi déposée par le MRP, Annexe au Procès-Verbal de l'Assemblée Nationale, J.O.*, 7 September 1951.
33. ibid., p. 2.
34. E. Dary, *Financement de la Construction, Avis et Rapports du Conseil Economique*, March 1950.
35. G. Houist, *Rapport présenté au nom du Conseil Economique, Avis et Rapports du Conseil Economique*, 25 July 1952.

36. *Rapport Général et Rapports Spéciaux Annexes de la Commission de l'Habitation du Ve Plan*, 1966, p. 160.

37. Debate of 18th March 1953, *J.O.*, *Débats* pp. 2031–37.

38. E. Halbout, *Rapport au nom de la Commision de la Production et des Echanges*, *Annexe au Procès-Verbal de l'Assemblée Nationale*, *J.O.*, 10 June 1965. This report conveniently summarizes changes in the terms offered which took place in 1959 and 1965, and contains figures demonstrating the failure of these schemes.

39. *Le Figaro*, 13 October 1969.

40. *Le Monde*, 20 March 1973.

41. P. Alphandéry, *Les Prêts Hypothécaires* (Que sais-je? No. 1326, P.U.F., 1968).

42. *Le Financement du Logement en France et à l'Etranger* (Centre d'Informations et d'Etudes du Crédit, P.U.F., 1966).

43. R. Chastagnol, 'Les Banques et le Financement à long terme du Logement', Part I in *Banque*, March 1971, p. 251; Part II in *Banque*, April 1971, p. 281.

44. *La Politique du Logement en France* (Études et Documents du Centre de Recherches Economiques et Sociales, May-June 1964), pp. 10–11. G. Ebrik and P. Barjac, *Logement: Dossier noir de la France* (Dunod, 1970), p. 19. In the 1950s the percentage of the French housing stock in owner-occupation was about four per cent above the British figure (France, 1954: 35.5 per cent; Britain, 1956: 31.1 per cent). Although owner-occupation has expanded in both countries, this process has been more rapid in Britain, so that the relative position of the two countries is now reversed.

# XIII

# The Owner-Occupied Sector: Britain

In examining the owner-occupied sector in France we have found it to be considerably less controversial than the other two sectors of housing provision. This is equally true of the British case, although both provide examples of political conflict and sufficient policy development to make the examination of the sector worthwhile. In both cases the examination of this sector tends to confirm the impressions which we have already formed in preceding chapters.

Since the Building Societies dominate the financing of the owner-occupied sector in Britain, it is useful, before beginning a discussion of policy, to recall the salient features of the Building Society system. The societies are non-profit-making and totally independent of the government. They collect savings from the public and many people simply use them as they would a bank. Each society, then, uses the resources thus obtained to advance loans on existing and new housing, each loan being secured by a mortgage on the property in question. Most societies are members of the Building Societies Association which represents them in discussions with the government, and also recommends the rates of interest to be charged by its members. Individual societies are in no way bound by these recommendations. Traditionally, therefore, the relationship between government and the Building Society movement has been indirect. The government has no direct control over their activities but, clearly, the societies are affected by the character of national economic policy.

The essential facts concerning government policy towards the owner-occupied sector during the earliest period under study, that of the Attlee Government, are already familiar to the reader [1]. The expansion of this sector was limited during this period by the system of local authority licences. The priorities of the Labour Government were clear and the owner-occupied sector suffered accordingly. Nevertheless, the events of this period bear witness to the great strength of the sector. No basic alterations were made whatsoever in the institutional framework upon which the sector had relied for its rapid development in the inter-war period, and these institutions were therefore intact and ready to operate as before, when the Conservatives returned to power and allowed them to do so. I am referring here principally to the Building Societies which, although their level of activity naturally remained low during the period, were not subject to any discriminatory legislation. The assets of the Societies grew satisfactorily during the period, although there was then, and has always been since, direct competition between the Building Societies and forms of government-controlled saving. In fact the rate of growth of Building Society assets exceeded that of the various forms of government saving [2]. Previously, I have stressed that policy in the 1945–51 period was sharply distinguished, for political reasons, from the policy pursued after 1951. The reference here to the immunity of the Building Societies from possible encroachment on their economic and financial strength is not intended to qualify in any important degree the conclusions previously reached. The point is rather that the pursuit of Labour's housing policies did not logically demand any modification in the position of the Building Societies. It is important to underline this for, had any important changes been necessary, they might well have inhibited the later expansion of the Societies under the Conservatives and, consequently, have interfered with the responsiveness of housing policy to political circumstances. In fact, however, the financial prestige and autonomy of the Building Societies have not proved a factor of rigidity since, in periods when the role of the private sector is diminished or even partly reduced, they simply expand less rapidly. When the unfavourable political circumstances have passed, the Building Society loan mechanism remains intact and available for a period of more rapid expansion. It is important to emphasize this factor because, as we have already frequently had occasion to observe, the institutions through which the State acts in France often operate as a restraint on government policy.

During the period of thirteen years of Conservative rule the sector was allowed to expand and did so rapidly, particularly during the early fifties [3]. The pace of advance was not even, but these irregularities were due to economic rather than political vicissitudes. In examining the development of policy in the public and private rented sectors during the period, we have distinguished a number of separate phases in policy development. This is not possible for the owner-occupied sector. This absence of dividing lines during a period of thirteen years is clear evidence of the non-controversial character of the sector, to which reference has already been made. The same point emerges from an examination of the important pieces of legislation of this period. Whereas private and publicly rented sectors are subject to important legislative modifications at fairly short intervals, the owner-occupied sector rarely receives such attention, and during this period only one statute of any importance can be found which deals primarily with the owner-occupied sector: the House Purchase and Housing Act 1959. An examination of the circumstances surrounding the passage of this Bill will serve usefully to show the limits of controversy affecting this sector.

It has become apparent in our discussion of the public sector that Conservatives are committed to owner-occupation as the most socially valuable form of housing tenure. But a constant difficulty which presents itself to activists within the Party is that there often seems little that can be done to encourage ownership. Much of what a Conservative Government may do in this direction simply consists in reducing the importance of the principal rival sector: council housing. By 1958 the Party had done what was possible in this direction by reducing the subsidies for council housing in 1956, and by providing for a much smaller public building programme. As the 1959 election approached it was natural that Conservative back-benchers should feel somewhat dissatisfied with this indirect form of assistance of the owner-occupied sector. It may also be noted in explaining the dissatisfaction of back-benchers that all that the Party had done in seven years, between 1951 and 1958, for the owner-occupied sector could not be regarded as directly beneficial to individual owner-occupiers. The decreasing size of current building in the public sector might increase the number of owner-occupiers but it could hardly affect directly the welfare of those already established in their own houses.

Responding to this sort of dissatisfaction, forty back-bench Conservatives signed a motion in May 1958 calling upon the Government to intervene actively in order to encourage home ownership [4]. This motion suggested that the form of aid to be adopted should be some additional tax concession to mortgagees on lower incomes. There has always been in Britain a tax concession allowing full deductibility of interest repayments but this aid is in no way concentrated on the lower-paid and is in fact highly regressive. There was no response to this call from the back-benchers and, therefore, Conservative MPs persisted with their campaign. A Home Ownership Committee was formed in addition to the normal Housing and Local Government Committee and it produced a report which was submitted to a Cabinet Committee under the chairmanship of R.A. Butler in August 1958 [5]. This report made three proposals; these were the abolition of Schedule A income tax, the abolition of the stamp duty on housing transaction, and most important of all, the establishment of a system of state guarantee which would allow the Building Societies to extend 100% mortgages instead of the 90% which was then customary as a maximum.

Mr Brooke, the Minister of Housing and Local Government was at first critical of these proposals. At the Conservative Party conference in October 1958 he spoke of the possibility of the availability of 100% mortgages and suggested that the development would be undesirable in principle since it was healthy that there be at least some element of self-sacrifice involved in the purchase of a house [6]. Only one month after this speech which gave no encouragement to those Conservatives who had been calling for action, the Minister published a White Paper which made several concessions all designed to encourage the wider spread of home ownership [7]. The Government proposals did not correspond exactly to the suggestions made earlier by the back-bench committee, but the objection which the minister had apparently entertained to 100% mortgages at the Conservative Conference was waived and local authorities were permitted to extend such mortgages to home buyers. This meant that the local authority had been selected as the means through which the new mortgage facility would be made available, in preference to the Building Societies on whose behalf the back-bench committee had earlier requested changes in mortgage regulations. But the Building Societies were not forgotten; a scheme was outlined in the White Paper under which the government would lend £100,000,000 to Building Societies for use as loans on older houses. The White Paper proposed that the Building Societies should advance up to 95% of their own valuation on pre-1919 houses, a category of property which they would normally have treated with some degree of circumspection. Since the Government would now be financing indirectly advances on this type of older property, the Building Societies would be enabled to redirect the money which they would have otherwise used in this sector to houses of more recent date. No concession was granted however on the question of Schedule A. In due course the proposals contained in the White Paper were enacted in the House Purchase and Housing Act 1959, and they constituted without doubt an element in the Conservative record to which Conservative candidates in the 1959 election campaign could point with pride.

From time to time between 1951 and 1964 Conservative backbenchers and speakers at party conferences expressed the view that the government was not doing enough for the owner-occupier. But only in the pre-electoral atmosphere of 1958–9, as we have seen, did these demands stimulate any governmental response. Once again as the 1961 election drew near, the government responded to demands, on this occasion from Labour as well as Tory members, and in the 1963 Budget abolished Schedule A income tax. This was a step which was no doubt very popular with owner-occupiers, but which could do nothing to encourage owner-occupation. Most informed comment on housing policy sees nothing but harm in this change, which has added to the tax privileges of the owner-occupier. Such a gain once conceded will be impossible to withdraw. It is significant that the demand for abolition was voiced by all three political parties [8] and that there has since been no one in the political world willing to advocate the re-introduction of Schedule A.

The development of the Labour attitudes towards this sector and more especially the idea of home ownership is particularly interesting since there has been a considerable change since 1951. If one were to attempt to summarize the attitude of the party when in office between 1945 and 1951, one would have to stress at one and the same time that the development of home ownership was not actively fostered and also that the party equally refrained from any intransigent doctrinaire opposition towards home ownership in principle. This attitude is admirably expressed by J. MacColl writing in the mid-fifties: 'There is no fundamental objection to a man owning his own house any more than to owning his own trousers. Private ownership of the personal property making up one's immediate environment has been accepted by even the most doctrinaire Socialists' [9]. But the acceptance in principle of home ownership does not mean that there was no distinction at this time between Labour and Conservative attitudes. Labour had not encouraged ownership actively when in power and they were critical of the expansion of building within the private sector which took place during the fifties, at least at the outset. MacColl goes on: 'The truth is, and we ought to have the courage to say it, that, for the great bulk of the people, the Tory gospel of a property owning democracy is not only a fraud but a dangerous and cruel one' [10]. He also disapproves of the attempt by the Conservative Government to lower the size of the deposit which a buyer normally requires, and feels that workers will be taking on dangerously heavy commitments and incumbering themselves with a wasting asset. Munby, writing at about the same time, expresses many of the same fears and exactly the same acceptance in principle coupled with considerable reserve in practice towards the institution of home ownership. He stresses particularly that owner-occupation complicates enormously the activities of an authority supervising central city re-development [11].

In order to appreciate the transformation in Labour Party attitudes one may contrast the foregoing with the electioneering of Labour Party politicians in the period immediately before the 1964 election and with the actions of the elected Labour Government. In the run-up to the election, as much emphasis was placed on the total annual production of houses by Labour as by Conservative politicians. In the early fifties Labour had scorned this approach and had emphasized that what was more important was the regional distribution of the accommodation provided and the form of tenure which would determine the social group for whose benefit the building was taking place [12]. In 1964 great emphasis was laid upon Labour's intention to bring down the mortgage interest rate. There were also firm undertakings to introduce some form of assistance to the buyer repaying his mortgage. No longer was there any reserve in the party's attitude towards owner-occupation. There was now no talk of excessive mortgage burdens, or of the need to encourage the mobility of labour or of the planning problems posed by owner-occupiers.

Once in power, Labour were as good as their word. The Option Mortgage Scheme was introduced, building for sale continued at a high level although expansion which was planned for failed to materialize, and no attack was made on the acquired privileges of the sector in the form of tax deductibility and Schedule A exemption. Labour's housing programme stressed the need to expand production in the public sector in the short term. But in contrast it was stated of the private sector: 'The expansion of building for owner occupation on the other hand is normal; it reflects a long term social advance which should gradually pervade every region' [13]. And again, adding arguments of convenience to those of principle: 'The Government strongly supports the movement towards extended owner occupation which brings with it a standard of maintenance and repair by no means always found in privately rented houses [14]. We have here a very profound transformation in attitude which goes a long way towards explaining the current political strength of the owner-occupied sector.

Relations between the government and the Building Societies are clearly of key importance in the owner-occupied sector. In the period prior to 1964 there was comparatively little interaction. It is true that the Building Societies were obliged to follow the trend towards higher interest rates which resulted from government policy, but despite occasional expressions of regret this did not cause any serious difficulties for the movement. But from 1964 onwards things began to change.

Between 1964–7 the international difficulties of the pound brought a higher bank rate. On occasions during this period the Chancellor appeared to be at logger-heads with the Building Societies Association in insisting that they reject calls for a higher recommended interest rate [15]. Generally the BSA was willing to cooperate and did, for example, delay an anticipated increase whilst interest rates were examined by the Prices and Incomes Board. Conflict between the Labour Government and the BSA about interest rates always contained a substantial element of shadow-boxing, and was apparently conducted mainly for political effect. Conservative and Labour Chancellors are aware that they cannot ask the Building Societies movement to do any more than delay slightly changes in the interest rate, unless the Government is willing to subsidize their lending more than hitherto and until the acute problems of 1973 neither party was prepared to do this.

The attempt in the early years of the Labour administration to establish a system of indicative planning was not without effect on housing. Mr Crossman made it clear during 1965 that he hoped to establish working relations with the industry and the Building Societies in order that they might work together to avoid the stop-go difficulties of earlier years. He hoped in this way to avoid the difficulties of the fifties and also the physical controls of the immediate post-war period [16]. In this connection the National Federation of Building Trade Employers (NFBTE) attempted to organize a joint approach to the Government with the Building Societies Association. These moves, whether on the part of the Government or by the NFBTE and BSA, did not develop as they were intended to, largely because of the abandonment of the National Economic Plan and the housing target associated with it. Nevertheless, a joint memorandum was submitted to the Chancellor of the Exchequer in January 1967 [17]. It did not receive a very positive response from the Government. The main demand upon which the NFBTE and BSA were able to agree was for a restoration of the 1959 scheme. This the Government felt unable to grant. The NFBTE was also particularly interested in the proposed distribution of the half-million target dwellings for 1970 between the private and public sectors. On this point again the Government was not persuaded to change its view which had been from the first that an approximate distribution of one private to one public dwelling should be maintained. The NFBTE had asked for a target of three hundred thousand houses for the private sector which would, of course, have left two hundred thousand for the public sector. The joint memorandum also asked on behalf of the NFBTE for government assistance to the Building Societies designed to enable them to advance 100% mortgages over a greater span of years and also perhaps at lower interest rates. These are constant preoccupations of the building industry, particularly at times when the private sector is not expanding, but they are not generally viewed sympathetically by either Conservative or Labour governments and the Building Society movement is itself reluctant to accept aid since, with good reason, it is of the belief that in the long term at least its independence would be compromised in this way. As we have already seen, any such tendency is strongly opposed by the movement. The only point on which the Chancellor was able to give any satisfaction, and it was a small point, was his willingness to recommend to the banks that they be as helpful as possible with bridging loans for house purchasers and also that they be prepared wherever possible to help out builders in temporary cash difficulties [18].

I have already drawn attention to the fact that from 1964 onwards, as a result of increasing economic difficulties, contact and interaction between the government and the Building Societies increased. The importance of national economic policy for the house-building industry and the Building Societies was once again underlined by events during the period of the Heath Conservative Government.

In May 1971 the Bank of England issued *Competition and Credit Control* [19]. This document explained new government policy which was now designed to encourage competition between the banks. Little notice was taken of this change by those interested in housing at first, but its importance became only too clear in 1973 when the Building Societies learnt that depositors with Barclays Bank were receiving a higher rate of interest than the Building Societies were offering. They explained to the Government, which was already worried about the unpopularity of rapidly rising interest rates, that if nothing was done to change the rate which Barclays were offering they would have to raise their own rates considerably [20]. They did not wish to do so and succeeded in persuading the Government to intervene to prevent competition developing between the banks and the Building Societies and thus reversing the policy adopted two years earlier [21].

This was a spectacular dimonstration, not of the political strength of the BSA as a pressure group, but of the willingness of a Conservative Government to sacrifice a great deal and make an about-turn in the interests of owner-occupiers. Despite the political importance of these events, there is no sign here of any change in the uncontroversial character of policies promoting owner occupation. The Labour Party, although ready enough to deride U turns, supported this intervention on behalf of the Building Societies.

Events in 1973 and 1974 have further underlined the political weight of owner-occupiers as a class. For the first time ever, a Conservative Government in 1973 made a cash grant to the Building Societies in return for an undertaking to delay an anticipated increase in the lending rate, and the 1974 Labour Government has continued this policy on a much larger scale [22].

We are now in a position, having examined the course of events in the two countries under study, to attempt an explanation of differing patterns of policy development with particular regard to those factors which are operative in the owner-occupied sector.

## References

1. *See* above p. 155.
2. *The Financial Times*, 9 March 1951.
3. *See* table IX.
4. *The Times*, 23 May 1958.
5. *The Times*, 1 August 1958.
6. *The Times*, 9 October 1958.
7. *House Purchase – Proposed Government Scheme*, Cmnd. 571 (H.M.S.O., November 1958).
8. *The Times*, 22 June 1960.
9. J. MacColl, *Policy for Housing* (Fabian Society, 1954), p. 13.
10. ibid., p. 15.
11. D.L. Munby, *Home Ownership* (Fabian Society, 1957).
12. *H.C. Deb.*, Vol. 494, cols. 2253–63, 4 December 1951.
13. *The Housing Programme 1965–70*, Cmnd. 1838 (H.M.S.O., November 1965), p. 8.
14. ibid., p. 13.

15. *The Times*, 20 January 1965.
16. *The Times*, 2 July 1965.
17. *The Times*, 24 and 26 January 1967.
18. *The Times*, 7 February 1967.
19. *Competition and Credit Control*, Bank of England, May 1971.
20. *The Times*, 2, 27 and 30 August 1973.
21. *The Times*, 12 September 1973.
22. *The Times*, 5 April 1973 and 15 June 1974.

# XIV

# The Owner-Occupied Sector: Conclusion

It will be the task of this chapter to analyse the differences in the patterns of policy development which may be observed with respect to the owner-occupied sector in Britain and France and to attempt some explanation of these differences. It is necessary first, however, to clarify exactly what is meant in the two cases by the owner-occupied sector since the parallel is not exact.

In the British case there is no difficulty as the sector, judged from the legal and financial point of view, is extremely homogeneous. The fact that in Britain at the more expensive end of the market some finance may be provided by insurance companies rather than the Building Societies, and at the other end that some may come from local authorities, has very little political importance and does not affect the basic homogeneity of the sector. The Building Societies dominate and, when other institutions lend, they do so on terms very similar to those offered by the Building Society movement.

The French situation, as we have already observed with regard to other sectors, is much more complicated. Without attempting to be comprehensive one may reasonably distinguish three subsectors within the owner-occupied sector. Starting at the lower level of income and price, one has the sector financed predominantly by the *Crédit Foncier* through the system of the Special and Family Loans the availability of which is limited by an income ceiling for the house buyer. Secondly, one has a sector, that of the Deferred Loans, in which the *Crédit Foncier* and private bank finance both play an important part. In this sector there is no restriction regarding the income of the beneficiary but there may be specifications affecting the type of construction. Thirdly, there is the unaided sector which relies entirely on various forms of privately available finance, predominantly the personal savings of the purchaser and the bank loans which he may obtain on mortgage.

The basic contrast which we have observed in other sectors holds for owner-occupation although, in this case, the differences are perhaps less marked. It will be remembered that we have already established contrasted patterns of policy development. In Britain, one sees political events impinging on housing policy, and this has meant that successive periods in time, each with its own characteristic policies, can be easily distinguished. In France, on the other hand, because of a variety of factors which make change more difficult to bring about, there is much greater rigidity of policy. The characteristically British pattern is observable in the owner-occupied sector in the late forties and early fifties but operates no longer because the Labour Party has ceased to be hostile to the expansion of home ownership [1]. This means that the sector is much less controversial than it was and, hence, tends to be insulated from political life. In the previous chapter we observed that there were some signs in the mid-sixties that the owner-occupied sector was being drawn back into the political debate. But as previously explained, much of the conflict between Conservative and Labour Governments on the one hand and the Building Society movement on the other has been more apparent than real, and the Option Mortgage Scheme, the operation of which began in 1968, was uncontroversial. It remains true, therefore, that the owner-occupied sector is now much less politically controversial than it was and, as a result, French and British patterns of policy development are now more similar in this sector. But convergence is far from complete. There is the same resistance to change in France that we have described in other sectors. In the owner-occupied sector the obstacles to innovation in France are illustrated particularly by the events surrounding the rising bank rate of 1957, the attempted reforms of late 1963, the intentions of which were largely contradicted by the reverse turn carried out by the Government in the summer of 1965, and most important of all by the interminable difficulties with which special savings schemes have been confronted. This impression is not perhaps as overwhelming in this sector as elsewhere since the picture of immobility must be modified by certain important and real innovations the equivalent of which it is difficult to find in other sectors. One thinks here particularly of the changes in the Bank of France's discount rules and the new legal provisions which have enabled the government to create, since 1966, a mortgage market for funds of private origin. Nor should one forget the *Logécos*, established in 1953 and abolished ten years later, and the fact that an effective special savings scheme has finally emerged. One sees then some of the same rigidities which had already been observed in the French system although they are less marked in this sector.

This chapter has so far been concerned to clarify what is meant by owner-occupation in Britain and France, and to summarize different patterns of policy development. We are now in a position to pass from description to explanation and this task is best begun by examining the role of general ideas, or ideology, as an influence on policy. In sectors previously examined we concluded that ideology was much more important in Britain than in France. This is also true of the owner-occupied sector.

We have already had occasion to remark on the British Conservative Party's insistence on the theme of ownership. It should be made clear that the Conservative approval of this form of tenure as being the most desirable, although no doubt connected with their attitude towards wider economic questions, should in no way be confounded with a generally liberal approach to economic problems. As far as housing is concerned, Conservatives applaud ownership not so much because the provision of housing within this sector is accomplished by the free enterprise system but much more because ownership is regarded as desirable for its own sake. The contrast between the two great British parties is not one of for and against. It is simply that, for the Conservatives, home ownership is a theme of party propaganda whereas for the Labour Party it is not. To the reader familiar with the British situation these attitudes may seem the natural form of the debate between Right and Left but an examination of the French case shows this to be not entirely true. One does not find the same insistence on the merits of ownership coming from French parties of the Right. There has never been, for example, an equivalent in France to the Tory slogan of the early fifties of a property-owning democracy. The speeches of the French Prime Minister and the Minister responsible for housing policy in the great debate in the National Assembly in June 1971 do not contain a single reference to the merits of home ownership as such [2]. The whole emphasis is on the achievements of the Government in terms of the quantity of housing which has been built, and on the practical reforms which are submitted for the approval of Parliament. The only intrusion of more general ideas and principles into a debate which throughout concentrated heavily on practical reforms was the approval by M. A. Chalandon of the principle of selectivity of aid. Some Gaullist back-benchers did introduce a more doctrinaire tone into the debate, but they concentrated not on the virtues of home ownership but on criticism of the unjustified privileges and inefficiency of the HLM organizations [3]. If one searches in France for attitudes equivalent to those which are widespread in the British Conservative Party, the best one can do is to distinguish a little-known group of Conservatively minded thinkers and economists [4]. This group, from time to time, does issue statements and attempts to persuade governments of the benefit of ownership and also of the practicability and desirability of encouraging house rather than flat construction. But it is significant that their views have not been endorsed by any major political group, and also that their ideas concentrate much more on the distinction between flats and houses than between renting and owning.

The attitude of the Right and moderate Right in France, regardless of party affiliation, appears to be that house ownership, though no doubt desirable, provides no magic solution, and that in fact tenure is largely determined by economic circumstances upon which the Government can only exercise limited influence. Whereas a British Conservative would always hold out the hope of continually expanding home ownership within the population, his French political equivalent would tend to argue, as have successive reports of the Housing Commission within the French planning organization, that a wide spread of incomes requires an equally wide variety of housing provision, each type of housing being financed in a manner appropriate to the income of intended occupants. In this way, it is argued, upward social mobility in the housing sector is encouraged since each sector is not too far, in terms of the necessary annual cost, from its neighbouring sector. In the French view, any attempt to rely too heavily on home ownership and to concentrate on making all new rented accommodation available for lower income groups, which is broadly speaking the British Conservative approach to housing problems, would risk creating impassable barriers between the rented and owned sectors. They would also stress that many reasonably wealthy families may not wish to tie themselves to a house or flat and also that their conditions of employment may demand a degree of mobility which is not easily compatible with home ownership.

The Left's attitude towards the owner-occupied sector also deserves attention. In neither France nor Britain do the parties of the Left attack ownership as in any way anti-social. The French Socialist Party under the Fourth Republic was always favourable to the development of this sector, although always more concerned with the HLM sector, and, when in power, the party observed a scrupulous neutrality as between the different sectors of housing provision [5]. The French Communist Party was never in favour of national ownership of all housing accommodation, even in the immediate post-war period and, as we have seen, although initially opposed to privately financed construction, the party now accepts both the unaided and the *Crédit Foncier* sectors [6]. There is, however, one point on which the Left challenges government policy with regard to the sector under discussion, and it is also a point which distinguishes the French Left from its British counterpart. We have already noticed that the banks have, especially since 1966, played a rapidly expanding role in the financing of housing provision in France. This activity arouses the hostility of the Left, not with respect to the tenure and type of housing provided, but because they object to the high rate of interest which banks charge, frequently 12% or above, and they also object to the concentration of power which, they allege, is involved in increasing banking involvement [7]. The occasion for the adoption of such an attitude does not arise in Britain because of the non-profit-making character of the Building Societies. Even the left-wing of the Labour Party is basically sympathetic to the Building Society movement, although it may be occasionally critical. One may judge the extent of intransigent left-wing Labour hostility to the Building Societies by the support given to a motion promoted on the back benches in 1966. This motion called for the nationalization of the societies but received only eleven signatures [8].

We may now ask ourselves whether these ideological differences can contribute to the explanation of different patterns of policy development. The evidence seems to suggest that, with respect to this particular sector, political attitudes, at least in the sense used here of attitudes of parties or currents of political opinion, are not of great importance. In Britain, both parties have left the sector very much alone and therefore such differences as exist between them have had no practical results. One might have thought that the clear and sincere preference of Conservatives for home ownership would have produced, at least from time to time, legislation designed to favour this form of tenure. This, with the minor exception of the House Purchase and Housing Act of 1959, has not proved to be the case. The main reason for this is certainly that the sector has flourished and that there is very little which its satisfactory development has ever demanded from government, except the maintenance of an extremely favourable status quo. The non-doctrinaire attitude of the French Right towards home ownership is naturally not such as to have an impact on policy. As for the Left, even the Socialist-dominated coalitions of the Fourth Republic allowed the sector to develop, believing that, given the seriousness of the crisis, any form of housing provision which could add to the annual total was worthwhile. The issue which has since become of some political importance, that of banking involvement, did not arise during the fifties as banks then used all their available funds for industrial investment, and the owner-occupied sector was almost entirely financed by the *Crédit Foncier*.

One of the obstacles to change in this sector in France – inability to resolve differences existing between different ministries – may be disposed of quickly since, although it has great importance in explaining the slow appearance of special savings schemes, it is not a factor which often proves decisive. This is not to say that the same sort of difficulty does not from time to time arise in other connections. For example, during the period of M. J. Maziol's responsibility for housing (1962–5), there were clear signs of differences of opinion between him and the Minister of Finance. These concerned the establishment of the mortgage market. The Housing Minister appeared to wish to move much faster and to open the market much more widely than the Minister of Finance thought advisable [9]. Another interesting example of the same general phenomenon may be taken from the period of M. P. Courant's responsibility in 1953 when the *Logécos*, and the first abortive savings scheme, were established. The spurt of innovation which was a consequence of his brief six-month period of responsibility at the ministry can be explained if one pays attention to the minister's earlier career. M. Courant had previously occupied a minor ministerial post at the Ministry of Finance and it would appear that he retained some of his personal influence within the ministry and some of his contacts among senior civil servants. These assets served him well when he arrived in his new post. With respect to differences of this sort which appear between different ministries, it is important to bear in mind, for comparative purposes, that a one-party government will always have substantial advantages over a coalition, and also that the clear ideological preferences of the British party make the resolution of personal or departmental differences within the Cabinet much easier than they might be in other circumstances.

Thus far we have rejected ideology as an important determinant of policy, and also concluded that interdepartmental differences, although occasionally critical, are not a factor the influence of which is constantly felt. But we are now in a position to examine what appears to be the most decisive element determining the manner in which the British and French governments develop their policies with respect to this sector. This factor is the character of the financial institutions principally involved and their relation with the public authorities.

The British case of the Building Societies is extremely clear. There was a time when difficult questions arose between the Building Societies and the Inland Revenue Commissioners, but these concerned taxation only and housing policy as such was kept out of these discussions [10]. The Building Societies never enter the debate on housing policy unless forced to do so by events outside their control. Such a posture is natural for institutions which consider themselves fairly treated and in a position to expand their activities without serious hindrance. The way in which the Building Societies have contributed to the uncontroversial character of the owner-occupied sector is well brought out if we compare them with the *Crédit Foncier*.

The French-British comparison is clarified if one compares the position of a borrower from a Building Society with that of a *Crédit Foncier* client. In the former case, the society includes in the conditions of the mortgage a clause which permits modification of the interest rate charged during the period of repayment. When modification becomes necessary in Britain, the rate is changed normally without serious political difficulties. The absence of popular resistance is due partly to a technical factor. The resources of the societies often permit them to offer mortgagees the possibility of an extended period of repayment rather than an increase in monthly charges. But there is also a political factor of great importance. The Building Societies are clearly private institutions. They advertise for customers and for investment in a way which clearly indicates to the general public that they are commercial institutions comparable to banks or other forms of business enterprise. Given this context, an aggrieved client of a Building Society is placed in a somewhat difficult situation. He, or those who represent him, cannot easily complain of the interest rate demanded. If he wishes to challenge an increased interest rate, he is bound to call into question not simply the rate of interest charged but the whole status of the lending institution and its relation to the State.

The situation of a *Crédit Foncier* client is quite different. He is aware from the outset, if somewhat vaguely, that the institution with which he is dealing is of a public character. Its name, the *Crédit Foncier de France*, clearly indicates this. The events of 1957 show clearly the difficulties for the government which arise from such a situation. The pattern of events on this occasion and the restraint on government action thus revealed are quite straightforward. The public is aggrieved, representatives feel that these complaints are justified, the government feels it necessary to make some gesture of conciliation, and the rules governing the operation of the *Crédit Foncier* are accordingly modified. The situation in the 1963–5 period is somewhat more complicated although the essential difference between the French and British cases remains constant. The complaints on this occasion do not come from a defined aggrieved group but from a variety of sources: the building industry and its representative institutions, currents of political opinion generally favourable to the interest of the middle classes and wealtheir sections of the community, and the political opposition as a whole which is able to criticize the Government for permitting a slackening of the expansion of house building in a pre-electoral period. The events of 1963–5, and the about-turn which the Government was then forced to make, are made more comprehensible if we recall a factor to which reference has already been made. This is the differing character of state intervention in housing in France, an intervention which has never been defended on the grounds of aiding the disadvantaged but which is rather justified on simple pragmatic grounds of efficacy or on the basis that aid is used to correct injustices existing between different groups none of which is perhaps in a position of absolute need. When intervention has this character, it is much more difficult for the government to resist pressure for its extension because the rationale for existing arrangements is much less clear-cut.

It may be objected against the above argument that it explains obstacles to change in France and the lack of controversy in Britain but not why some French initiatives have been successfully carried through. This objection turns on the most important recent innovation, the inauguration of the mortgage market, open to a number of private banking institutions and controlled by the *Crédit Foncier*. In fact this initiative was distinguished from most other changes in housing policy in two important respects, both of which help to explain the Government's success. Firstly, the innovation did not change existing arrangements or impose new burdens on the existing system. The innovation was only designed to supplement existing arrangements and perhaps make available new facilities for those groups who could afford them. Logically, of course, any change must involve a transfer of some sort. But there is an obvious difference between the sort of adjustment which the Government had previously made in interest rates and lending terms, and the establishment of a system whereby the banks might shift some resources from industrial investment into housing. In 1957 and again in the events of 1963–5, vested interests were threatened, whereas the establishment of a mortgage market did not affect any identifiable group or institution adversely.

The second important difference concerned the character of the institutions through which the State was working. The private and semi-private French banks are accustomed to constant cooperation with the Bank of France. They naturally enjoy some autonomy but also accept, as a necessary part of their day-to-day working, the influence of the Bank of France which must supervise their activities in the interest of the economy as a whole. The relation is therefore one of constant managerial supervision rather than one of occasional important innovation from above. A relation of this sort is obviously much more conducive to rapid adaptation.

But there are other ways in which the character of financial institutions affects politics. We have already seen that banking intervention in France attracts left-wing hostility, whereas the non-profit-making status of the Building Societies protects them from this sort of criticism. Again, the French government must make decisions which affect in a most direct manner the way in which the banks distribute their funds between housing and industrial investment. The government can affect banking decisions by altering the discount facilities for different types of loan made available by the Bank of France. The British government possesses much less direct means for affecting this balance, since money invested by a saver in a Building Society can only be channelled into house purchase.

Although it is true that the private status of the Building Societies and the fact that they invest only in loans for house purchase are two powerful bulwarks protecting them from political controversy, they are not a sufficient protection in the most difficult circumstances. As we have already seen, there was occasional conflict over the interest rate between Labour and the Building Societies in the mid-sixties, and acute anxiety about Building Society rates on the part of the Tory Government in 1973 which led finally to a grant of fifteen million pounds. In my view this was a period of exceptional economic instability and in future there will be less important interaction between government and the Building Societies and the sector is likely to avoid government intervention and the controversy which inevitably surrounds it.

But, perhaps, of all the forms of interaction between financial institutions and politics, the most important is the conflict which existed in France, particularly in the 1950s, between the financial interests of the State and the needs of the housing market. We have already seen how the vested interest of the State in the *Chèque Postaux* and the *Caisse Nationale d'Epargne* for many years blocked the development of an effective savings incentive scheme for housing. A very similar conflict of interest limited seriously the rate of expansion of the operations of the *Crédit Foncier* during the 1950s. These were years of unbalanced budgets when the government often had to borrow on a large scale. It is little to be wondered at if, in these circumstances, the resources of the *Caisse des Dépôts et Consignations* were used firstly to finance government borrowing in general and only after this need had been satisfied, to provide funds for the *Crédit Foncier* [11].

It is true, of course, that any government must decide on a priority, balancing its own general needs against those of particular policy sectors. But different institutional arrangements in Britain render the conflict between housing investment and other forms of investment less acute. There has always been a tacit convention, greatly reinforced by the prestige of the Building Societies and the political saliency of housing, according to which the Building Societies should not suffer unduly from competition, either from private or public institutions, in attracting savings. Tory intervention in 1973 to protect the Societies against competition from the banks bears witness to this. Once savings have been placed with a Building Society, there is no way in which the government can avoid their being employed to finance house purchase.

In France, the State has more responsibility for financing housing and a more direct say in the way in which resources are allocated. This means, in certain political and economic circumstances, that housing suffers. In Britain, intervention cannot so easily allocate resources as between sectors because the Building Societies are only involved in housing and because there is no politically feasible way in which savings can be directed away from the societies into other hands.

How do the findings in this chapter relate to those concerning the other sectors of housing provision? In both countries we have observed that this sector arouses less emotion that the other two. This absence of fundamental political conflict reduces the role of the political parties, which can be decisive in other sectors. We also find in the owner-occupied sector that there is an absence of clearly articulated interests and opposed groups whose presence would complicate the government's task. We have discovered some interesting differences, on the Right and Left, in the ideological approach to the problems of the sector but have concluded that these differences do not have a direct impact on policy. On the other hand, interdepartmental conflict, already shown up as an important factor, is particularly influential in this sector. This is clearly because owner-occupation involves substantial private borrowing and therefore the departments responsible for the housing programme and for general economic policy are both concerned.

But perhaps the most important conclusions concerning the owner-occupied sector have been those which relate the working and structure of financial institutions to the facts of political life. I think it especially important to stress these institutional factors because a policy study such as this is particularly well adapted to revealing their significance. A study which confines itself to those processes and institutions, which are most obviously recognized as political, will often fail to show up the importance of other factors. Conventionally, political analysts have seen institutions like the Building Societies or the banks, whether private or public, as only marginally relevant to the study of politics. If any account was taken of them at all, it was as instruments for the execution of policy. What I have tried to show is that they are fundamental in the policy formation process, not in the direct political manner described by the pressure group theorists, but because they are the environment in which government policy must work, and hence they constrain it.

This chapter has attempted to examine one sector and to explain its political characteristics. It has, I think, made clear that in some respects one may observe the operation of factors which had already been indentified earlier on, but it also brings to the surface some new elements in our understanding. It will be the task of the following chapter to integrate findings and produce conclusions of a more general character which may serve to illuminate the British and French policy-making process.

*References*

1. *See* chapter XIII.
2. Debate of 10 June 1971, *J.O.*, *Débats*, pp. 2642–3 and 2643–9.
3. Speech by M. Henri Collette (UDR), Debate of 11 June 1971, *J.O.*, *Débats*, pp. 2747–8.
4. '*L'Académie des Sciences Morales, Combat*, 11 June 1963.
5. R.H. Duclaud-Williams, 'The Politics of Housing in Britain and France', D. Phil thesis, University of Sussex, 1974, pp. 195–9.
6. *Le Monde*, 24–25 October 1963. The PCF even accepts the institution of the ILN: *L'Humanité*, 4 March 1966.
7. *Changer la Vie—Programme de Gouvernement du Parti Socialiste* (Flammarion, 1972), p. 145; *Parti Communiste Français, Changer de Cap — Programme pour un Gouvernement Démocratique d'Union Populaire* (Editions Sociales, 1971), pp. 201–4.
8. *The Times*, 16 December 1966.
9. *Le Monde*, 17 September 1965.
10. A. Nevitt, *Housing, Taxation and Subsidies* (Nelson, 1966), pp. 50–4.
11. G. Houist, *Rapport présenté au nom du Conseil Economique, Avis et Rapports du Conseil Economique*, 21 August 1953; *Rapport Général et Rapports Spéciaux Annexes de la Commission de l'Habitation du Ve Plan—Rapport Special relatif au Financement*, 1966.

# XV

# The Politics of Housing in Britain and France

It has proved convenient in this study to compare the housing policies of Britain and France sector by sector. Consequently it will be my aim in this chapter to draw together the conclusions which have already been stated with respect to the three sectors examined, and also to raise certain questions relating to housing as a whole. I shall attempt to concentrate particularly on those explanatory factors whose importance, it seems to me, is made apparent by a comparative analysis of policy-making.

Traditionally, students of politics have asked themselves the question: 'Where does power lie?'. In more contemporary terms, observers of British politics, for example, may ask themselves whether the power of the Prime Minister has grown at the expense of the power of the Cabinet. Writers on contemporary French politics, in much the same vein, attempt to assess to what extent new constitutional arrangements, in force since 1958, have produced a transfer of power from the National Assembly to the presidential executive. I have been concerned here not to describe political systems in their entirety but rather to observe and attempt to explain their operation in a particular policy area. It might seem at first that such a change in focus does not necessarily imply an alteration in the basic question which has to be answered. If one is to explain the course of policy development, it might be argued, it is clearly necessary to locate power since it will be those institutions or individuals exercising power which will influence the development of policy.

On occasions, I have found it useful to follow this approach. For example it was observed when discussing the development of policy in France with respect to public housing that the UNFO–HLM, acting as a representative of the HLM movement as a whole, had considerable influence on the way in which public housing policy developed. There have been other occasions when it has been possible to point to pressure groups that have some influence. Such influence was clearly observable in the French decisions respecting forms of housing finance taken in the summer of 1965 which proved so popular with the building industry and with groups who saw themselves as defenders of the middle class. On the other hand it was concluded after an examination of the privately rented sector that, for various reasons, landlord and tenant interests were not particularly influential in either Britain or France in affecting rent control legislation. I have also pointed to the importance of the political party as a crucial determinant of policy in Britain although this is not a factor of great significance in the French case. These examples have been cited in order to show that, in a comparative study of policy development, it is useful to follow the traditional path in political analysis and attempt to locate power. But other aspects of this study have pointed to the limitations of this approach. Instead of asking who has power or what institutions are capable of exercising power, it has often been necessary to ask, instead, to what factors we can point in order to explain the pattern of policy development. The answers given to this question have proved to be the most important and interesting part of this study and it therefore seems proper to enlarge here on the general type of explanation which has proved most appropriate in a policy-making study.

The examination of policy in a particular area has pointed in the first place to the extent to which policy development is affected by the special characteristics of the subject of policy. In general studies of policy-making this is a factor which tends to be ignored [1] but if the focus, instead, is on a particular sector of policy, such as education, health or housing, the question naturally arises as to whether this particular policy area does not possess characteristics which influence the way in which policy develops. There has been ample evidence in earlier chapters of the existence of such factors in the case of housing although their impact is different in the British and French cases.

In any modern industrial society housing is likely to be seen as divided into three sectors: owner-occupation, public housing, and privately rented housing. Each of these sectors stands in a different relation to the State and poses different problems for policy-makers. At a number of points this study has brought out the importance of this division into different sectors and also of the interaction between sectors. In the British case we have observed that the question of

income distribution is always inextricably involved with conflict
over housing policy and that therefore tension is constantly created
by the comparison of the respective financial advantages and dis-
advantages enjoyed by each sector. The most important example of
the significance of this sectoral interaction is found in the British
case in the origins of the rent allowance and rebate scheme established
by the Conservative Government to provide financial assistance
for private and public tenants. The 1957 Conservative Rent Act
adopted as a final aim the establishment of an uncontrolled market in
privately rented accommodation. This implied that private tenants
would eventually pay the full market price for their accommodation.
At the same time existing subsidies provided for the public sector
continued in operation and, in 1961, a general subsidy was re-
established for the public sector. In this way Conservative policy
created an anomaly because the private tenant was losing the benefit
of rent control, whilst the council tenant contined to receive some
subsidy.

It seemed for a time as if the 1965 Rent Act had dealt with this
problem by providing security of tenure in the private sector and
bringing to an end the free market. But, although public and private
tenants were now placed on a more equal footing, differences remained, which were not easy to justify. While at least some public
tenants were entitled to rent rebates from their local authorities,
there was no comparable provision whatsoever in the private sector.
When, therefore, the Conservative Government of 1970–74 decided
to establish a national Rent Rebate Scheme for the whole of the
public sector, it was inevitable that some comparable provision be
made for tenants of privately rented accommodation and this was
done through the 1972 Housing Finance Act. In 1957 the Conservatives seemed to be moving towards a position in which neither
private nor publicly rented sectors would receive special advantages.
But the operation of disengagement proved politically unfeasible
in both sectors. Once a turnabout had been accepted in the public
sector and it was admitted that subsidies would continue to be important for council housing, the future of decontrol in the private
sector was compromised. Again, once both sectors were clearly taken
out of the free market, as they were after 1965, it was inevitable that,
if rent rebates were appropriate to the public sector, then they must
eventually be also in the private sector. What one is observing here
is both a process of sectoral interaction and also the working out of
the logical implication of principles generally accepted or decisions
taken [2].

I should not wish to give the impression that the division of housing provision into three sectors will produce the same political consequences in one system as in another, but it would appear that the factor of sectoral interaction will have some effect in almost any situation. Clearly, in Britain there is a particular sensitivity to the broad comparisons which may be established between one sector and another. In France, for a number of reasons the factor of sectoral interaction is much less important. It may be useful here to summarize some of our earlier findings on this point. In the first place, it is clear that in Britain, at least with respect to the council and owner-occupied sectors, interaction becomes particularly important because of the association with class. In the French case, such an association is difficult since the public sector is much smaller and can in no sense be regarded by the French as a typical form of housing provision for working-class families. It is also important to remember that, although the basic threefold division exists in French housing just as it does in the British case, it is overlaid in France by a much more complicated structure of financial, legal and administrative arrangements. The consequence is that whereas in Britain one has broad categories of housing provision which in many cases can be associated with class loyalties and ideologies, in France one has a more complicated situation in which such simplifications are less easily made. The fact that sectoral interaction is less important in France than in Britain helps to explain the greater stability of French housing policies.

There are other factors which should not be overlooked in any explanation of why sectoral interaction is less important in France than in Britain. The French State remains much more *dirigiste* than the British and this factor, coupled with the traditional weakness of private forms of finance for house purchase in France, means that much state intervention, which is justified in Britain as a form of social aid, is regarded in France as necessary for economic management. Such an attitude has a stabilizing effect. The question of who is benefiting from particular forms of state aid is secondary since the aim of intervention is to promote construction rather than to aid any particular social group. Since such a wide variety of groups benefit in some degree from this state aid and intervention, it is correspondingly difficult to find any social group or section of political opinion which will support reduction and concentration of state aid. Liberal doctrines on social and economic policy are traditionally weak in France and do not find even today automatic acceptance even within the ranks of the most conservative political parties.

I have paid considerable attention to the special character of housing as an area of policy-making, its division into three major sectors of provision, and the political consequences of such divisions, because I believe that these are the sort of factors which a policy study can bring out but which can be easily overlooked in other studies. The same may be said with respect to the structure of executive institutions in the field of housing. At numerous points in this study I have had occasion to refer to the importance of this factor. Institutions which are conceived of as being concerned only with the execution of policy do in fact have an important effect on its formulation. Numerous examples of this process at work may be found in both Britain and France.

I have described how the Labour Party in 1953 and 1954 came to adopt a policy of the municipalization of privately rented accommodation as a policy designed to deal with the problem of poor standards of repair and maintenance. In this connection it is important to remember that the adoption of this policy was not an ideological gesture. It was a policy which, although in a moderated form, was approved at this time by the Conservative Minister for Housing and Local Government, Mr Macmillan. It was a policy which was realizable because it based itself on the local authorities and their experience in the building and managing of existing houses on a large scale. It was in fact a policy which some local authorities, within the limits of the finances available to them, had begun to apply under the Attlee Labour Government, although at that time the policy received no official encouragement from the minister with responsibility.

The adoption of municipalization was not only a radical policy in itself but it also had the effect of stiffening Labour's opposition to the 1957 Rent Act. Labour was able to oppose this Act in uncompromising fashion because the party believed that it had an answer to the repairs and maintenance problem. Had this not been so, it would have been more difficult to oppose moderate increases in rents after almost twenty years of fixed private rents. The Labour argument was that it would be necessary to raise rents in order to assist in the provision of repairs and a decent standard of maintenance but that these higher rents should be paid to a local authority which alone could be trusted to carry out the necessary work. One may conclude, therefore, that the character of the local authorities as executive institutions in the field of housing policy, their national coverage, and, above all, their experience in house-building and managing, made municipalization a credible alternative policy and thus greatly assisted in its becoming, for a time, official Labour policy. The French Left has never adopted a policy of municipalization, the means not being to hand, and it has therefore been less well equipped when attempting to oppose rent increases.

In France the nature of executive institutions had tended to restrict rather than enlarge the range of policy choices available to political leaders. In this respect the HLMs are a particularly interesting case. Whereas in Britain the responsibility for the execution of public housing programmes is placed on the elected local authorities, in France the HLM organizations, which have much the same function, are bodies whose leading personnel are appointed by the government. The HLMs were conceived of when first created as bodies outside politics and, despite ample evidence to the contrary, they continue to proclaim that they are not involved in politics. An observer of the very different executive structures which exist in Britain and France would be tempted to conclude that, since the executive authorities, in the former case, are elected and must therefore be under the control of a political party, politics would play a considerable part in local central relations. He might deduce that in France, where HLM officials are not directly responsible to local politicians, relations between centre and locality would be less politicized. In fact, as any reader of this study will by now be clearly aware, the contrary is the case. The leaders of the HLM movement are not only established and experienced operators in the political field but seem also to enjoy considerable power, if only of a negative character. Outside the public sector in France, whether one considers the *Crédit Foncier* or the private banks upon which the State relies increasingly for housing finance, the relation between government and its executive institutions has been much more co-operative and these institutions have therefore had correspondingly less impact on the course of policy development.

Before leaving this subject, one more example of the impact of the character of executive institutions on policy development deserves mention. We have seen how the conspicuous rectitude and non-profit-making character of the Building Societies protect the owner-occupied sector from political controversy in Britain. The Building Societies have deep roots in English social history and, much as it would like to, the French government cannot create even remotely similar institutions. In their absence it must rely on the *Crédit Foncier* and private banks. In the former case, as we have seen, the semi-public character of the institution exposes the government to political pressure coming from borrowers. This pressure, both in 1957 and 1958, and again in 1964 and 1965, had considerable impact on the development of government policy.

No attempt to summarize the most important conclusion of this study would be complete without some reference to pressure groups. I suggested in chapter I that, if one was concerned to explain policy outcomes, it was illogical to focus study on only one of a number of possible explanatory factors. My approach has sought to avoid this difficulty and also the lack of perspective which arises from the use of a case method. But the adoption of this point of view did not presuppose any particular conclusion as to the possible influence on policy of pressure groups. What are, then, the most important findings of the study on this point?

I have first observed that in many areas of housing policy the relevant organized groups do not exist. Owner-occupiers as a group have no organized representation in either Britain or France. Tenants of public and private housing are organized to some extent in France, although rather ineffectively, but almost not at all in Britain. Perhaps an even more significant point than this is that many of the choices facing policy-makers do not involve discriminating between clearly defined groups of citizens. A critical case of this sort is found in the early post-war years, when French politicians preferred to ignore the housing problem and concentrate investment in the so-called productive spheres of investment. Decisions on the allocation of investment were essentially political but it would be very difficult to find an organized group, or even a definable group of individuals, whose interests would have been served by investment in housing and damaged by a concentration on industrial investment. All social classes suffered from the shortage of housing, although naturally to different degrees, and all certainly stood to benefit from an expansion of French industry. Any association such as the CNPF, representing industrial employers as a whole, must inevitably find it extremely difficult to recommend the encouragement of investment in one branch of industry rather than another: in this case in the building industry rather than manufacturing. Our account has made it clear that the answer given to this question of whether to invest in industry or to balance investment as between industry and housing was quite different in the French and British cases. As I have suggested, the difference in the course of action followed is best explained by reference to the traditionally low saliency of the housing problem as an issue in French politics and its high saliency in Britain since at least 1918.

Although I have suggested that many issues of housing policy are not intrinsically capable of being influenced by pressure groups, there is a particular case, that of landlord-tenant legislation, in which decisions clearly do affect easily defined groups. If there is one area of policy in which we would expect to discover influential pressure groups, it is here. In chapter IV I described how, with great hesitation, French policy has slowly but steadily developed towards a system which is now very favourable to the landlord. Throughout the post-war period, the organizations representing French landlords have of course constantly campaigned for a return to the free market. But it is not the level of their activity, which has been fairly constant, which can explain the way in which policy has evolved. Nor can it be said that tenants have had any influence on policy since the trend of development has been continuously unfavourable to them. It is of course true that tenant opinion has been an important restraining influence on government policy. Any account of events in this field of policy-making, covering the period of the 1950s and 1960s, shows that the government has pursued its aim of disengagement with extreme caution. But the factor which has finally proved decisive in the French case is the need for the government to attract housing investment by high rents. In the British case, since new construction of privately owned housing for rent has long ceased, a quite different solution, and one much more favourable to the tenant, has been possible. Again, although the antagonistic groups are clearly defined, they have not significantly influenced the development of policy. Instead, in the British case, each of the major parties is identified with one of the two groups in question and policy has alternated accordingly. But these alternations have now settled down on a compromise position very different from that which has been reached in France. We have here, in the case of the privately rented sector, another example of the way in which a policy study can bring out factors which are unlikely to emerge in other sorts of political enquiry. Any observer of politics will be concerned with parties and pressure groups, and even to some extent government policy, but he is much less likely to take sufficient account of the political importance of the way in which new housing is financed.

I have often referred to the high political salience of housing in Britain and its relative obscurity as an area of political controversy in France. This difference affects policy-making in many ways, but in particular it obviously sustains stability, or if one prefers, rigidity, in France, and encourages change in Britain. It is therefore one of the most important factors giving rise to the contrast in patterns of policy development which we have observed. Why is there this difference of salience?

Some of the points which need to be borne in mind in answering this question have been suggested by earlier discussion. Salience is clearly sustained by the polarized character of provision in Britain and its association in many people's minds with the issues of class and income distribution. It is also clear from figures provided by Hampton's study of politics in Sheffield that the existence of public housing itself stimulates its occupants to contact political representatives in housing issues [3]. This is relevant because publicly owned housing constitutes about one third of the British stock, which is twice the French figure. It is also clearly important that housing in Britain is a major local government function, whereas it is largely kept out of local politics in France. In this connection it should particularly be borne in mind that the subsidies or income transfers between owner-occupiers and council tenants are much more visible when the tax used to do this is the rates. As many people see it, A is asked to pay more for his house in order that B should pay less for his [4]. Although this process operates in essentially the same way in France, greater reliance on national sources of finance means that it will more often be seen as a process in which all contribute something to a national pool from which all receive something.

Again anyone who is familiar with the day-to-day political debate in Britain and France will have remarked on the policy-centred character of the former, and the necessarily greater concentration on tactical considerations in France. This is a result of the British two-party system which eliminates the tactical element from party relations. The simplification of the French party system which has taken place since 1962 has not as yet attenuated this contrast between British and French politics. Time spent on inter-party relations and their analysis, whether it be between Socialists and Communists, or between Gaullists and their coalition partners, is time that might otherwise be spent on political debate about policy between government and opposition.

Something needs also to be said here about professionalization [5]. Some areas of policy-making have been partially insulated from the party-political world by the claims of professionals to a special competence. This is particularly noticeable in most countries in the educational and medical fields. It is not the case in housing. The absence of professionalization in the field is not particularly significant in France since other mechanisms, already described, reduce the impact of politics on policy, or succeed in making it purely regative. In Britain, however, the importance of this factor is greater, since it seems probably that if housing were more professionalized, this would insulate it to some extent from politics.

This chapter has been so far concerned to emphasize particularly those explanatory factors the importance of which is made clear by a study of policy. But the picture which has been presented would be incomplete if no reference were made to the significance of factors which have always played an important part in political analysis. Little reference has been made in this study to the legislatures. In the British case the explanation for this is that government legislation has seldom been modified in any important respect as a consequence of parliamentary debate. In the French case, the reasons for the comparatively small importance of the National Assembly are different. First among these are the extensive delegated powers which the French government possesses. For example, the government is capable of changing the terms on which the *Crédit Foncier* may grant finance, or altering the rules governing HLM tenant selection, or changing the terms of financial assistance within the public sector, or affecting the size of the free market in privately rented housing, without needing to have recourse to the Assembly for new legislation. There is of course one important exception to this general rule which must be noted and that is the 1948 Rent Act, the content of which was considerably affected by parliamentary discussion and amendment.

At numerous points in this study it has been necessary to refer to the importance of the political party as an influence on policy. This is a factor which is traditionally considered as important and such indeed has proved the case with respect to both British and French post-war housing policies. In the British case the role of the party is too obvious to need underlining. In France the link between party and policy is less obvious but still important. I have pointed to the historical origins of the Gaullist Party and tried to emphasize that its identity was framed essentially in response to colonial and constitutional questions. In both these areas it adopted stands that were markedly different from those of its predecessors and succeeded in introducing important changes in policy. In the social and economic sphere, however, the party differs from other European parties of the moderate Right in that it lacks a clear social and economic identity. There are sharp differences of view within the party as to the direction which future housing policy should take and this inhibits any decisive policy initiatives. The tendency to carry on as before is reinforced by the feeling of precariousness which seems to prevail still in French political life and the lack of discipline within the party. I have also tried to argue that, even when the party is united on the course of action to be followed, it lacks the self-confidence necessary to put through unpopular measures. Such has been the case with respect to the lifting of controls over privately rented accommodation.

It is no easy matter to attempt, as one must, to synthesize the most important conclusions relating to the different patterns of policy development to be observed in French and British housing policy. One can, however, point to a number of factors, all of which appear to reinforce the flexibility and susceptibility to change which we have observed in Britain and which explain the rigidity and stability of policy in France. A fundamental factor is the lower level of political interest in housing as an issue in France, which means that politicians, whether in government or opposition, see less political capital to be made out of the issue. In Britain housing is constantly a subject for political controversy. There is also the apparent weakness of the French state in the face of determined opposition whether based in executive institutions or social groups whose interests seem threatened by new policy initiatives. In France one may also point to intellectual traditions, associated with and embodied in institutional arrangements, which favour a high level of state intervention in the economy in order to encourage economic expansion. When the State sees economic expansion as its basic preoccupation and it is largely succeeding in this aim, there is likely to be only intermittent pressure for substantial changes in economic and social policy. No comparable consensus of economic doctrine concerning the role of the State exists in Britain and the same lack of agreement and consequent instability manifests itself in housing policy. It is also the case that many important changes of housing policy in Britain do not demand accompanying institutional adjustments since the framework provided by the local authorities and the Building Societies is capable of responding to widely different policy orientations. The high level of political interest in housing in Britain makes it impossible to isolate housing issues from general issues of social and economic policy, and politicians in both major parties see many housing issues as raising important questions of income redistribution. These factors, taken in conjunction with others I discussed earlier in this study, reinforce each other and produce the different patterns of policy development which we have observed. The aim of this study has been to describe and explain policy development in two advanced industrial countries. For this reason I have not attempted to judge the success of housing policies and to suggest possible improvements, but it would be wrong of me altogether to ignore some of the wider questions which are inevitably raised by a study of this sort. Housing is something of vital concern to all citizens and a student of housing policy cannot be content with explaining policy decisions. He must also ask himself how what he has observed relates to the functioning of a healthy democracy. In this respect the most obvious question which needs to be answered is: have the more favourable political conditions for the development of housing policy observed in Britain resulted in the British people being better housed than the French?

Without for the moment attempting to say why, it is certainly true, and has been for many years, that the British are better housed than their near neighbours. If one compares for example the amount of space available per thousand of population in the British 1961 and French 1962 censuses, one finds that there were 1423 rooms per thousand in Britain as against 955 in France. This means that the British population enjoys more than 40 per cent more space than the French [6]. This lack of space in France is reflected in more recent figures of acute overcrowding. In the 1962 census, 12.7 per cent of all households were registered as suffering in this way and this figure had only fallen to 8.9 per cent by 1968 [7]. This figure is of course an overall one for the nation as a whole and rises, for example, to 17.4 per cent for young married couples [8]. These housing difficulties are not equally shared by all sections of the population. For example, the liberal professions and senior management have a level of critical overcrowding which is approximately one-seventh of that to be found in the working class [9]. The figures for overcrowding in Britain are of quite another order. In 1966, as measured by a stricter overcrowding standard than that used in France, there were only 1.2 per cent of British households considered overcrowded [10]. Nor is the gap in standard of provision closed if one considers quality rather than quantity. In the early 1960s, 46 per cent of the British housing stock had been built before 1914, as compared with a figure of 62 per cent in France [11].

But it would be wrong to suggest that this difference in level of current provision is solely the consequence of different political circumstances. It is certain that much of the difficulty faced by French policy-makers in recent years is the consequence of neglect between the wars. Even if there had been a political will to improve the housing situation at that time, it is doubtful whether the stagnant French economy could have supported a housing achievement in any way comparable to that of Britain in the 1920s and 30s. Nevertheless, it is significant that the failure to tackle the housing problem between the wars did not cause serious political problems for the public authorities. The Popular Front, for example, showed no particular interest in housing and cannot be credited with any notable legislative achievements in this area. In contrast to this, interwar Labour Governments were much concerned with housing and one of the main achievements of the 1923–4 Government is considered to have been the Whetley Act which involved the long-term planning and provision of subsidy for the public sector. I would suggest, then, that the different level of political concern which we find in Britain has borne fruit in the form of a higher level of housing provision, but that it would be going too far to attribute higher building rates and better housing entirely to political factors. Although, as we have remarked, there has been no period in recent French history when there has been a decisive move to increase investment in housing, there has been a steady increase in the level of state aid and in the size of the housing programme throughout the 1960s and, if this effort is pursued and expanded, it will bear fruit, at least in the long term. At present French housing completions are running well above the British level and, between 1962 and 1970, the share of the French gross national product devoted to investment in housing rose from 5 per cent to 6.6 per cent [12]. The British figure for 1965 was only 3.5 per cent [13]. These figures show that housing is now receiving a much higher priority in France than in the past and the current building programme cannot fail to assist in raising the general level of housing provision, although progress in this field is always extremely slow.

I should like, however, in conclusion, to return to the political aspect of the problem because it seems to me that, in the absence of political changes in France, the scope for improvement in housing conditions will be limited regardless of the expansion of the French economy. Economic progress may render possible the beginning of an attack on the quantitative problem but political change will be necessary if any substantial improvement in the quality of housing is to be achieved. In saying this I refer particularly to our discussion of improvement and repair policies in chapter XI. Although this is a matter which has recently received more attention in France than in the past, there is no sign as yet that the government intends to launch any substantial project of slum clearance, as distinct from urban redevelopment, nor has the decision yet been taken to provide capital grants from public funds to aid towards repair and conversion. Subsidies for this work are available on a small scale but the size of operations is only sufficient at present to scratch the surface of this enormous problem. Publicly financed capital grants to help owners and landlords to improve their property have been a feature of housing policy in Britain for more than 25 years and spending under this head has increased considerably recently. Effective repair and improvement policy is by its nature undramatic. For this reason it is likely to be left alone by government and policies which do not reach to the root of the problem may still continue to be applied. In Britain this danger has been overcome because of the exceptional political importance of housing, but in France this seems unlikely.

I would conclude, therefore, that the greater consciousness of the importance of the housing problem among political leaders in Britain has greatly assisted in the effective search for solutions to the housing problem. Rapid economic expansion in France will not alone be sufficient to remedy housing difficulties. There is here, however, no cause for complacency with regard to the British situation. In some ways the concern which the political parties manifest for housing problems is itself the cause of particular difficulties. The Labour Party champions the development of the council-house sector whilst the Conservatives support owner-occupation. The system which these two parties between them have created favours the development of a polarized form of housing provision which may cater reasonably well for most people but which is crude and inflexible. It has been noted for example that, of the three million dwellings built in the council sector between 1945 and 1966, only 2.3 per cent had more than three bedrooms and were therefore suitable for large families [14]. Nor has there as yet been a sufficient governmental response to the problem of the homeless in central city districts. Nor have any of the British political parties faced up to the problem of discrimination against racial minorities in public and private housing. Perhaps the housing politics of the future in Britain and France will be more concerned with the housing needs of minorities. One can only hope so.

*References*

1. B. Smith, *Policy-making in British Government* (Martin Roberts & Co., 1976).

2. The operation of this process is described in O. Macdonagh, *A Pattern of Government Growth 1800–60* (MacGibbon & Kee, 1961).

3. W. Hampton, *Democracy and Community* (Oxford University Press, 1970), p. 141.

4. This argument was first brought to my attention by Professor Alan Potter.

5. David Donnison and Jim Bulpitt have both made this point in discussion with me.

6. D.V. Donnison, *The Government of Housing* (Penguin Books, 1967), Table I, p. 49.

7. *Rapports des Commissions du VIème Plan 1971–75 – Rapport de la Commission de l'Habitation*, Vol. I, p. 36.

8. *Les Cahiers Français* (La Documentation Française, Nov.–Dec. 1970).

9. P. Consigny *Rapport sur l'Aide Publique au Logement* (Groupe de Travail sur l'Aide Publique au Logement, 1969), p. 15.

10. *Council Housing – Purposes, Procedures and Priorities – Ninth Report of the Housing Management Sub-Committee of the Central Housing Advisory Committee* (H.M.S.O., 1969), p. 8.

11. D.V. Donnison, *The Government of Housing* (Penguin Books, 1967), Table 3, p. 54.

12. *Tendances et Politiques Actuelles dans le domaine de l'Habitation, de la Construction et de la Planification* – Monographie Nationale de la France (Ministère de l'Equipement et du Logement, Juillet 1971), Table Cl.

13. G. Ebrik et P. Barjac, *Logement – Dossier Noir de la France* (Dunod, 1970), p. 77.

14. *Council Housing – Purposes, Procedure and Priorities – Ninth Report of the Housing Management Sub-Committee of the Central Housing Advisory Committee* (H.M.S.O., 1969), p. 92.

# Bibliography

## France

Alphandéry, C., *Les Prêts Hypothécaires* (Coll. 'Que sais-je?' No. 1326, Paris, P.U.F., 1968).

Alphandéry, C., *Pour une Politique du Logement* (Paris, ed. du Seuil, 1965).

Baschwite, J., 'La Lutte contre l'insalubrité', *Notes et Études documentaires*, No. 4051, Jan. 1974.

Bodin, J.J., and Séligmann, N., 'Les changements d'affectation et l'amélioration des logements de 1962 à 1967' *Economie et Statistique*, No. 16, Oct. 1970.

Chaigneau, Y., 'Le Groupement interministériel pour la resorbtion de l'habitat insalubre', *Equipement, Logement, Transport*, Vol. 92, Feb. 1975.

Champion, P., *Le Crédit Foncier de France* (Paris, Editions de l'Epargne, 1966).

Chastagnol, R., 'Les Banques et le Financement à long terme du logement', *Banque*, March and April 1971.

Cosigny, P., *Rapport sur l'Aide Publique au Logement* (Paris, Groupe de Travail sur l'Aide Publique au logement, 1969).

*La Construction et l'Habitat* (Coll. Technique et Démocratie, Paris, Ed., Eyrolles, 1966).

Crivelli, E., and Bouret, J., *Les HLM* (Ed. de l'Actualité Juridique, 1975).

Dary, E., *Financement de la Construction* (Avis et Rapports du Conseil Economique, March 1950).

Dresch, M., *Le Financement du Logement* (Berger-le-Vrault, 1973).

Durif, P., 'Fin 1960, un cinquième des logements loués relèvent de la loi de 1948', *Economie et Statistique*, No. 43, March 1973.

Durif, P., 'Propriétaires et Locataires en 1967', *Economie et Statistique*, No. 3, July-August 1969.

Durif, P., and Allaire, E., 'Le niveau des loyers en 1967 et leur évolution depuis 1963', *Études et Conjoncture*, Vol. XXIII, II, No. 9.

Durif P., and Berniard, S., 'De quelques inégalités entre locataires', *Economie et Statistique*, No. 25, July-August 1971.

Durif, P., and Berniard, S., 'Le logement des jeunes ménages', *Economie et Statistique*, No. 5, October 1969.

*Le Financement du Logement en France et à l'Etranger* (Paris, P.U.F., Centre d'Informations et d'Études du Crédit, 1966).

Hans, M.-E., 'Les conditions de logement au centre des agglomérations', *Economie et Statistique*, No. 55, April 1974.

Hirsch, A., 'Le Logement' in A. Sauvy (ed.), *Histoire Economique de la France entre les deux guerres* (Paris, Fayard, 1972).

Houdeville, L., with Dhuys, J.-F., *Pour une Civilisation de l'Habitat* (Paris, Ed., Ouvrières, 1969).

Houist, G., *Logement des Travailleurs de Faible Revenu* (Avis et Rapports du Conseil Economique, 25 February 1956).

Houist, G., *Rapport présenté au nom du Conseil Economique* (Avis et Rapports du Conseil Economique, 21 August 1953).

*Livre – Politique de l'Habitat.* Table Ronde, 25 September 1969.

*Logements – Immeubles* (Paris, INSEE, 1972).

Malignac, G., 'Le Logement des Faibles: Evincement Progressif et Formation d'un Sous-Prolétariat', *Population*, April-June 1957.

Mathieu, G., 'L'Anarchie des Loyers', *Le Monde*, 4–7 May 1966.

Mathieu, G., *Peut-on loger les Français?* (Paris, Ed. du Seuil, 1965).

Meynaud, J., and Lancelot, A., 'Groupes de Pression et Politique du Logement', *Revue Française de Science Politique*, Vol. VIII, No. 4.

Nora, S., and Eveno, B., *L'Amélioration de l'habitat ancien* (La Documentation Française, 1975).

Pascal, F., *Economie de la Production de Logements* (Paris, Thèse de Sciences Economiques, Université de Paris I, 1971).

*La Politique du Logement en France* (Documents et Études du Centre de Recherches Economiques et Sociales, May-June 1964).

*Rapport Barré, Revue de l'Habitat social*, No. 5.

*Rapport de la Commission de l'Habitation du IVème Plan* (Paris, Imprimerie des Journaux officiels, 1961).

*Rapport du comité habitat du VIIème Plan* (La Documentation Française, 1976).

*Rapport Général et Rapports Spéciaux Annexes de la Commission de l'Habitation du Vème Plan* (Paris, Imprimerie des Journaux Officiels 1966).

*Rapports des Commissions du VIème Plan 1971–75 – Rapport de la Commission de l'Habitation* (Paris, La Documentation Française, 1971).

Riboud, J., *Libéralisme et Financement – Le cas particulier du crédit au logement* (Paris, Ed. de l'Epargne, 1965).

Sauvy, A., 'Les mal-logés', *Population*, Oct.-Dec. 1957.

Stavridis, L., 'Souhaite-t-on être propriétaire ou locataire de son logement?' *Economie et Statistique*, No. 47, July-August 1973.

*Tendances et Politiques Actuelles dans le domaine de l'Habitation, de la Construction et de la Planification* — Monographie Nationale de la France (Paris, Ministère de l'Equipement et du Logement, July 1971).

## Britain

Allaun, F., *Heartbreak Housing* (London, Hodder and Stoughton, 1968).

Barnett, M.J., *The Politics of Legislation: The Rent Act of 1957* (London, Weidenfeld & Nicholson, 1969).

Barr, J., 'Status Village', *New Society*, No. 370, 30 March 1969.

Bowley, M., *Housing and the State 1919–44* (London, Allen & Unwin, 1945).

Burney, E., *Housing on Trial* (London, Oxford University Press, 1967).

Corfield, V.F., and Rippon, G., *Target for Homes* (Conservative Political Centre, 1965).

*Council Housing – Purposes, Procedures, Priorities – Ninth Report of the Housing Management Sub-Committee of the Central Housing Advisory Committee* (London, H.M.S.O., 1969).

Crossman, R.H.S., *The Diaries of a Cabinet Minister* (Hamish Hamilton and Jonathan Cape, 1975).

Cullingworth, J.B., *Housing and Local Government* (London, Allen and Unwin, 1966).

Cullingworth, J.B., *Housing in Transition – A case study in the city of Lancaster, 1958–61* (London, Heinemann, 1963).

Cullingworth, J.B., *Housing Needs and Planning Policy* (London, Routledge and Kegan Paul, 1960).

Donnison, D.V., *The Government of Housing* (London, Penguin Books, 1967).

Donnison, D.V., *Housing policy since the war*, Occasional Papers on Social Administration, No. 1 (London, Codicote Press, 1960).

Donnison, D.V., 'A Housing Service', *New Society*, No. 476, 11 Nov. 1971.

Donnison, D.V., Cockburn, C., and Corlett, T., *Housing since the Rent Act*, An Interim Report from the Rowntree Trust Housing Study, (London, Codicote Press, 1961).

Donnison, D.V., Cockburn, C., Cullingworth, J.B., and Nevitt, A.A. *Essays on Housing*, (London, Codicote Press, 1964).

Eversley, D., *Rents and Social Policy* (London, Fabian Society, 1955).

*Fair Deal for Housing*, Cmnd. 4728 (London, H.M.S.O., July 1971).

*Furnished Rented Accommodation and the Rent Act (1968)*. Labour Party Evidence to the Francis Committee (Dec. 1969).

Gelting, G.H., 'Economic effects of rent control in Denmark', in A.A. Nevitt (ed.), *The Economic Problems of Housing* (London, Macmillan, 1966).

Greve, J., 'Housing policies and prospects', *Political Quarterly*, Vol. XL, No. 1.

Greve, J., *The Housing Problem* (London, Fabian Society, 1961).

Greve, J., *London's Homeless*, Occasional Papers on Social Administration, No. 10 (London, G. Bell and Sons, 1964).

Greve, J., *Private Landlords in England*, Occasional Papers on Social Administration, No. 16 (London, G. Bell and Sons, 1965).

Hampton, W., *Democracy and Community* (London, Oxford University Press, 1970).

Harlow, M., Issacharoff, R., Minns, R., *The Organization of Housing – Public and Private Enterprise in London* (Heinemann, 1974).

*Help towards Home Ownership*, Cmnd. 3163 (London, H.M.S.O., Dec. 1966).

*House Purchase – Proposed Government Scheme*, Cmnd. 571 (London, H.M.S.O., Nov. 1958).

*Houses, The Next Step*, Cmnd. 8996 (London, H.M.S.O., Nov. 1953).

*Housing*, Cmnd. 6609 (London, H.M.S.O., March 1945).

*Housing*, Cmnd. 2050 (London, H.M.S.O., May 1963).

*Housing – Action* (Labour Party, 1967).

*Housing Finance – Present Problem* (O.E.C.D., 1974).

*Housing in England and Wales*, Cmnd. 1290 (London, H.M.S.O., Feb. 1961).

*The Housing Programme for 1947*, Cmnd. 7021 (London, H.M.S.O., Jan. 1947).

*The Housing Programme: 1965–70*, Cmnd. 2838 (London, H.M.S.O., Nov. 1965).

*Increases in Rents of Local Authority Housing*, National Prices and Incomes Board Report, No. 62, Cmnd. 3604 (London, H.M.S.O., April 1968).

*Is the Rent Act Working?* A Transcript. (Shelter, 21 June 1969).

Jennings, J.H., 'Geographical implications of the municipal housing programme in England and Wales, 1919–39', *Urban Studies*, Vol. VIII, No. 2.

*London – Employment, Housing, Land*, Cmnd. 1952 (London, H.M.S.O., Feb. 1963).

MacColl, J., *A Plan for Rented Housing* (London, Fabian Society, 1957).

MacColl, J., *Policy for Housing* (London, Fabian Society, 1954).

Merritt, A.J., and Sykes, A., *Housing Finance and Development – An analysis and programme for reform* (London, Longmans Green, 1965).

Morton, J., 'The defence of ATACC', *New Society*, No. 441, 11 March 1971.

Morton, J., 'Direct Labour', *New Society*, No. 358, 7 August 1969.

Morton, J., 'Raising council rents', *New Society*, No. 359, 14 August 1969.

Morton, J., 'Selling-off council houses', *New Society*, No. 220, 15 December 1966.

Morton, J., 'Selling to tenants', *New Society*, No. 495, 23 March 1972.

Munby, D.L., *Home Ownership* (London, Fabian Society, 1957).

Nelson – Jones, J., *Home Truths on Housing, Costs, Rents and Subsidies*, (The Conservative Political Centre, 1966).

Nevitt, A.A., 'Conflicts in British housing policy', *Political Quarterly*, Vol. XXXIX, No. 4.

Nevitt, A.A., (ed.) *The Economic Problems of Housing* (London, Macmillan, 1966).

Nevitt, A.A., *Housing Taxation and Subsidies – A Study of Housing in the United Kingdom* (London, T. Nelson and Sons Ltd., 1966).

Nevitt, A.A. (ed.), *The Economic Problems of Housing* (London, Macmillan, 1966).

Nevitt, A.A., 'The State of the Social Services: Housing', *New Society*, No. 262, 5 Oct. 1967.

*Old Homes into New Homes*, Cmnd. 3602 (London, H.M.S.O., April 1968).

*Our Older Homes – A Call for Action, Report of the Central Housing Advisory Committee* (London, H.M.S.O., 1966).

*Rents and Security of Tenure*, Cmnd. 2622 (London H.M.S.O., March 1965).

*Report of the Inter-Departmental Committee on the Rent Restriction Acts*, Cmnd. 3911 (London, H.M.S.O., July 1931).

*Report of the Inter-Departmental Committee on Rent Control*, Cmnd. 6621 (London, H.M.S.O., 1945).

*Fifth Report from the Select Committee on Estimates – Housing Expenditure*, Session 1945–46 (London, H.M.S.O., 1946).

*Report of Inquiry: Rent Act 1957*, Cmnd. 1246 (London, H.M.S.O., Dec. 1960).

*Report of the Committee on Housing in Greater London*, Cmnd. 2605 (London, H.M.S.O., Feb. 1963).

*Fourth Report from the Estimates Committee – Housing Subsidies*, Session 1968–69 (London, H.M.S.O., 1969).

*Report of the Committee on the Rent Acts*, Cmnd. 4609 (London, H.M.S.O., March 1971).

*Tenth Report from the Expenditure Committee*, Session 1972–73 (Improvement

276      POLITICS OF HOUSING IN BRITAIN AND FRANCE

Grants), Environment and Home Office Sub-Committee (H.M.S.O., 1974).

Rex, J. and Moore, R., *Race, Community and Conflict*, (London, Oxford University Press, 1967).

Rose, R., *The Problem of Party Government*, (London, Macmillan 1974).

Wilson, D., *I Know it was the place's fault* (London, Oliphants, 1970).

# Index

The *Letter-by-Letter* system of alphabetization has been adopted and acronyms have been freely used, the solutions for which will be found on pp. ix and x. The following abbreviations have also been incorporated to identify the subject being discussed: (B) for Britain, (F) for France, (Pte) for Private Sector, (Pub) for Public Sector, and (OO) for Owner-occupied Sector; where no note has been indicated the entry is common to all, unless the entry is obviously French.

ABBÉ PIERRE, 94, 132–3, 146–7
AHANE, see FNAH
Aide à la personne (F Pub), 197
Aide à la pierre (F Pub), 197
AMA, AMC, see Association of Municipal Corporations
Amery, Julien, 91
ANAH (F Pub), 203–4
Arrêté (1968) (F Pub), 135
Association of Municipal Corporations, (B), 166, 183–4

BANK OF FRANCE, 221, 231, 246, 253
Barre Committee, 1975 (F Pub), 136, 140, 168, 188, 193, 195, 225–6
Bevan, Aneurin, 115–6, 205
Bibliography, 272–6
Brooke, Sir Henry, 72–3, 75, 84, 161, 163, 171–2, 238
Building Societies (B), 18, 22, 91, 223, 235–43, 245, 251, 253–5
Butler, R.A., 238

CAISSE D'EPARGNE, 141, 219, 254
Caisse des Depôts et Consignations, 254
Caisse des Prêts aux HLMs, 137, 140
Callaghan, James, 205
CGL (F), 94, 96, 221
CGT (F), 46
Chalandon, Albin, 58, 94, 139, 142, 203, 247
Chambre Syndicale des Propriétaires de Paris, (F), 97
CHANE (F Pub), 203

Channon, Paul, 84
Chochoy, Mons., 49, 51
Class differences (B Pub), 194
Claudius-Petit, Eugéne, 45, 47–9, 147, 216, 219, 227
Clay Cross defiance (B Pub), 175
CNL (F), 94–6, 221
CNPF (F), 263
Communist attitude (F), 33–7, 42–3, 46, 218–19
*Competition and Credit Control* (Bank of England), 242
Conservative policy (B): (1951), 64–5; (1951–55), 156–60, 160–5; (1957), 66–79; post 1970, 170–6; on repairs and improvements, 205–10; (OO), 237–8
Consigny, Mons., 134, 150–1
Contract Companies (F), 90
Contrat de Programme (F), 135–6
Couinaud, Mons., 221
Council Houses (B), 20–1, 89, 161; sale of, 168; see also Public Sector
Council/Private ratios (B), 155, 159
Courant, Pierre, 49, 100, 147, 219–20, 226, 250
CPACT (F Pub), 203
Crédit Foncier (F), 17–18, 22, 91, 151, 186, 191, 196, 215–26, 230, 245, 249–52, 262
Cripps, Sir Stafford, 158
Crosland, Anthony, 175
Crossman, Richard H., 79, 81–2, 98, 101, 166, 196

Dary, Mons., 227
Décret Loi (1954) on points system for HLMs (F Pub), 133
Denington Report (B), 207
Differed loans (F OO), 225
Dominjon, Mons., 42
Donnison, David, 7
Dumont, Mons., 125, 215
Dwellings: boom in building (F Pub), 147; new construction, see Completions and Targets, both under Housing; policy of re-allocation of (F Pub), see Sur-Loyer; Private/Council ratios (B), 155, 159; rationing policy for (B Pub), 156; rented and unfurnished, distribution of (F Pte), 60–1; table of completions (B Pub), 177, (F Pub), 148–9; targets for (B), 164–5, 269, (F), 215, 219–20, 269

Economic and Social Council (F), 215
Economic Council Report 1953 (F Pub), 132
Employer and worker relationship, 28–9
Epargne Logement (F OO), 226–7, 230
Equivalents Superficiels system (F), 40

Fair rent (B Pte), 79–80; (B Pub), 170–1
Fair Rent Committees (B Pub), 170
Family Allowances, 196
Faure, Edgar, 39, 129
Fifth Plan (F), 195, 208, 228
FNAH (AHANE) (F Pub), 201–4, 207
FNB (F OO), 224
Foreign workers, housing for (F Pub), 135
Formula for Tenant selection (F Pub), 130–1; see also Selection under Tenant
Fourth Plan (F), 52, 99
Francis Committee (B), 75, 84, 91

Giscard d'Estaing, Valérie, 55, 136, 185
Grants for improvements and repairs (B), 204–10
Greenwood, Arthur, 84, 168–9
Greve, J., 163

Hill, Dr Charles, 163
HLM System (F Pte), 19, 23, 89, 93; (F Pub), 124, 126, 127–38, 139–40, 141, 180–3, 262; financing of, 140–1; sale of, 142; when differentials, 143–6
Homelessness (B), 75, 163

Houist, Mons., 48, 143, 227
House Purchase and Housing Act, 1959 (B), 237–8, 249
Housing, see Dwellings
Housing Act, 1952 (B), 156
Housing Act, 1961 (B), 162, 172
Housing allowances (B Pte), 101; (F Pub), 144
Housing Associations, voluntary (B Pte), 75
Housing Commissioners (B Pub), 175
Housing completions (B Pub), 177, 269; (F Pub), 148–9, 269
Housing Corporation (B Pte), 91
Housing (Finance) Act, 1971 (B), 184
Housing (Finance) Act, 1972 (B), 13 21, 100, 101, 117, 168, 170–6, 259
Housing (Financial and Miscellaneous Provisions) Act, 1946 (B), 156
Housing (Improvement) Act, 1964 (B), 184, 207
Housing (Improvement) Act, 1969 (B), 206
Housing investments (B Pte), 73
Housing Policy, (B and F compared), 15–22; (B), 20–2; (F), 15–19; summary, 22–3
Housing, politics of (B and F compared), 257–70
Housing Repairs and Rent Act, 1954, (B), 20
Housing (Subsidies) Act, 1952 (B), 158, 160
Housing (Subsidies) Act, 1956, (B), 100
Housing targets for construction, (B Pub), 158, 164–5; (F Pub), 215, 219–20, 269; see also Dwellings; Housing Completions

Improvements (Pub), see Repairs and Improvements, Public Sector
Indexing of Savings (F OO), 228

Joseph, Sir Keith, 75, 91, 163–6, 184, 207

Labour policy (B Pte), 79–85; (OO), 239, 243; (B Pub), 155–8, 205
Labour's Plan for Older Homes (B), 206
Lambeth Borough Council (B), 174–5
Landlords: and tenant relationship (Pte), 27–8, 56; powers of (F Pte), 88, 95; organizations of (F Pte), 97; powers of (B Pte), 92–3

Langlet, Mons., 129, 144–6
Laniel, Mons., 128
Lasswell, Harold, 5–6
Legislation (B) 20–2 but see also individual titles of acts; on repairs and improvements 204; (F) primary of 1948, 16–17; establishing Crédit Foncier, 17–19, 217, 220; establishing HLMs, 19; see also Crédit Foncier; HLMs
Lemaire, Mons G., 129
Letourneau, Jean, 125
Loans (F), see Crédit Foncier; (B) see Building Societies
Logécos (F OO), 219–3, 246
Logement et Famille (journal), 96
Loi Krieg (F), 96
London (B): effects of 1957 Act on, 72–4; rent freeze (Pte), 80; shortage of rented accommodation in (Pte), 77–8
Loyer d'Equilabre (F Pub), 128–30

MacColl, J., 239–40
Macmillan, Harold, 65, 71, 158–60, 205, 261
Maintenance coefficients (F), 53
Marie, André, 33
Mathieu, Mons., 225
Maziol, Jacques, 55, 99, 104, 183, 223–4
Milner Holland Report (B), 76–8, 83, 92, 101, 163, 176
Mollet, Guy, 50–1
Morane, Mons., 202–3
Morrison of Lambeth, Lord (Herbert), 71
MRP (F), 34–9, 42, 46, 94, 227
Munby, D.L., 240

National Association of Property Owners, (B), 92
National Institute for Statistical and Economic Studies (F), 34, 208
National Rent Rebate Scheme (B Pte), 101–2; see also Rebates under Rents
NFBTE (B OO), 241–2
Nora Report (F Pub), 204
NRP (F), 216
Nungesser, Mons., 137, 197–8, 202

Option Mortgage Scheme (B), 206, 240, 246
Owner-occupied Sector: (B) 235–43; (F) Crédit Foncier, 215–26; other forms of aid, 226–30; semi-public sector, 215–26; summary and conclusion, 231–

2; summary and comparison (B and F), 245–55

Parkin, Ben, 75
PCF (F), 129
Pennock, J.R., 7–8
Pflimlin, Mons., 222
Pierre, Abbé, see Abbé
Pinay Plan (F), 185
Pisani, Edgar, 55, 104
Plan d'Epargne Logement, 230 see also Epargne Logement
Plan Monnet (F), 125
Plans of French Government, see Fourth; Fifth; Sixth
Points system for HLMs (F Pub), 133
Policy: see Conservative; Housing; Labour; Subsidy; TUC; and French Political Parties by individual acronyms
Politics of Housing (B and F compared), 257–70
Pompidou, Georges, 99
Powell, J. Enoch, 71, 73
Préaumont, Mons. De, 197–8
Prêts Différés (F OO), 225
Prices and Incomes Board (B Pub), 168, 184
Private/Council ratio (B), 155, 159
Private Rented Sector: Introduction, 27–32; (B) 64–85 (1945–56, 64–5; 1956–65, 65–79; Rent Act, 1965, 79–85; (F) 33–62 (Rent Act, 1948, 33–43; its application 1948–58, 43–51; post 1958, 51–62); summary and comparisons (B and F), 87–106; see also Owner-occupied Sector; Public Sector; Repairs and Improvements, Public Sector
PRL (F), 47
Property Investment Companies (F), 90
Public Sector: introduction, 111–23; (B) 154–78 (1945–51, 154–8; 1951–55, 158–60; 1955–61, 160–2; 1961–64, 162–5; 1964–70, 165–9; post 1970, 170–6; tenant selection, 176–8); (F) 124–51 (1945–53, 124–7; Abbé Pierre, 146–7; finance for HLMs, 140–6; housing completions, table of, 148–9; rent levels, 127–30; Sur-Loyer, 138–40; tenant selection, 130–8; summary, 147–51); summary and comparison of B and F, 180–99; see also Owner-occupied Sector; Private Rented Sector; Repairs and Improvements, Public Sector

QUEUILLE, MONS., 47

RACHMANISM (B Pte), 75–6, 101
Rent Act, 1948 (F), 33–43, 87
Rent Act, 1957 (B), 17, 21, 31, 66–79, 101, 259, 261
Rent Act, 1965 (B), 17, 21, 31, 76, 79–85, 87, 259
Rent Assessment Committee (B Pte), 80–1
Rent levels, public (F), 127–30
Rent Officers (B Pte), 80–2
Rent Rebate Scheme (B Pte), 101–2
Rents: appeals against (B Pte), 80; (B Pte) ceilings, 82–3, 84; (F Pub), 134–5; (F OO), 225; (B Pte), control of, 20, 64; (F Pte), commitment to end, 50, 52; (B and F), 29–30; (B Pub), council house, political issue over, 168; (B Pte) decontrol of, 66–74; (F Pte) decontrol of, 56–61, 99, 104; differential (F Pub), 143–6; Fair, what is a? (B Pte), 79–80; freezing of, (B), 80, (F), 16–17; (F Pte) raising of under 5th Rep., 53–6; (B Pub), rebates of, 171, 174, 259; (F Pub), for self employed, 144; (B Pte), what is an exorbitant, 74
Rent strikes (B), 72; (F), 60
Repairs and improvements, (Pub), (B) 204–8; (F), 201–4; summary and comparison, 208–10
Ridley Report, 1945 (B), 64, 68, 70, 82
*Right Road for Britain* (Conservatives) 65
Rueff–Armand Report (F), 52

SANDYS, DUNCAN, 65–74, 84, 100, 160–1
Savings Incentive Scheme (F OO), 226–7
Savings, indexing of, (F OO), 228
SFIO (F), 34
Sixth Plan (F), 96, 134–6, 195, 208, 215, 230
Société d'Economie (F), 191
Sociétés Conventionées (F), 90
Sociétés Cooperatives d'HLMs (F), 190
Sociétés Immobilières d'Investissement (F), 90
Special loans (F OO), 225, 245

Speculation (F), 225
*see also* Rachmanism (B)
Strike, threat of (B), 72; (F), 60
Study, approach to and justification of this, 3–13
Subsidy policy: (B Pte), 71, 91; (B Pub), 156–7, 160, 163, 165–6, 172, 173–4; (F Pub), 136, 138
Sudreau, Mons., 31, 49, 51–3, 143, 145, 202, 208
Surface Area Equivalents (F Pte), 40, 53; (F Pub), 127, 181
Surface Corrigée System (F) *see* Surface Area Equivalents *above*
Sur-Loyer (F), 138–40, 195

TAITTINGER, MONS., 224–5
Targett, A.J., 184
Tenant: and landlord relationship, 27–8, 56; organizations (B), 92, 96–7; (F) 94–7; selection (B Pub), 176–8, 181; selection (F Pub), 130–8, 181; (F Pub), selling of HLMs to, 142; (F Pub), sitting, 142
Tenure, security of: (B) 67, 69, 83, 84, 98; (F Pte), 56
Tillon, Charles, 33
Tribunals, rent (B Pte), 79
TUC policy, 173

UDR (F), 103–5
UDSR (F), 34, 39, 45
UNFO-HLM (F Pub), 128, 142, 144–5, 182–3, 257–8
UNPI (F), 60, 97
UNR (F), 142

VALEUR LOCATIVE (F Pte), 40–1, 45–6, 50
Vivien, Mons., 55, 99, 104, 203
Voluntary Housing Associations (B Pte), 75

WALKER, PETER, 84, 172
Weighted Surface Area System (F Pte), 37, 39, 181
Wilson, (Sir) J. Harold, 76, 196
Worker and employer relationship, 28–9

Margaret Morris